MACKERELS IN THE MOONLIGHT

MACKERELS IN THE MOONLIGHT

Four Corrupt American Mayors

Gerald Leinwand

McFarland & Company, Inc., Publishers
Jefferson, North Carolina, and London

LIBRARY OF CONGRESS CATALOGUING-IN-PUBLICATION DATA

Leinwand, Gerald.
    Mackerels in the moonlight : four corrupt American mayors /
Gerald Leinwand.
        p.   cm.
    Includes bibliographical references and index.

    ISBN 0-7864-1845-1 (softcover : 50# alkaline paper) ∞

    1. Mayors—United States—Biography.   2. Thompson, Wil-
liam Hale, 1869–1944.   3. Hague, Frank, 1876–1956.   4.
Walker, James John, 1881–1946.   5. Curley, James Michael,
1874–1958.   6. Political corruption—United States—Case studies.   7. United States—Politics and government—Case studies.
I. Title.
    E176.L498   2004
    364.1'323'092273—dc22   2004007594
British Library cataloguing data are available

On the cover: (from top left to right) Mayor Jimmy Walker, 1929;
Frank Hague, 1925 (courtesy Library of Congress); William Hale
Thompson, 1909 (courtesy Chicago Historical Society); Governor
Curley, 1936 (courtesy Library of Congress); background image of
moon ©2004 PhotoSpin; background image of mackerel ©2004
Stockbyte.

Manufactured in the United States of America.

McFarland & Company, Inc., Publishers
    Box 611, Jefferson, North Carolina 28640
    www.mcfarlandpub.com

For my grandson Spencer Maslin.

With thanks to my research assistant,
Dan Prosterman, whose talent and
diligence made this a better book.

Contents

PART IV
James Michael Curley: America's Fourth Worst Mayor

Preface

What does it take to be Mr. or Ms. Clean in politics?

It is said of pornography, "It is difficult to define, but I know it when I see it." Political corruption, on the contrary, is easy to define; it is the use of public office for private gain. But not so readily seen.

As the president of a state-supported public college, may I use public funds to take an alumnus to lunch? Am I no longer Mr. Clean if I allow the alumnus to buy lunch for me? Does it make a difference if the above-mentioned lunch is in the college cafeteria or in an expensive French restaurant? Am I compromised if an alumnus buys me an airplane ticket to give a speech at a conference held in a distant city? If a coach ticket is acceptable, is going first class also acceptable? If the alumnus thinks I need a new suit in order to give the speech and buys one for me, is that OK?

If I were president of a private college, not a state-supported institution, I could do most of those things with no one questioning my behavior. If I were CEO of Enron, Worldcom, or some other private enterprise, would my ethics even be challenged? The answer — not likely — explains the massive unseemly behavior by corporate America's imperial and imperious CEOs. Thus, when I allow an alumnus to pay for my lunch in the school cafeteria, do I take my first step down a slippery slope making me a politically corrupt state employee? Is political corruption merely the price paid for a political favor?

Following the example of Arthur M. Schlesinger, who, in 1945, had distinguished historians rate the best and worst American presidents, Melvin G. Holli, in 1993, conducted a parallel study in which political scientists rated the best and the worst American big-city mayors.[1] In that survey, William H. Thompson of Chicago had the dubious distinction of being rated the first of the worst, followed, in order, by Frank Hague of Jersey City, James Walker of New York, and James Michael Curley of Boston.

These four worst mayors in America are all firmly ensconced in America's political hall of shame.

Yet, if these are shameful politicians, why then were they elected, reelected and, sometimes, elected yet again? If none are so blind as those who will not see, were the voters of Chicago, Jersey City, New York, and Boston so blind that they could not see the shortcomings of the men they elected as their mayors? Or, quite the contrary, did the ordinary voters on election day know better than scholars and pundits what was good for them? Scoundrels though they were, one and all, they were perceived as the people's scoundrels who derived their legitimacy precisely because, like the ordinary voters, they wallowed in a no-man's land in which honest and dishonest practices sometimes appeared indistinguishable from one another.

In this book about the four worst mayors, you will find that at some point they crossed the line between "acceptable" and "unacceptable," corruption or what George Washington Plunkett of Tammany Hall described as honest vs. dishonest graft. As an example of honest graft, if a politico receives a cash payment but the city incurs no extra cost, or imposes no burden on the taxpayer, is anybody hurt? Should anybody care? An example of this may be the choice of banks a city uses to deposit funds. If the charges for banking services are roughly the same, who is hurt if a public employee is bribed to select one bank over another? Dishonest graft, however, costs the city money. The city buys what it does not need or pays a higher price than it should for inferior merchandise, building materials, or workmanship.[2]

"Big Bill" Thompson, who was born in Boston to wealthy parents and moved to Chicago while he was still quite young, is considered America's worst mayor, having, among other things, accepted the support of gangster boss Al Capone. He died with an estate estimated to be worth almost $2 million. There is little evidence that, having been born to wealth, he profited hugely from thrice being elected mayor of Chicago. Yet somewhere he crossed the line and was, in due course, viewed by Chicago as a corrupt mayor to be gotten rid of.

Mayor Frank Hague of Jersey City described his town as the "moralest city in the nation." What he meant was that vice, prostitution, bordellos, porno shops, and porno movies had been banished from his city. But inasmuch as he, like William Bennett, America's virtue guru, saw no evil in gambling, Jersey City became a gambling Mecca for many.

Jimmy Walker of New York was a "good time" mayor and did well when the city prospered. He was, however, the wrong man at the wrong time, when the Great Depression struck. He cared little for money, his or the city's; he was more careless than consciously villainous, but his activities were corrupt by almost any standard.

James Michael Curley of Boston openly asserted, "Politics is my business," and he proceeded with deliberation to make money from the offices he held as Boston's mayor and as governor of Massachusetts. He flaunted a lavish home built entirely at public expense. Yet, he was elected again and again — once while still in jail.

In an op-ed piece in *The New York Times* of September 30, 2002, Alan Ehrenhalt quoted John Randolph of Virginia, who, in the 1820s, complained that his colleague, the distinguished Senator Henry Clay of Kentucky, was brilliant yet so corrupt that "like a rotten mackerel in the moonlight, he both shines and stinks." In this biographical approach to America's four worst mayors you will find that they were not altogether without achievement, but like rotten mackerels in the moonlight they both shine and stink.

Attempt no more good than the nation can bear.

Solon in Ancient Athens

There is no kind of dishonesty into which otherwise good people more easily and frequently fall than that of defrauding the government.

Benjamin Franklin

Prologue:
Four Funerals

William Hale Thompson (1869–1944)

William Hale "Big Bill" Thompson, one of the most picturesque figures in Chicago's political history, died on March 19, 1944, in the Blackstone Hotel at the age of 74. Only brother Gale Thompson and his sister, Mrs. Helen Nelson Pelouze, were at his bedside. As mayor he had been alternately laughed at and cursed. Although he had been elected mayor three times, there were few mourners at the North Side funeral parlor where Bill Thompson's body was laid out. For two days and two nights it lay there and few came. A reporter wrote, "Just thirty-two persons stopped at the chapel last night. Mayor Thompson lay in a solid bronze casket. There was not a flower nor a fern to be seen."[1]

But on the day of "Big Bill's" funeral Chicago's politicians were moved to act. Entrances to City Hall were hastily draped in somber crepe and the city council held a memorial service. Those who attended the service included aldermen too young to have known Thompson personally, and there were old enemies and friends who came to pay belated respects. Oscar De Priest, an African-American admirer of Thompson, observed, "He had a real love for my people in his great heart. We will never forget him."[2] A funeral service was held at the Thoburn Methodist Episcopal Church on the South Side, and he was buried at Chicago's Oak Woods Cemetery. As the momentum of mourners slowly built, there were 1,000 who attended the church services while another 2,500 thronged in the streets outside. Governor Green was among the mourners, as were others from Thompson's political life. His friend, supporter, and pastor, the Reverend John Williamson, delivered the eulogy — "By the time people had

5

recovered from the shock of his crudeness and quit their laughing at what appeared to be silly, William Hale Thompson had achieved what he was after."[3]

Frank Hague (1876–1956)

He had hoped to die, so he said, in the "Horseshoe" slum of Jersey City where he was born, but he died instead on January 1, 1956, of complications from arthritis in his expensive apartment at 480 Park Avenue in New York City, where he was hiding out from a subpoena that would surely have been served him had he ventured to cross the Hudson River to Jersey City. Frank Hague was sued by the Jersey City administration for $15 million for alleged kickbacks from city employees in the amount of 3 percent of their salaries for the years 1917 to 1949.

The body of Jersey City's erstwhile mayor was taken to the Lawrence Quinn Funeral Home at 298 Academy Street in Jersey City. On Thursday, at 10:00 A.M., a high requiem mass was sung at St. Aedan's Roman Catholic Church where in the 1930s he had donated a $50,000 altar. Few were the tears that were shed and fewer still the eulogies that were delivered at the funeral services for this once-powerful political satrap.

As the eight professional pallbearers hefted the 700-pound hammered casket out of Lawrence Quinn's Funeral Home in Jersey City, a solemn voice ordered, "Hats off," as a final gesture of respect. Of the hundred curious onlookers, only four did as they were told. The sparse floral tributes disturbed the undertaker but, as he explained to one who was attending the funeral, "When the Big Boy goes, it means he can no longer do anything for anybody." Some bosses endeared themselves to posterity. Not Mayor Hague. Thus, the bitterness Frank Hague generated as mayor lingered at his death. As the funeral procession went by, an elderly woman held aloft an American flag and a sign that read, "God have mercy on his sinful, greedy soul."[4]

Jimmy Walker (1881–1946)

Death came to James J. Walker at 6:25 in the evening on Monday, November 18, 1946. "The gay and flashing wit of the 1920's" had been mayor of New York for seven glamorous years.[5] This symbol of a once-glittering New York drew crowds to the flower-banked chapel at the Campbell Funeral Home, at Madison Avenue and 81st Street, to pay their last respects. From every walk of life they came — 8,400 of them in a day, nearly

30,000 in all — New Yorkers for whom Jimmy Walker's death reminded them of a time they fondly remembered.

Jimmy Walker did not create the nightclub era, the bootleg lairs, and the free and easy twenties, but he mirrored the era for the people of the city of New York. In his reflected light they remembered participating vicariously as he enjoyed the nightlife, the worlds of sports, theater, movies, song, and dance. His was the very essence of the lush, glamorous boom years the young could not remember and the middle aged and elderly could not forget.

At the nadir of his career, New Yorkers, like the rest of the nation, were ground down by depression and joblessness. During World War II they had sacrificed life and treasure to defeat Hitler and his Axis partners, Italy and Japan. So the mourners could be excused, as they filed by his bier, if they reflected upon a less grim and more innocent time which they knew was forever lost.

New York City's mayor, Bill O'Dwyer, ordered flags in all public buildings to be lowered to half-staff for the mourning period. New York State Governor Joe R. Hanley designated the entire membership of the state senate, where Walker had served twenty years ago, as a committee of the whole to attend the interment at the Gate of Heaven Cemetery at Valhalla, New York.

Two close friends, humorist Arthur Baer and restaurateur Toots Shor, were sitting in the latter's restaurant when they heard the news of Walker's death. They tried to drown their sorrow and hide their tears in illicit booze, but, at 4:00 A.M., the two went to the Campbell Funeral Home to pay their respects to their dead buddy. "Jimmy, Jimmy," Shor cried out, "When you walked into a room you brightened up the joint."[6] The distinguished attorney Louis Nizer more soberly yet sympathetically said of Walker: "He met success like a gentleman and failure like a man."[7]

James Michael Curley (1874–1958)

"It was the biggest wake the old city had ever seen.... The biggest wake was followed by the biggest funeral. A crowd of one million ... lined the sidewalks to watch the hearse carrying James Michael Curley pass through the streets of the city he had led and to which he had given life and laughter, sorrow and scandal, for over fifty years."[8] Death had come to this legendary Boston politician just eight days short of his 84th birthday. Only the assassination of President John Fitzgerald Kennedy five years later would capture more local media attention.

He lay in state in Boston's Hall of Flags, a rare tribute paid only to three other sons of Massachusetts. Long lines wound through the State House to bid farewell to this "Mayor of the Poor," as he liked to be called. Flowers stood at the foot of each of the sixteen marble columns in the Hall of Flags. Among the many floral tributes, one came from "Jack and Jackie Kennedy."

Archbishop Richard J. Cushing had flown to Boston from Washington, D.C., to deliver absolution, but the celebrant at the requiem mass was Father Francis Curley, S. J. — James Michael Curley's youngest son. A guard of honor surrounding the polished mahogany coffin was composed of the Knights of Columbus, Fourth Class. "They stood there, plump and middle-aged, in silk capes, their hands on their sword hilts, white plumes covering their heads."[9] The Archbishop prayed over the body, and when the prayer ended he tried to comfort the family. There was no eulogy.

James Michael Curley was buried atop a hill in Mt. Calvary Cemetery in Roslindale beside his first wife and seven of their nine children. As he dropped the dirt on his father's casket, Father Francis intoned in Latin: "Remember, man, that thou are dust and in dust returneth."

Part I

BILL THOMPSON:
AMERICA'S WORST MAYOR

Hog Butcher for the World,
Tool Maker, Stacker of Wheat,
Player with Railroads and the
   Nation's Freight Handler;
Stormy, husky, brawling,
City of the Big Shoulders

"Chicago," 1916
Carl Sandburg

1

From Home on the Range to Hat in the Ring

Between Sunday, October 8, 1871, and the early morning of October 10, 1871, fire destroyed the heart of Chicago. Its impact on the city was greater than that of the terror of September 11, 2001, which destroyed the huge twin tower skyscrapers in New York City. Three years before the fire, in 1868, "Big Bill" Thompson's parents, Medora Gale and William Hale Thompson Sr., had moved from Boston to Chicago where the already well-to-do Thompson Sr. sought to do even better in Chicago real estate. William Hale Thompson was born in Boston, on Beacon Street, the first son of a wealthy man with a distinguished lineage.

"Big Bill's" father continued in the family's naval tradition by going to sea when he was nineteen. He rose to be a ship's second officer, but severe injuries from a fall into the hold while in dock at San Francisco forced him to give up active naval duty. He returned to New England and entered the counting room at Cummings and Lee, East India Commission merchants. He did well in business and bought a mansion on Boston's elegant Beacon Street. When the Civil War broke out he applied for a commission in the navy and did well enough on the examinations to be assigned as a lieutenant on the sloop-of-war *Mohican*, on October 2, 1861, and became its paymaster. Eight months later he was promoted to lieutenant commander and assigned to the staff of Admiral David G. Farragut, the hero of the Battle of Mobile Bay, who, lashed to the mast of his flagship, bellowed, "Go ahead—full steam—and damn the torpedoes." As a candidate for public office "Big Bill" was not above wrapping himself in the mantle of the admiral's and his father's courage. Thompson Sr. was promoted to paymaster for the fleet and, in 1866, was honorably discharged from the navy.

While on leave in January 1864, Commander Thompson married Medora Gale of one of the first families in Chicago. Her father, Stephen, had been one of the thirty-eight incorporators of the town of Chicago. The couple's first child, Helen, was born in 1866 and on May 14, 1867, William Hale Thompson, Jr., was born. There were two more male additions to the family, Gale in 1871 and Percival in 1876.

Where Jimmy Walker, New York's mayor, came from an immigrant family in modest circumstances, Chicago's William Hale "Big Bill" Thompson, mayor of Chicago from 1915 to 1923 and again from 1927 to 1931, came from a wealthy family with deep roots among the early settlers of New Hampshire and Boston. Where Jimmy Walker was the living symbol of New York and Broadway during the Roaring Twenties, prohibition, and the age of jazz, "Big Bill" put a live face on Chicago as the brawling "city of the big shoulders," as Carl Sandburg described it. If the Thompson family had remained in Boston, "Big Bill" (Republican) and James Michael Curley (Democrat) might have been political rivals. But "Big Bill" Thompson thoughtfully left Boston to the predatory tactics of Curley, to feed at the political trough of Chicago. "Big Bill" could not be a proper Bostonian, but in Chicago he could be noticed, and he was.

The Man Who Never Grew Up

Journalist and author William Allen White had this to say about "Big Bill" Thompson, mayor of Chicago, as he made his appearance at City Hall to begin his third term in 1927:

> His voice had a resonant clarion quality, his oratorical voice is throaty, authoritative, penetrating.... His jaw and mouth and nose indicated strength without purpose, power without intelligence, force without humor or charm. But his eyes, rising above his lower face, explained why "Big Bill" Thompson stood there, three times Mayor of Chicago.... For out of his eyes looks the eternal boy — beaming forth, not the innocence of youth but its shiny inexperience! His eyes give a certain puerility to his face. This bland, blithe, deceptive puerility makes it clear why he attracts and holds for a time with passionate loyalty the millions who follow him.
> They are worshiping Pan!
> Here is the man who never grew up.[1]

"He must have been a big, fat, wrinkled-wristed baby."[2] He was a lumbering youth but athletic. Because of his wealth he could "throw his weight around," and among his youthful peers he could bully them into allowing him to assume some leadership among his intimates. By the time the future mayor of Chicago was fourteen, it became evident that the discipline and routine of school were not for him.

Bill's father was determined to send his son to a school providing greater discipline, but Bill prevailed upon him to let him take his chances with the cowboys in the American West. Moreover, he would pay his own way with money he would earn from a new job in a grocery store. Both Bills kept their promise. That is, Bill's father would allow his son to try his fortune in the "wild west," and young Bill would stay at his job earning enough to try to realize his fantasies of cowboy life on the western plains. For the next several years, Bill Thompson would alternately work at the business of being a cowboy, but he would return to Chicago for part of the year to attend the Metropolitan Business College.

The Cowboy Years

Bill Thompson was younger and stayed longer than the 26-year-old Theodore Roosevelt, who likewise looked to the American West to find new beginnings in the strenuous life on the cattle frontier. With eighty dollars in his pocket, this big fourteen year old sat in the caboose of an empty cattle train and made his way to Cheyenne, Wyoming, where, miners, ranchers, cowboys, and railroaders came together to raise hell, make a fortune, and get out. Young Bill, with his father's help, did just that.

Cheyenne was an expensive town where meals were a dollar each and a cot in the Inter-Ocean Hotel cost four dollars. The eighty dollars "Bill" Thompson had saved from his job did not go far. Despite his lack of experience Bill sought and obtained a job at one of the Standard cattle ranches as a wagon driver and cook's helper. With the few cents he had left, he bought a cookbook. He was paid twenty dollars a month plus meals and a place in the wagon to sleep. When the Standard provision wagon left Cheyenne, Bill was aboard riding the high spring seat. On the trail, he awakened at three o'clock in the morning, rebuilt the fire, hauled water, gathered wood, helped cut the meat, and baked the day's supply of fresh bread.[3]

For each of the next six years, Bill spent three winter months attending business college in Chicago and the rest of the year on a ranch out west. He learned how to build and hold a fire, spot a water hole, pack cooking gear for the trail, bake bread, broil steaks, handle a gun, rope a calf, and wrestle a steer for the branding iron. He learned to wear, unselfconsciously, a bright wool shirt, blue denim pants, a beaver Stetson hat, and cowboy boots. When he visited Chicago, he thrilled his friends when he regaled them with stories of his education on the western prairie. His experiences made theirs seem pallid by comparison. Did he know more or less than those who were attending Harvard or Yale? One thing we can know, he was not jealous of them. As it turned out, the education he received among the cowboys was the best education for him, and it is something to the credit of his father who did not insist upon Exeter and Yale, where he had gone, but helped his son realize his own, very different, ambitions.

In the spring of 1888, while at Cheyenne, Bill received a telegram from his father: "Bought a ranch at Ewing, Nebraska ... You take over." A father could not make a son happier.

As a ranch manager, Thompson improved his herds, the bunkhouses, and the yields from his hay and cornfields. At the end of three years, he showed a profit of $30,000. But happy days as manager of his own ranch did not last. In 1891, his father died of pneumonia. Bill arrived in Chicago in cowboy dress but outfitted himself in appropriate mourning attire and attended his father's funeral, where he heard his father eulogized as one of Chicago's finest citizens. Although Thompson Sr. had left his widow a fortune of over $2 million, she exacted Bill's reluctant promise that he would remain in Chicago.

While a Spartan life was imposed on most cowboys who lived on the pittance they received as ranch hands, "Big Bill" could enjoy the cold nights on the prairie or the hot and dusty trail, secure in the knowledge that he need not, indeed could not, support himself out of his earnings. When his prairie colleagues recognized that, unlike them, this was a wealthy young man, they were initially skeptical of the reasons that he lived and worked among them and they were uncomfortable in his presence. But they were seduced by his gregarious ways and were forever in his debt as he treated them to another round of whiskey at the bar. In time they gained a general respect for his ability to master cowboy skills, withstand harsh weather, endure back-breaking work, and hold his own in the inevitable brawls. For this man who never grew up, his years as a cowboy must be deemed a success.

One cannot determine what skills or attitudes "Big Bill's" cowboy experiences contributed to his actions as politician or as mayor. But, as did Theodore Roosevelt before him, he never let the public forget that he had been a cowboy. To the extent that the cowboy life continued to trigger the imagination of an urban and immigrant people, Thompson's youthful experiences did surround his upbringing with a sense of romance and a degree of adventure most of those who would compete with him could not share. When he campaigned in his cowboy hat he reminded voters not only that he had had experiences of which they could only dream, but also that through those experiences he had transformed himself from his patrician origins to a servant of humble citizens.

Although he was manager of his father's business, that business required little of Bill's additional supervision. Free of the daily grind, what glamorous pursuit could possibly take the place of the cowboy life he sorely missed? He would find that outlet in athletics.

The Athletic Years

Through his wealthy friends Willie and Gene Pike, Bill Thompson was invited to join the Chicago Athletic Association, where he quickly was recognized for his athletic talent — first in water polo and later in football. In those days the C.A.A. competed not only against other private clubs but also with teams from Harvard, Yale, Princeton, and leading midwestern colleges. While most of the athletes of the C.A.A. had learned their skills while stars on college teams, Thompson had to learn and play the games without the benefit of university coaching staffs. But, in the stadium as on the prairie, he learned quickly and before long became captain of the water polo team and led it to victories over Yale, Harvard, Princeton, and the Boston and New York Athletic Clubs. Nor was water polo the only sport in which he excelled. He became a star baseball player and won the club handball championship. He won several swimming and diving trophies and even became skilled in trapeze exhibitions. But the athletic fame for which he is best remembered was on the football field.

In 1894, he was the C.A.A.'s left tackle and the football team's strongest player. In that year the team lost to Yale and Harvard but defeated Princeton and Dartmouth. In 1896, now as captain, Thompson put together an exceptionally strong team of former college football stars. He acted "not only as captain but as coach, strategist and manager," and the team responded with victory after victory. On Thanksgiving Day the team was scheduled to play the Boston Athletic Club for the national championship, when Captain Thompson learned that another member had been providing free meals for six of the C.A.A. players, thus violating the rules of the Amateur Athletic Union. Captain Thompson, to his credit, took the only honorable course open to him and expelled the six who had broken the rules.[4] Despite the expulsion of six important players, the C.A.A. football team won the game handily as Boston remained scoreless, and Thompson was toasted at a victory banquet later that night.

Bill Thompson was an athletic hero and an important man in national

William Hale Thompson, as sportsman, sitting at the wheel of a boat in 1909. Courtesy of the Chicago Historical Society (DN-0054139A, *Chicago Daily News*).

athletics. He was elected to the vice-presidency of the C.A.A. but was sorely disappointed when he lost the election for the presidency. To lick his wounds, he took an extended hunting trip to Montana, Washington, and Oregon and spent most of the summer at his family's summer estate at Oconomowoc, Wisconsin, where he sailed his boat, the *Myrone*, and was vice-president of a local yacht club made up of other millionaires.

In Chicago, he shared bachelor quarters in the Metropole Hotel with Gene Pike, his wealthy friend from childhood. Business affairs failed to interest him, and he was genuinely pleased when Pike became an alderman on the Chicago City Council but as yet had no thought of entering politics himself. Pike kept prodding him to do so and pointed out that he could easily be nominated for the second aldermanic slot. Thompson was not easily persuaded. As Thompson, Pike, and a mutual friend, George Jenney, sat around a card table at the C.A.A., Pike told Jenney:

> "I think Bill should run. He'd be great, don't you think?"
> "He's scared!" cried Jenney. "He's afraid to run!"

Then Jenney pulled out of his wallet and pushed a fifty-dollar bill toward Pike. "This money says Bill Thompson is scared!"

Before Pike could speak, Thompson covered the bill with his big palm. "I'll take this one myself," he bellowed. "George Jenney, you've got yourself a bet."[5]

2

The Playboy as Politician

"Big Bill" Thompson did not enter politics as a career move. He did not seek to reform government or to improve the lots and lives of Chicagoans. He had plenty of money and so financial gain could not have been a factor. He had no background in the law and no concept of what may be required of a person in public service. The extent to which vanity played a part cannot be known. Did he guess that the life of a cowboy was forever closed to him and that an athletic career, given its demands on the body, could not last? "Big Bill" Thompson may be the only politician in the country to enter politics because of a bet! In 1900, at age thirty-one, he "strode into the fray as an adventurer, because a friend told him he did not dare."[1]

Plunging into Chicago Politics

Freiburg Hall, a meeting space owned by Ike Bloom, "King of the Brothels," and frequented by Chicago's community of vice, including thugs, gamblers, pimps, bootleggers, knaves, thieves, and prostitutes, was where Bill Thompson was nominated by acclamation on February 17 as the candidate of the Republican Party as an alderman for the Second Ward. In celebration he treated those in the meeting room to twenty-cent whiskey, not five-cent beer or ten-cent rotgut, all served by scantily clad waitresses.

In 1900, the Second Ward extended from the south branch of the Chicago River to Lake Michigan. It contained the homes of the wealthiest, including the Thompson home, to the shacks of newly arrived African-Americans from the southern states and, alarmingly, a growing number of upscale brothels. Thompson was new to politics but not new to Chicago.

His cowboy background gave him a common touch; his success on the athletic field made him a widely known and much appreciated sports hero, and his skill in yachting gave him that touch of class that set him off from Chicago's *hoi polloi* without offending them. He was one of the boys, a back slapper, a card player, a glad hander, a big spender, and big drinker.

In his acceptance speech he declared,

> I aim to be a first-class representative of this fine ward. What the Second Ward needs is decent streets and enough lights at night to protect citizens from holdup men. I want to pledge myself to work for better condition of the streets. It is time the aldermen of this ward pay some attention to the demands of those who employ them![2]

Chicago's Municipal Voters League (MVL) thought they saw in Thompson an electable Republican who, as alderman from the Second Ward, would help the cause of political reform in Chicago. The MVL recognized the shortcomings of their man but thought he would, in the end, do their bidding. "The worst you can say of him," an unenthusiastic MVL member declared, "is that he's stupid."[3] The reformers, however, did not really know their man.

Thompson's opponent as alderman from the Second Ward was a well-known, old-time politician, Charles F. Gunther, but despite respectable political support he could not overcome the upstart's popularity. During the campaign the reform groups attacked the Democrats in "the Harrison Gang," among whom were "Bathhouse" John Coughlin, once owner of a circus zoo and proprietor of a Turkish bath, and "Hinky Dink" Michael Kenna, former newsboy and operator of gambling houses. They won repeated election as aldermen of Chicago's First Ward by protecting the bootleggers as well as the owners and girls of the bawdy houses of the Levee. The two aldermen of Chicago's First Ward, lawless and ruthless, by virtue of seniority controlled the Chicago City Council. But "Bathhouse" John and "Hinky Dink" Kenna felt power slipping away as the vice district spread from the Levee in the First Ward to the Second Ward. These two savvy, if unsavory, politicians knew they could get the cooperation of a political novice if they could but get him elected as an alderman of the Second Ward. This they did, and later Thompson rewarded them by voting himself out of political office.

Although he ran as a reformer, Thompson ran his own kind of campaign. He made few speeches but bought good whiskey and visited every one of the 270 saloons in his ward, where he shook hands, slapped backs, and enjoyed himself. "I'm spending $175 a day ... I've worn out two pairs of shoes, and I've gained fourteen pounds. Fellows, politics is really the life," he told his cronies at the Chicago Athletic Club.[4] On election day fine carriages drove up to the polling stations, businessmen closed their shops, and Thompson won 2,516 votes to 2,113 for Gunther.

Why did William Hale Thompson win?

He won because "Hinky Dink" and "Bathhouse" preferred a less-sophisticated alderman in the Second Ward just so they could wrest that ward away from him. The reformers of the Second Ward thought they saw in Thompson one of their own and of like mind. He wasn't, but they rallied to his support — a vote for Thompson was an expression of their distaste for their current mayor, Carter Harrison the Younger. Thompson was also able to make inroads into the vote of African-Americans who came to Chicago in large numbers, many of whom lived in the poorer sections of the Second Ward. By exaggerating his father's role in serving the Union cause, he had a message that he could use to encourage their support and obtain their vote. He was an aggressive candidate and not above name-calling; his opponent, he declared, was a "sneak" and "Jack Rabbit." Thompson, moreover, had an engaging personality both on and off the hustings. To what ordinarily would have been a lackluster election, he added a measure of enthusiasm.

Thus, Bill Thompson won his bet with his friend George Jenney. But, having won office, what would he do with his victory? As he would again and again, he turned to the least desirable elements in his party for advice and guidance.

Alderman Thompson served as a member of the Chicago City Council for two years. But instead of listening to the voices of the MVL, he allowed himself to be flattered, encouraged, and mentored by "Bathhouse" John Coughlin, who was always at his side during Thompson's infrequent presence at council meetings. Thompson's interest in civic reform was minimal, and he was not even present when he was appointed to various committees, including those on gas, oil and electric lights, City Hall, police stations, and Bridewell city jail. He successfully fought for the establishment of the city's first public playground that would primarily serve the African-American children of his ward. As a sportsman he also fought for the establishment of an athletic commission to regulate boxing.

Thompson would rather sail his yacht than legislate; he would rather campaign than govern. With a cowboy hat or yachting cap he would visit a neighborhood saloon or watch a card game and thereby win the admiration of his constituents as a man of wealth and class who mixed so effectively with ordinary people.

Bill Thompson was a man's man rather than a ladies' man. By no means a misogynist, he did not seem to have a great interest in women. So it was something of a surprise when Bill Thompson took time from his aldermanic duties to marry Mary Walker Wyse, a member of his real estate office staff. "Maysie," as she was called by her friends, was described as "one of the most beautiful women of her day."[5] He was thirty-two; she, twenty-six. In an attempt to keep the wedding secret from Bill's mother, who opposed a marriage she thought unworthy of her son, the couple married quietly in St. Joseph, Michigan, on December 7, 1901, in the Evangelical Lutheran Church. The Thompsons had no children and after a time drifted apart.

"Bathhouse" and "Hinky Dink" did not offer their mentoring skills for nothing. They did not flatter without expecting a payoff. What they wanted was a piece of the Second Ward to which vice had expanded so that they could continue to control the often pivotal "flop house" vote. To accomplish this they required Thompson to agree to a redistricting plan that would, in effect, leave the latter without a constituency. But Thompson, who now liked to call himself "Big Bill," either did not care or did not know the consequences of the redistricting proposal. The purpose of the redistricting ordinance, declared a Republican alderman, "is to give control of the city back to the boodlers."[6] Thus it was that when Mayor Harrison ordered a roll call, he grinned broadly at "Hinky Dink" as Gene Pike and Thompson, Republican reformers of the Second Ward, voted to support the redistricting measure. Thus, Alderman Thompson, unknowingly, legislated himself out of a ward!

The people of the Second Ward were not amused. They could not understand how their two aldermen, Pike and Thompson, could have been so duped. Pike remained indifferent to the criticisms since he did not visualize a further political career for himself. The *Chicago Evening Journal* derisively remarked, "The Gray Wolves ("Bathhouse" and "Hinky Dink" and their allies) rule again. They have eaten the sheep who wore the clothing of reformers!"[7]

Thompson was genuinely embarrassed. He learned to love public life and delighted in campaigning even more. No sooner had he been elected alderman than visions of higher office danced in his head — mayor of Chicago, United States senator from Illinois, even president of the United States did not seem to be out of his ambitious reach. Thompson, humiliated, was determined to fight back.

He threatened to challenge "Bathhouse" Coughlin in the First Ward, but the threat was empty; the candidate, the newspapers, and the voters knew it. How to remain in the political arena was the challenge he now faced. Again at the crossroads of his political career, "Big Bill" Thompson leaned for guidance on the "Blond Boss" and the "Poor Swede," the worst elements among Chicago's Republicans.

The Blond Boss

In the spring of 1902, in Mickey Conlon's saloon on West Madison Street, a West Side furniture dealer and a dabbler in politics, John M. Smyth, introduced Thompson to William Lorimer, known as the "Blond Boss" and the most powerful Republican in Chicago. Political novice though he was, Bill Thompson's natural skill as a campaigner came to the attention of Lorimer who prevailed upon Thompson not to run against "Bathhouse" John. When Lorimer spoke, Thompson listened. "We need men like you in the [Republican] Party, Bill. We need men of good connections.... Tie to me Bill," urged Lorimer.[8] And, Bill Thompson did so.

In all things political Lorimer was essentially amoral. He viewed politics and morality as a contradiction in terms. He did not believe one could have political aspirations and be honest as well. With the money of Charles Yerkes, the traction baron, and in Edward Hines, the lumber king, Lorimer's political machine was financially well oiled.

Lorimer was a master of political intrigue, at reconciling ethnic interests, and in developing a political organization. A superb political organizer, he was a dismal campaigner. Nevertheless, he longed for public office and was rewarded with six terms in the House of Representatives (1895–1901 and 1903–1909) and, in May 1909, the Illinois General Assembly broke a four-month deadlock and elected him to the United States Senate.[9]

In July 1912, Lorimer's colleagues in the Senate repudiated his election because there was substantial evidence that he had bribed his way into that august body. On July 14, 1914, the Senate voted overwhelmingly to oust him. Lorimer would never be the factor in political life he once was, but he remained in politics and was an unhealthy influence on "Big Bill" Thompson, his protégé.

Lorimer was determined to remain in politics, and Thompson was eager to make his mark in politics. Lorimer was a poor campaigner and Thompson an unpolished one, and so both needed the help of yet another political coach.

The Poor Swede

Between 1902, when he voted himself out of a job as alderman of Chicago's Second Ward, and 1915, when he became Chicago's mayor, Bill

Thompson sharpened his political techniques when he paid attention to another political mentor, Fred Lundin, pitchman for patent medicines.

Lundin was twelve years old when, shortly after the Chicago fire of 1871, his parents brought him from Sweden to America. He peddled newspapers and shined shoes, sold clothing and, finally, pills. Convinced that he could make more money if he mixed his own medicine, he scraped together enough money to buy a horse and wagon. In the kitchen of his parents' home, he mixed a drink from juniper berries that he sold as a fine alternative to alcohol. Lundin's Juniper Ade, a kind of Gatorade of its day, sold well and became widely known by 1893.

Lundin, colorfully dressed in what passed for the Bohemian style of the day, was likewise well known and easily recognized. How could it be otherwise? He drove through the streets of Chicago and set up his stand from which he extolled the virtues of his "alternative medicine." As described by Thompson biographers Lloyd Wendt and Herman Kogan:

> His long black frock coat was tight at the waist and it flared around his thighs. On his head was a black plainsman's hat. He wore a black Windsor tie and a black, low-cut waistcoat, ornamented with an enormous gold watch chain. His round eyes hid behind amber spectacles. When, in a burst of oratory, he swept his broad-brimmed hat from his head, a home-shorn shock of wheat-blond hair tumbled over his forehead. His rickety wagon was decorated in flamboyant style and equipped with kerosene torches. Before he made his flamboyant sales talks to the crowds that quickly assembled, two Negro boys strummed guitars and sang popular songs of the day. The music was his signal.
>
> "Step right up, folks!" Lundin cried. "It's all free. It costs you nothing to hear these sweet singers of the South directly from New York's matchless Academy of Music! They sang there for the nabobs of Fifth Avenue! They are offered here for the first time as an open-air attraction under the auspices of that wholesome, delicious, incomparable, refreshing, foaming but non-alcoholic beverage — Juniper Ade! Juniper Ade, my friends, that human boon! Delightful and refreshing to young and old! Recommended by all doctors, too."[10]

Quack medicine though it was, Juniper Ade did little good but apparently little harm and when mixed with gin was a welcome cocktail. But, using the skills of the medical huckster, Lundin became a favorite of Chicago's German and Scandinavian organizations and won a seat in the United States House of Representatives, thus becoming a factor in Chicago politics. Using the florid tactics of a huckster of patent medicine, he forced Bill Lorimer and eventually Bill Thompson down the throats of Chicagoans.

At Sea in Politics

For William Hale Thompson the taste of politics was in his mouth and he liked it. The lure of yachting on the Great Lakes was also irresistible, and in the years between 1903 and 1915, Thompson remained a political amateur, a playboy politician. When Lorimer floated the idea of running Thompson for mayor, the latter insisted, on November 7, 1902, "I have no political ambitions—at least not so far as the mayoralty is concerned."[11] He was probably not telling the truth. But, what was the truth?

With Lorimer down, the "Poor Swede" Lundin worked tirelessly to rebuild the Illinois Republican Party in his image. Dissension among Democrats seemed to auger well for a Republican victory in Chicago, but who was the candidate who could unite the various constituencies? "A candidate who hoped to win in 1915," pondered Lundin, "would have to be good-looking to attract the ladies, pleasing to the varied elements in his new organization, and a man who would speak firmly for reform and purity in politics."[12] Lundin thought he found his man in William Thompson.

Lorimer was not to be pushed aside so easily. In August 1914, as the "Guns of August" were booming in Europe, the Republicans held their annual picnic in Kolze's Electric Park. Although he had been ousted from the U.S. Senate, although the Illinois state bank examiner had closed his LaSalle Street Trust and Savings Bank—and he and fourteen associates were awaiting trial on charges of embezzlement—Lorimer emerged from political oblivion.

On the hottest day of the year, Lorimer urged his sweating listeners to support William Hale Thompson as the next mayor of Chicago. Bill Thompson, likewise dripping with perspiration, welcomed Lorimer's support, promised to fight those who "tried to ruin the name of an honest and honorable man," and announced that Bill Thompson "will be your candidate for mayor!"[13]

Fred Lundin was furious. He thought he had weaned the party away from Lorimerism, but Thompson's pledge to redeem the reputation of the "Blonde Boss" seemed to undermine Lundin's efforts to attract progressives and reformers to the Thompson bandwagon.

> "From now on," said Lundin, "you don't make speeches unless I know about them — and write them for you. We can't take chances."
> "You know best, Congressman," was Thompson's meek response.[14]

With the "Poor Swede" as his mentor, Thompson went on to win the Republican primary and, in the general election, defeat the better-known

William Hale Thompson (center) and his wife (left) voting during mayoral primaries on February 23, 1915. This was the first Chicago mayoral election in which women were allowed to vote. Courtesy of the Chicago Historical Society (DN-0064113, *Chicago Daily News*).

Democratic candidate, county clerk Robert Sweitzer, to become Chicago's mayor. Despite the fury of the campaign, the Chicago newspapers did not initially give the rival candidates front-page space. There was, after all, a war in Europe going on and in Havana, Cuba, Jess Willard was training for his prize fight with the champ, Jack Johnson. The Thompson-Sweitzer contest was often a poor third in coverage to the war between France and Germany and the fisticuffs between Willard and Johnson. With all that was going on could Thompson's campaign slogan, "All for Chicago and Chicago for All," make a hit with the voters? Not imaginative, but apparently adequate.

On election day the polls opened at 6:00 A.M., and at the polling places long lines had already formed. The police were hard pressed to control the more than usual violence that prevailed at the polls. Thompson, Lundin, and the other major players in the Thompson entourage went to their suite of rooms in the LaSalle Hotel to await the election returns. When the vote was counted there were 398,538 for Thompson and 251,061 for Sweitzer. Lundin's strategy had clearly worked; his estimate of the extent of the Thompson victory had been uncannily accurate.

Early the next morning, with the cowboy hat he had never been without during the campaign, Thompson posed for pictures, including one with Mrs. Mary M. Conrad, Chicago's oldest voter, who at 102 was a great supporter of the mayor-elect. "Then our hero went for a walk with the Missus, in the course of which he bowed 433 times and shook 77 hands."[15] At that moment, nothing seemed beyond the political reach of "Big Bill" Thompson. "You'll be President someday," many of his loyal supporters assured him.

Charles Wheeler, the *Chicago Tribune's* political expert wrote: "No mayor ever entered the city hall with such a backing, such apparently universal good will and sincere spirit of cooperation. If he doesn't make good he will be the most despised mayor of the whole lot."[16] Although Bill Thompson had three opportunities to "make good" as mayor, he failed to do so. Instead, he went on to be rated as the worst mayor in American history.

3

To Hell with the People

On April 26, 1915, Mayor Thompson bounced into his office, put his elbows for the first time on the new mahogany desk presented to him by the yacht club, and in a burst of energy promptly went about the business of being mayor of Chicago.

Although the *Chicago Tribune* failed to endorse him, one of Bill Thompson's first acts as mayor was to send a thank-you note to its editors. "I desire to thank you for the fair manner in which you gave me an opportunity through the columns of your paper to present my candidacy and the principles for which I stood."[1] For its part, the *Tribune* urged its readers to reserve judgment. Despite the ballyhoo of the campaign, the outbreaks of violence, the extravagant rhetoric, the bigger-than-life parades, the *Tribune* asserted, "We are not headed for the bow-wows."[2]

The attempt at making peace with Victor Lawson, the owner of the *Daily News*, was less successful. In a meeting at Chicago's LaSalle Hotel, Lawson listened as "Big Bill" repeatedly assured him that "I'm gonna be a good mayor." To which Lawson replied, "Mr. Thompson, everything you do as mayor that is beneficial to Chicago will meet with the approval of the *Daily News*. I should be lacking in frankness, however, if I did not say to you now that I have no confidence in either you or your chief supporters."[3]

The Mayor's Political Honeymoon

During the early days of his administration, the new mayor surprised his critics and perhaps himself with the success of his initiatives. Among the first of these was his settlement of the strike of streetcar and elevated railway workers. Unable to prevail on the traction barons to augment pitifully small wages, their labor leaders took 15,000 traction workers off their jobs on June 14, 1915. "Big Bill" knew that Chicagoans would not long be content with getting to work on foot, bicycle, buggy, or horseback, and his first inclination was to end the strike by force and encourage the traction owners to hire strikebreakers. He ordered his new chief of police, Charles Healey, to issue 500,000 additional rounds of ammunition and planned to hire additional police. But, as violence appeared unlikely to get the strikers back to work any time soon, he listened to the advice of the transportation committee of the city council and wisely sought negotiation instead.

He orchestrated a meeting in his office of union leaders, traction owners, and members of the transportation committee. Before long the group agreed that the mayor would serve as arbitrator. Bill locked the door, sent out for coffee and sandwiches, and insisted that the group meet throughout the night. To distract them and make their negotiations less controversial, "Big Bill" fell back on what he knew best — yacht racing. He filled a tub of water, placed several toy boats in it, and urged the negotiators to bet on which of the toy boats would reach the end of the bathtub first. By morning, the group knew each other better. They knew that the mayor needed a settlement, the public would not long tolerate the inconvenience of a strike in transportation, and the strikers needed better wages. A settlement was agreed to, and the workers went back to work after an absence of but fifty-three hours. The new mayor was triumphant and wallowed in the praise heaped upon him. *Chicago Commerce* magazine thanked him in a front-page editorial.

However, Bill Thompson was no friend of labor. When Sidney Hillman, representing garment workers, sought a meeting with him to protest police action against pickets, Thompson refused to see him. Thompson opposed labor unions among civil servants and municipal employees such as police, sanitation workers, and teachers. He was eager to settle the strike of workers not out of sympathy for the motormen, conductors, and maintenance workers and the merits of their cause, about which he cared little and knew less, but because he understood the political implications of a prolonged work stoppage so early in his administration and the danger of such a stoppage on his long-term plans for further political office.

In response to the support he had received from temperance and reform groups generally, this hard-drinking mayor moved to enforce a state law, unenforced in Chicago since 1870, requiring saloons to be closed on Sunday. In accordance with a city ordinance, deplored by "drys" and lauded by "wets," many saloons had in fact been open on Sunday. As he was empowered to do, the mayor closed the saloons beginning on the first

Sunday of October 1915. So that they would not be fined up to $200, as the law required, saloon owners kept the doors of 7,150 saloons closed for the Lord's Day, and Chicagoans deplored "the demise of friendship's social glass."[4] The president of the Women's Christian Temperance Union, Anna Gordon, exulted, "We thank you, Mayor Thompson, we thank you." The evangelist Billy Sunday praised the mayor for his "grit" and was sure that Bill Thompson's courage sent "the devil [to] bed with pneumonia."[5]

The euphoria of the reformers did not last. Police Chief Healy's flying squad of police enforcers discovered that Sunday saloon closings were being selectively applied in many cases in that the saloons of prominent criminals were often allowed, quietly, to open. But William Hale Thompson was not a man to be troubled by doubts or fears of inconsistency. The saloons had been at least temporarily closed on Sunday, he had won at least the temporary praise of the reformers, and he could say at least that he had fulfilled one of his campaign promises. As he began his mayoralty administration, "Big Bill" was content.

He likewise savored the praise heaped upon him when he returned from a journey to the West Coast to attend the Chicago and Illinois days at the Panama Pacific International Exposition in San Francisco. Three trainloads of politicos headed for California. On the William Hale Thompson Special, a hundred of the most distinguished politicians had the privilege of sharing the train with the mayor. On the second train was the first regiment of the Illinois National Guard and the entire band. The third train carried other distinguished politicians, mostly from Governor Edward F. Dunne's entourage. "The Thompson" rolled slowly through the countryside giving the nation a chance to see the new and popular mayor of Chicago, and one who had at least one eye cast in the direction of the White House. On this triumphal train ride nothing seemed impossible and Bill Thompson's political future looked cloudless.

"We're at the Feed-Box Now"

The mayor appeared ready to build upon his early record of accomplishments by making appointments to his administration of able and competent people. For his chief of police he chose Captain Charles C. Healey, head of the Chicago police department traffic division and a man who had allegedly never tasted liquor. He was as decent and honorable a police chief an under-financed police department could afford. But the love affair with Healey would not last, and before long Healey resigned under pressure. During the Thompson administrations the office of police chief would become something of a revolving door.

Thompson appointed his millionaire friend and companion, Eugene R. Pike, to the position of city comptroller, and another millionaire, William R. Moorehouse, as commissioner of public works. To his long-time associate and Lundin confidant, Dr. John Dill Robertson, went the position of health commissioner despite protests from the medical community. James Hamilton Lewis, a fine lawyer, was appointed corporate counsel. The appointment was a complete surprise because Lewis was a Democrat and had contributed nothing to the Thompson campaign. Lewis, too, resigned in a year and a half and was replaced by the more flexible Samuel Ettelson. But the lion's share of responsibility for distributing political plumbs was given to the gray eminence behind Thompson's reach for political stardom — Fred Lundin.

"Here it is, you play with it," asserted the new mayor as he handed over the city payroll to Fred Lundin.[6] To his inner circle, of patronage handlers the "Poor Swede" offered the following advice, "To hell with the public. We're at the feed-box now."[7] The political honeymoon of Thompson's early days as mayor was made-to-order for Lundin, who used the mayor's early favorable press and public popularity as a cover for building the Thompson political machine.

Shrewd enough to stay away from city hall and out of the mayor's cabinet, Lundin, in the "second city hall" as his office in the Sherman Hotel was called, kept careful tally of who could be relied upon to rally in times of stress, to march in parades in times when showmanship appeared to be in order, or to demonstrate at a mass meeting when that tactic was called for. In dispensing jobs Lundin ran roughshod over the civil service law requiring that appointments be made on the basis of merit as objectively measured. Lundin's chief instrument for making such appointments was to designate them as "temporary" and to renew the appointment periodically so long as the incumbent continued to demonstrate loyalty to the Thompson political machine rather than performance on the job.

The most tragic victim of the Lundin system of making appointments may best be illustrated in the case of Dr. Theodore B. Sachs, an expert in pulmonary medicine and godfather of the Chicago Municipal Tuberculosis Sanatorium, which he had pioneered and led for many years. Although he enjoyed a national and international medical reputation, this distinguished physician could not escape the greedy reach of the Lundin machine, which sought to replace the good doctor with a political appointment more amenable to the discipline of party politics.

Mayor Thompson, under pressure to reappoint Sachs, reluctantly did so. But Lundin and his political lackey, Hospital Commissioner Robertson, would not be so easily thwarted. At the insistence of Lundin and

Robertson, the mayor did an abrupt turn around and proceeded to vilify Sachs for incompetence, extravagance, and inefficiency, with a view toward removing him from office. Demonstrating his servility to Lundin, an unthinking mayor demonstrated his indifference to the public weal, and absurdly asserted that Dr. Sachs had been "the worst [appointment] which I have made thus far." Thompson's badgering of Dr. Sachs continued mercilessly until this gentle, able man took his own life. In his suicide note addressed "To the People of Chicago," Dr. Sachs wrote, "The community should resist any attempt by unscrupulous contractors to appropriate money which belongs to the sick and the poor. Unscrupulous politicians should be thwarted."[8]

While the dismissal of Sachs as head of the Chicago Municipal Tuberculosis Sanatorium stirred anxiety among Chicago's Jews, it was not anti-Semitism that motivated the mayor's attack on Dr. Sachs but the opportunity, insensitive as it was, to secure yet another position for the insatiable need for patronage, power, and reelection. While the Sachs scandal became something of a rallying cry for Chicago's reformers, Thompson, under the tutelage of Lundin, politicized and debased everything he touched.

"Big Bill" and Ethnic Chicago

In September 1917, from a lamppost in Chicago's Grant Park, the fat figure of Mayor William Hale Thompson was hanged in effigy by the Society of Veterans of Foreign Wars. What had he done? The United States had been at war with Germany for five months. But there were those for whom American participation in the World War was a mistake at best and probably a disaster.

Because World War I involved the homelands of hundreds of thousands of immigrants, Chicago's religious and ethnic rivalries surfaced and created a situation made to order for ethnic appeals and manipulation of the city's political rivals. When Thompson recognized the large numbers of Germans and their descendants in Chicago, he won their friendship and often their vote. The "solid" Jewish wards were for Thompson as were the "solid" Irish ones. Thompson had the capacity of successfully uniting these groups behind him during his early mayoral campaigns.

However, ethnic groups in Chicago were fickle, bipartisan, and in no party's pocket. William Hale Thompson could not keep their loyalty for long nor was it ever total, except perhaps among African-Americans. When Thompson ran in 1915, with World War I as the backdrop to his first campaign, no one was better in playing to ethnic interests than Thompson. The once and future mayor's essential demagogic character may best be seen in his use of ethnicity to his immediate advantage, now solicitous of ethnic groups, then hostile. "Big Bill" played to ethnic stereotypes and prejudices with the zeal and practiced skill of the political demagogue.

Using data based on school census reports, Bill Thompson asserted in April 1917 that Chicago was "the sixth largest German city in the world, the second largest Bohemian, the second largest Norwegian, and the second largest Polish."[9] There were, in fact, in "Big Bill's" Chicago about 450,000 Germans; 400,000 Poles; 300,000 Irish; 200,000 Italians; 200,000 Czechoslovaks; and 125,000 Swedes. Most of these groups opposed the war with varying degrees of intensity. German-Americans deplored their homeland being pilloried as a land of "barbaric Huns" who committed unspeakable atrocities on women and children. Irish-Americans were opposed to American soldiers fighting in alliance with England, the country that, in their view, was holding their Irish homeland in thrall. In his stance in support of the meeting of pacifists, Thompson was serving the cause of freedom of expression and assembly, but he was also playing to the ethnic interests of Chicagoans who opposed a war against their former homelands.

The mayor cared for little other than securing the German vote. Labeled "Kaiser Bill" by those who resented what they perceived to be his support for the enemy, he incidentally performed a service for them in mitigating the anti–German hysteria which was characteristic of the war years in Chicago and in America generally. German-Americans saw through "Big Bill's" condescension, but well after the war was over many Chicagoans of German background continued to support him, albeit with less and less enthusiasm. As one voter commented, "Damn him, we know he's no good, but he made life livable for us in 1918, and he gets our votes."[10]

Chicago had never been a city of brotherly love. Ethnic rivalries were the rule rather than the exception, and frictions among ethnic groups, often based on prejudices and stereotypes from their former homelands, proved common. When the war was over, repressed tensions exploded and were difficult to resolve inasmuch as proximate causes were not necessarily the real ones.

Whereas Poles and Jews once shared Douglas Park on Chicago's West Side, in 1919 Jews charged Poles with harassment and blamed them for the pogroms (anti–Semitic attacks against Jews) which continued in Poland. On June 8, 1919, about 8,000 Chicago Jews gathered at Twelfth Street and Kedzie in anticipation of an attack in Douglas Park by 5,000 Poles. An extra 250 police were required to keep a temporary peace. However, when a rumor spread that a Jewish grocer had killed a Polish boy, friction between Jew and Pole spread to southeast Chicago, where 3,000 Poles milled about the streets for three days around the Fourth of July. Eighteen of the Polish rioters were fined. "Big Bill," however, was careful to praise the part the Polish people and their officers had played in bringing independence from England to the American colonies.

"Big Bill" and Black Chicago

Between 1916 and 1919, some 50,000 Southern blacks settled in Chicago, and during the 1920s the city became the home of an additional 120,000. To African-American migrants Chicago held the promise of a level of economic well-being of which they could only dream in the South. In the South, as sharecroppers or tenant farmers, blacks could earn but $2 to $3 a week, while workers in Chicago in 1916 could earn between $2 to $2.50 a day. Migrating Southern African-Americans found jobs in Chicago's steel and meat-packing industries and as Pullman railcar porters and in Pullman repair shops. African-Americans worked in laundries and tanneries and took jobs as janitors, servants, elevator operators, and waiters. However menial the employment, it seemed to the migrants far better than the poorly paid, back-breaking work on a Southern farm cultivating tobacco or cotton.

Moreover, whatever the city's shortcomings, to migrating blacks the trek to Chicago promised relief from unbearable racial discrimination. In Chicago, most blacks enjoyed a degree of freedom they dared not expect in the South. In Chicago, they could vote and could send their children to better, if still segregated, schools. One African-American recalled her experience when she boarded a Chicago streetcar for the first time and took a seat next to whites: "I just held my breath for I thought any minute they would start something. Then I saw nobody noticed it, and I just thought this is a real place for Negroes."[11] To recent migrants of African-Americans from the South, Chicago was a "promised land," a land of milk and honey and a land of freedom and opportunity.

The *Chicago Defender*, a black-owned newspaper, was not unaware that migrating blacks faced many obstacles in Chicago, not the least was living in one of the most segregated black ghettos in America. But the writer Langston Hughes, who grew up in Chicago's Black Belt, recalled its vibrancy in 1918: "South State Street was in its glory then, a teeming Negro street with crowded theaters, restaurants, and cabarets. And excitement from noon to noon. Midnight was like day. The street was full of workers and gamblers, prostitutes and pimps, church folks and sinners."[12]

Mayor Bill Thompson shared the racial and religious prejudices of his time and place, but votes were votes and that's all that mattered. The mayor's commitment to African-Americans was largely politically motivated and did not draw on genuine concerns for racial justice or against racial inequality. That Thompson's commitment to African-Americans was severely proscribed was evident when he did not protest when, in February 1917, a Cornell-trained black physician, Dr. Roscoe Giles, was removed six hours after taking the job at the municipal tuberculosis sanitarium because white patients objected to the doctor's color. When, in the same year, African-American alderman Oscar De Priest was arrested on vice charges, Mayor Thompson did not hasten to his support.[13] Little wonder then that Chicago's blacks felt that while they were better off in Chicago than in the South, their living conditions and job opportunities were still not good enough. Many whites, on the other hand, felt that blacks were having it too good in Chicago.

Nevertheless, African-Americans, mostly newly arrived in Chicago, were likewise among Thompson's supporters, and by mutilating civil service, he was free to reward this constituency as well. Since they were good Republicans and had carried the Second Ward for Thompson, he felt obligated to reward them for their loyalty, and he did so. By September 1915, there were 700 black municipal employees, an increase of 200 from the previous administration. At a time when racism was the rule rather than the exception, the increase in the number of African-American appointments to positions in Chicago's municipal government was widely noted and not well tolerated. A parody described Thompson's city hall as "An Amazingly Stupendous Production of the Pathetic Melodrama Uncle Tom's Cabin in Many Acts" with "Big Bill" Thompson portrayed in the role of Uncle Tom.

Regardless, three months after he began his second term as mayor, one of the greatest race riots of urban America burst forth. The race riot of 1919 would test the mettle of the mayor, and he would barely pass.

Chicago's Wentworth Avenue was the boundary that separated the South Side's Black Belt from the adjoining Irish neighborhood. To cross the line was to risk one's life. On Sunday, July 27, 1919, with the temperatures soaring well into the 90s, several black teenagers were swimming in Lake Michigan from their segregated Twenty-fifth Street (blacks only) beach when they drifted over into the Twenty-ninth Street (whites only) beach. A man on shore began throwing rocks at the black children, and one, Eugene Williams, was hit in the forehead and drowned. His terrified companions reported what happened to a black policeman at the Twenty-fifth Street beach. The boys and the black policeman apprehended the man who had killed Williams at the Twenty-ninth Street beach, but Daniel

Callahan, a white policeman on that beach, refused to arrest him and prevented the black policeman from doing so. When the boys reported the miscarriage of justice to black adults at the Twenty-fifth Street beach, an angry crowd of blacks invaded the white beach; rock throwing ensued, gun shots rang out, one black man was arrested, and city-wide rioting began.

Mayor Thompson was in Cheyenne, Wyoming, for the Frontier Days celebration when the riots began, but when he returned by train to Chicago the race riot was fully blown and entirely in his lap. Advised early on that the Chicago police were inadequate to the task of stopping the riot and that the state militia needed to be called upon, Mayor Thompson initially rejected the advice. However, when the bloody nature of the rioting became clear to him, he urged Governor Frank Lowden to mobilize the state militia and hold them in readiness. Some 3,500 militiamen were assembled in Chicago's armories, but the mayor was still reluctant to use them despite the obvious inability of the Chicago police to restore peace to the city. It was not until July 30, and only after repeated urging by Chicago's African-American leadership, that Thompson called upon the governor to release the state militia.

The 1919 race riot ended after six days and required the arrival of the Illinois National Guard. The result was that 15 whites and 23 blacks had been killed and 500 Chicagoans injured. More than 3,000 city residents were left homeless because their homes had been set on fire.

Despite his uneven, unsure handling of the race riot of 1919, the political love affair between Thompson and Chicago's African-Americans continued. While Chicago's blacks recognized the shortcomings of their mayor, "Big Bill" remained one of the few whites they felt they could count on, and they continued to support him throughout his political career. Despite some backing and filing on race questions, African-Americans of Chicago viewed Mayor Thompson as a staunch friend. When, in 1919, he began his campaign for a second term as mayor of Chicago in a speech in Chicago's Second Ward, Thompson said: "Enemies have tried to divide us—they are trying to divide us now, but we have always stood together and we always will. I've given you a square deal and you've given a square deal to me."[14] An African-American in the audience was moved to cry out, "You're my brother." The overwhelming majority of Chicago's blacks agreed with the expressed sentiment.

Thompson was justifiably proud of his association with Chicago's African-American community. By the time he ended his third term as mayor, 14 percent of the city's legal department, including 6 assistant corporation counsels, would be black, and the number of African-American policemen rose from 50 in 1914 to 137 in 1930. This increase in the number of African-American employees placed on the payroll of the city of Chicago could not have been accomplished without bending the civil service regulations of the city. "Thompson niggers," as they were derisively referred to by heads of various agencies, were clearly unwelcome and often resented in the agencies for which they worked, but Thompson stood by black municipal employees throughout his mayoralty and was more loyal to them than were some of the reform mayors who followed him.[15]

In 1927, as he launched his campaign to serve as Chicago's mayor for the third time, Thompson, before an African-American audience of 10,000, struck a sympathetic note when he deplored "police terror" as when police, with excessive zeal, more vigorously enforced prohibition violations among Chicago's blacks than among Chicago's other ethnic groups. Moreover, Thompson stunned Chicago's whites by embracing an African-American child. A cartoon showing Thompson kissing a black child was distributed by the Democratic Party with the warning, "Do you want Negroes or White Men to Run Chicago?"[16] In defense, Thompson was quoted in the *Chicago Defender* as saying, "The black finger that is good enough to pull a trigger in defense of the American flag is good enough to mark a ballot."[17] In 1919, Thompson won 78 percent of the African-American vote and 93 percent in 1927.

"It Is My Duty ... I Will Run"

On November 30, 1918, with the war now over, Lundin and a delegation of Thompson supporters called upon the mayor to run for a second term:

> "Because you have given Chicago a clean, constructive and economical administration, because honesty has been the rule and not the exception in municipal service, because you have appointed competent administrators and heads of departments, because you have followed the law yourself and enjoined its obedience on others; because you have stood against the encroachment on human rights of all powerful interests and thereby incurred enmity and vengeance as reflected in Chicago's daily newspapers, we join in urging you to become a candidate for reelection!"
> "Big Bill" proudly responded, "I am honored that you ask me. It is my duty to obey. I will run."[18]

When "Big Bill" won reelection as Chicago's mayor in 1919, he knew that he had some political life left. When he prevailed upon the Republican

Party to hold its presidential nominating convention in Chicago in 1920, "Big Bill" knew that despite his antiwar stand, his rehabilitation as a good Republican and a patriot was well on its way. When at that convention he thwarted Governor Frank O. Lowden's bid for the presidential nomination, he knew that he had retained some political clout.

Bill Thompson's nomination for a second term as Chicago's mayor was, in fact, a consolation prize offered by Fred Lundin in view of his candidate's failure to secure the Republican nomination for the United States Senate. In 1918, Lundin thought that he could make Bill Thompson a United States senator despite Thompson's unpopularity in view of his many-times-expressed lack of enthusiasm for American efforts during the world war. Lundin believed that voters had short memories, and if his protégé would adopt a posture of unqualified Americanism, the voters of Illinois would readily forget his foot dragging during World War I. With this strategy in mind, Mayor Thompson told an audience meeting in the lodge of the Loyal Order of Moose in Rockford, Illinois, in 1918, that when the war was over he wanted America to be free of all foreign alliances: "I'm for America first!"

This campaign mantra was, however, not enough to overcome the hostility of those who supported the war and to whom William Hale Thompson was still remembered as "Kaiser Bill." The "Poor Swede's" view was that anti–Wilson Democrats, antiwar Republicans, and Chicago's large pro–German population would support William Hale Thompson in the Republican primary and in the campaign that followed. But, this time, Fred Lundin was wrong.

The manager of a theater in Edwardsville canceled Thompson's engagement to speak since the candidate was not "a hundred percent" loyal American. In Kankakee, mobs jeered and pro–Thompson banners were destroyed. In Springfield, former president Theodore Roosevelt asserted that Thompson's nomination would "give satisfaction to Germany ... and be hailed with joy ... by disloyal people here and enemies abroad."

In the primary, Thompson lost the Republican nomination for United States senator to Congressman Medill McCormick, the brother of the owner of the *Chicago Tribune* and one of Thompson's severest critics. McCormick, without the support of Chicago's Republican mayor, went on to defeat the Democratic senatorial incumbent, J. Hamilton Lewis. While Illinois Germans and African-Americans supported Thompson's senatorial ambitions, those votes were not enough to ensure his nomination.

While Fred Lundin had misjudged the temper of Illinois voters, he guessed the feelings of Chicago's voters with reasonable accuracy. Thompson handily won the primary to become the Republican Party's candidate for Chicago's mayor for a second time. As in 1915, his Democratic opponent was a Catholic of German origin, Robert Sweitzer, who had the support of George E. Brennan, boss of Chicago's Democrats. Maclay Hoyne, who had steadily inveighed against "Big Bill," was disappointed in Brennan's choice and unwisely presented himself as a third-party candidate.

In a clever campaign, Fred Lundin had his candidate concentrate his efforts in African-American wards and in wards containing large numbers of disaffected anti–British Irish and those of German birth or descent. The latter remembered Bill Thompson's sympathies during the war, and the Irish appreciated the mayor's call for Irish home rule. Through these strategies "Big Bill," on April Fool's Day, won a squeaker of an election by a margin of but 21,000 votes, of which 11,000 came from the wards in which African-Americans lived. When the votes were tallied, Thompson won with 259,828; Sweitzer was right behind with 238,206; and Hoyne with a respectable 110,851. Thompson won his second term as mayor a mere seven months after his defeat in his race for a seat in the Senate against McCormick.

Chicagoans, perhaps, were not surprised by the repeat victory of William Hale Thompson. Fred Lundin appeared to be a more subtle political boss than George E. Brennan, his opposite number in the Democratic Party. Moreover, the votes of Democrats had been split by the ill-advised Hoyne candidacy. But Thompson's reelection caught Americans outside Chicago, at least as expressed in their newspapers, quite by surprise. How could a "Kaiser Bill" possibly be reelected mayor of America's second largest city? "Poor Old Chicago!" was the headline in the *Kansas City Star*. "CHICAGO'S SHAME!" was the rueful headline in the New Haven *Journal-Courier*. *The New York Times* rather pompously found in the reelection of Thompson "a state of mind very close to that out of which Bolshevism arises overseas."[19]

On the other hand, *The Republican,* the paper of Chicago's Republican Party, was sure that Bill Thompson's reelection as that city's mayor was a victory for all Chicagoans. He was a man who "could be neither BOUGHT, BOSSED NOR BLUFFED."[20]

The year 1920 would be a good one for Republicans. "Big Bill" was already Chicago's mayor, and by November, Warren G. Harding became president of the United States in a landslide. Len Small became the Republican governor of Illinois, and Robert Emmet Crowe became the Republican state's attorney in Cook County, Illinois. Every county and every office in the state went to the Republicans. Outside his office in city hall, "Big Bill" exulted, "The roof is off!" "We ate 'em alive!" Thompson shrieked,

"We ate 'em alive with their clothes on!" [21] In New York Michael J. Faherty, in a speech to the American Road Builders Association of which he was president, told a rapt audience, "William Hale Thompson is the greatest statesman Illinois has ever had since Abraham Lincoln! As a politician he is without peer and we believe he will be President in four years!"[22]

However, the omens for a bright and perky start to "Big Bill's" second term as Chicago's mayor were not good. Candidates and voters alike had to fight a massive epidemic of influenza, and in 1919 the White Sox were favored to win the World Series against Cincinnati, but seven White Sox players decided to throw the game in one of baseball's great scandals. His second term as Chicago's mayor would, likewise, prove to be one rocked by political scandal.

A Second Term for "Big Bill"

As he began his second term as Chicago's mayor, William Hale Thompson was beginning to show his age. As an observer noted, his eyes were "heavy and somewhat sad, mouth lax and heavy and not reassuring except when he smiles, and then the smile irradiates the whole face ... [his] complexion still florid as in the old days, eyebrows heavy and give the face strength; on the whole a massive head, poised on a powerful neck."[23] If he was losing his youth, and if his movements already gave the impression of indolence and inertia, his political power was at its zenith. He formed an alliance with the obedient and fawning Len Small, the Republican governor of Illinois, and with Robert E. Crowe, who had been the youngest chief justice in the history of Chicago's criminal court, as state's attorney. But with power in their hands, the Lundin/Thompson alliance began to fray and then to break.

Acting on his own initiative, and without consulting Lundin, "Big Bill" appointed his secretary, Charles E. Fitzmorris, as his chief of police with orders to "clear out the crooks." The new police chief, at 36 the youngest in Chicago's history, was appointed in response to cries that crime in Chicago had grown worse as rival gangs were busily carving up their turf to sell illicit wine, beer, and whisky in defiance of the Volstead Act, which went into effect January 16, 1920.

The *Chicago Tribune* filed a suit charging George F. Harding, Michael J. Faherty, and "Big Bill" Thompson in a scheme to defraud the city of $2,876,063. These were allegedly overpayments and kickbacks to so-called experts who were brought in to provide advice on the building of the Michigan Avenue Bridge. The "experts' fees" case, as it was called, dragged on for two years, involved over 100 witnesses, and required 11,000 pages of testimony and 3,000 exhibits. Judge Hugo Friend in circuit court was hardly friendly when he ruled that Thompson and his codefendants were to return to the city the sum of $2,245,604. Thompson, in an hysterical outburst, declared, "They've ruined me! They're going to take everything I've got! The sonsofbitches have ruined me."[24]

Lundin and Thompson nominated a new list of judges that they confidently expected to be elected. But the Democrats and the Chicago Bar Association drew up their own list of judicial candidates. In an election that ordinarily aroused little interest, the election of judges piqued the interest of Chicago good-government types, and with the cry, "Stop the City Hall from Seizing the Judiciary," the voters, to Lundin's astonishment, did just that. His judicial nominees were decisively defeated. Did the defeat of the Lundin/Thompson judicial candidates represent a breach in the armor of a heretofore almost invincible political machine, or was it just a temporary setback?

The next stop in what Lundin/Thompson hoped would be a comeback effort was in Springfield, Illinois, where the duo sought passage of their proposed "five-cent fare" transportation bill. The Corporation counsel, state senator and ally of Lundin/Thompson, Samuel Ettelson, assured the pair that the transportation bill would easily pass, but the pattern of defeat dogged the now vulnerable Republican political machine. When the five-cent transportation bill came up for a vote, it fell short by two votes of the required majority. Scurrying around in the corridors of the state capitol to round up additional votes availed nothing but additional humiliation. With a view toward further embarrassing "Big Bill's" ally, Governor Len Small was indicted for allegedly embezzling $2 million when he had been state treasurer. Had the Lundin/Thompson machine not suffered a series of highly visible defeats, Governor Small might never have been indicted. Even *The New York Times* noted the decline in Thompson's political fortunes and was moved to editorialize with considerable satisfaction that the Chicago City Hall machine "of which Fred Lundin is the brains and William Hale Thompson was the figurehead" was coming to a close.[25]

State's Attorney Crowe, although elected with substantial help of the Lundin/Thompson crowd, had an independent streak and, sensing the machine's weakness, made a bid to separate himself from the grubbiness of machine politics in Chicago. After he complained initially that Fitzmorris, Thompson's chief of police, after a good start, had become ineffective in reducing crime in Chicago, Crowe launched an independent investigation of Chicago's police. Crowe asked for forty police to be assigned to the state's attorney for the purpose of investigating the activities of the police department. While Fitzmorris understandably resisted the request, he was forced to comply by Mayor Thompson, who thought that Crowe would be mollified. Under Crowe's supervision, a character with a less-than-sterling reputation for probity, the investigation essentially came to naught. But Crowe was not through taking advantage of the obvious weakness to the Lundin/Thompson forces and the growing tension between the two men that a series of defeats only exacerbated. Crowe thought he found a fruitful field upon which to launch a further attack in the scandals of the Chicago Board of Education.

The investigation into scandals in the administration of Chicago's public schools led by Crowe linked Fred Lundin directly to financial abuse in the management of the city's schools. The whiff of scandal was strong enough to prompt Lundin to leave town in haste and to leave a bewildered Mayor Thompson to declare that he had no further plans to run for reelection. On the day after "Big Bill's" announcement that he would not run for mayor again, the grand jury charged that Lundin and twenty-three other conspirators had robbed the school treasury of over a million dollars. They stole the money by faking contracts, overpaying for school supplies, graft, bribery, and shakedowns, thereby defrauding the taxpayers of Chicago. The trial that followed provided a sordid overview of assorted political manipulations for personal gain and provided further evidence that under Thompson civic virtue had suffered a near-mortal blow.[26]

Lundin remained "on the lam" in Minnesota, then in Havana, but eventually he showed up in court with Chicago's finest criminal lawyers—Chris Erbstein and the famous Clarence Darrow. In a trial that lasted three months the jury heard how the school board, under the presidency of a Lundin acolyte, Edwin S. Davis, had approved paying $7,500 for boilers that could easily be bought for $4,000 and renting buses for handicapped children for $28.50 a day that could be rented for less than half that amount. For potato peelers the school board paid $133, for kitchen tables $106, and for electric hand driers $133. Phonographs worth $70 had been bought from a "preferred" dealer for $187. Doors for new school buildings could be bought only through Lundin's own Central Metallic Door Company. Board President Davis, the jury heard, had received 50 cents for each ton of coal bought by the city, and Lundin received 30 percent of the insurance premiums paid by the schools.

Despite the massive evidence against him, Lundin sat serenely in the courtroom and played with his black string tie. He gloated when his high-priced attorneys brought hostile witnesses to tears and was assured when Darrow asserted that the case was "a conspiracy engineered by the enemies of William Hale Thompson and Fred Lundin." Darrow admitted that Lundin had engaged in business enterprises but that he did no business with the school board.

Despite the growing tension between them, "Big Bill" hurried back from a vacation in Hawaii to testify in Lundin's behalf. On the stand and without blinking, he asserted that Lundin had never interfered with city business and that the Republican Party was on guard against politics in the police and on the school board. In his testimony he developed the amazing theory of personnel administration according to which it is more important to have appointees who are "serviceably sound" rather than perfect. This was a lesson he had gleaned when, as a young cowboy, he sought to buy a perfect horse but could not find one until an old Texas rancher assured him that he would never find a perfect horse but that his choices would be much greater and he would be better served if he found one that was "serviceably sound."

Lundin, the only one of the twenty-three defendants who was permitted to testify, played to the hilt the role of the "Poor Swede" and "Insignificant Me" and was unerringly led to reveal his humble beginnings as a shoeshine boy, peddler of pills, hawker of newspapers, and distributor of Juniper Ade. Bill Thompson, he assured the jurors in a soft but confident tone, was "a man of strong character, integrity and courage, and so few have that in public life." Before leaving the courtroom to deliberate, the jurors once again heard Darrow intone, "This is an infamous conspiracy against the liberties of man!"

In four hours, the jury found Lundin and his fellow defendants not guilty. Upon hearing the verdict, a grinning Lundin said to his weeping wife, "C'mon kid, let's go home."

Despite the acquittal of the "Poor Swede," the load of scandal was too much even for the broad back and thick skin of "Big Bill" to bear. Reluctantly, he withdrew from the 1923 campaign, but in a flatulent, prolix statement he promised, "I wish to make plain my continued interest in public affairs and my willingness to lead or follow in any contests as the people may make manifest their desire."[27]

4

America First

"Big Bill" Thompson out of office was more dangerous than "Big Bill" in office. The now former mayor determined, first, that he would not be forgotten and would remain in the public eye and, second, that he would build a network of allies to whose political success he had contributed by supporting candidates for other state and city offices. But in order to achieve these objectives he took increasingly demagogic positions with such bluster, flamboyance, and political buffoonery that, in the eyes of many Chicagoans, made their city rife for ridicule and caricature. Surprisingly, despite seemingly absurd projects and bizarre conduct, or because of them, a slim majority of Chicago voters in 1927 returned him to office for yet another term.

Because of the break with "Poor Swede" Lundin, Thompson resumed consulting his one-time idol and mentor, the deposed Senator Lorimer. The latter suggested that one way Thompson could climb back into the political hustings was to propose, yet again, building a Great Lakes to the Gulf of Mexico waterway which would make Chicago a massive internal port. But in the ballyhoo years of the 1920s, the decade of flagpole sitters, goldfish swallowers, marathon dancers, freak shows, bathing beauty contests, yellow journalism and lurid headlines, bootleg whiskey and gangland "rubouts" followed by ostentatious funerals, how best to dramatize the need to keep "Big Bill" in the klieg lights of public perception?

In this environment, the former mayor announced that he would lead an expedition into the South Seas to hunt for a tree-climbing fish! William Hale Thompson did not seriously believe in the existence of a tree-climbing fish, but he did believe in the waterway project and he was not about to overestimate the intelligence of Chicago voters by appealing to their reason. Instead, he appealed to their sense of awe and fantasy.

After a few shakedown cruises on the Great Lakes, the *Big Bill*, as the ship especially built for him was called, set out on July 5, 1924, on its expedition. Thompson bet $25,000 on the success of his venture, but there were no takers. Thousands of Chicagoans watched from the Michigan Avenue Bridge as the vessel, adorned with a full-faced portrait of "Big Bill," sailed down the Chicago River into Lake Michigan. Despite its seemingly frivolous nature, the proposed journey was blessed with a supportive letter from President Calvin Coolidge, and his secretary of labor, James Davis, was among the curious who watched the cruise get under way.

The *Big Bill* never sailed the South Seas, and Chicagoans would never see a tree-climbing fish. Long before the ship reached New Orleans Thompson and his companions headed home. The project was, however, at least a partial success in that it helped Chicagoans remember "Big Bill" Thompson and dramatized the need for a Great Lakes–to–Gulf waterway, a project first envisioned by the explorer-priest Father Marquette in 1674 and kept alive by William Hale Thompson 250 years later. Under Thompson's flamboyant leadership the idea of an Illinois waterway was kept before Congress, and President Calvin Coolidge signed the bill for the waterway appropriation. "Big Bill" treasured the pen with which the president signed the waterway appropriation bill and which the president presented to the former mayor of Chicago in recognition of Thompson's leadership.

The "Comeback Kid"

Because the rift with Lundin could never be repaired, Bill Thompson knew that should he choose to run for mayor yet again he would have to build a new political network without the seemingly magical skill of the "Poor Swede." To the surprise of many, his campaign to become Chicago's mayor once again would be remarkably successful and merit him the title "Comeback Kid." But Thompson's third term would be perhaps one too many. During his last term as mayor his more-notorious and ill-conceived deeds and words would contrive to mark him as one of the worst American mayors. He would suffer a nervous breakdown, have an attack of appendicitis, and be ineffective for long periods of time. If he could have peered into a crystal ball, he might not have run. But the taste of political blood was in his mouth, and he yearned to thumb his nose at his enemies and reestablish his reputation as a politician and vote getter.

To lay the foundation for a return to politics, Thompson, toward the end of his second term as Chicago's mayor, published and distributed a pamphlet entitled, "Eight Years of Progress," in which he cited among his many building projects: 89 streets widened, 832 miles of streets paved,

402 miles of sewers constructed, 55 new playgrounds built, the Michigan Avenue bridge completed, and a fish hatchery established in Lincoln Park. He pointed out that the two "Pageants of Progress" he had sponsored had been enormously successful. He did not, of course, say that for much of the building he had undertaken Chicagoans had been overcharged or that the first of the two "Pageants of Progress" was vastly more successful than the second. But, as he left office he concluded, "I bear no ill will toward any person or persons. I shall forget my apparent injuries and shall ever remember all friendships and kindness."[1]

To launch his return to politics, William Hale Thompson used some of his own fortune to establish a radio station on the top of his building, the Wrigley Tower, with the call letters WHT. The purpose of the radio station was to build support for his projects such as the Lakes-to-Gulf waterway, to provide entertainment, and to promote himself. Thompson also sponsored a picnic at the Great Lakes Training Station where 75,000 people enjoyed baseball, music, food, soccer, band concerts, dancing, fireworks, and a vaudeville show. These efforts of buying mass support appeared to be ineffective as by 1926, a year for primaries, no important political faction was as yet supporting his campaign for reelection as mayor.

In order to set the stage for his political comeback in a more systematic fashion, Thompson needed to build a new organization to promote a popular platform. He cemented relationships with former political foes, "men who had called one another 'skunk' and 'rat' and 'thief' and 'crook' and 'liar' and 'bluffer' and worse were allies in a grand union to win power and help 'Big Bill' return to the City Hall."[2]

Early in his precampaign efforts to regain city hall, "Big Bill" formed a political strategy in which he would fight against American membership in the League of Nations and participation in the World Court. His "America First" strategy was a clever political ploy that took advantage of the predominant isolationist sentiment in Illinois and gave him issues against which he could rail rather than assert what he would attempt to achieve as mayor. To establish his "America First" bonifides, he and his new colleagues invited Senator William Borah of Idaho, the chief spokesman for American isolationism, to speak against American involvement in the World Court.

The senator arrived on Washington's Birthday and was greeted at the railroad station by "Big Bill," State's Attorney Robert Crowe, ten bands, and two thousand decorated automobiles. At the Field Museum, where the procession ended, Borah was honored with a seventeen-gun salute. Another parade followed as Borah was installed in Hotel Sherman's palatial presidential suite. Later that night, in Fred Mann's Rainbow Gardens,

Borah took aim at England, the World Court, and the League of Nations. "We cannot trust Europeans," he told a cheering crowd of 15,000. "We have many problems," he asserted, "but the problem most vital to the happiness and to the perpetuity of our American institutions, the policy most essential to peace and justice throughout the world is the preservation of the policies bequeathed by George Washington."[3] The good senator intoned before leaving Chicago for Washington, "Thank God for Chicago." The *Evening Post*, an anti-Thompson journal, grudgingly acknowledged, "It was a big and highly successful show."[4]

As the break with Lundin became bitter, Thompson resorted to ever more demagogic tactics to elbow his way back into politics. Thus it was that he invited Chicagoans to a "debate" at the Cort Theater on April 6, 1926, eight days before the Republican primary between Thompson, his former mentor Fred Lundin, and his former hospitals commissioner and Lundin ally, Dr. John Dill Robertson. Thompson saw to it that his erstwhile allies and current enemies did not appear, instead they were represented by two huge, caged rats from among those that roamed Chicago's meat packing plants, which "Big Bill" brought to the stage and introduced to the audience as "Fred" and "Doc."

> "I want you to meet a couple of fellows you've heard about. This one here on the left is Doc. I can tell him because he hasn't had a bath in twenty years." Waggling his finger at the other rat, "Big Bill" bellowed, "Fred, let me ask you something? Wasn't I the best friend you ever had? Isn't it true that I came home from Honolulu to save you from the penitentiary?... I have learned, Fred, that you are going to flood Chicago with 500,000 copies of lies about me. I know that for many years you have been referred to as 'The Fox' in politics. But now I think this justifies my saying that your moniker ought not to be 'The Fox' but 'The Rat.'"[5]

With encouragement from an appreciative but hardly sophisticated audience, "Big Bill" turned his attention back to "Doc."

> "[D]o you remember how thousands came to me to protest the appointment of yourself as health commissioner? Do you remember, Doc, how a newspaper said I was sacrificing the lives of Chicago children to fulfill a political debt by appointing an incompetent health commissioner? Do you remember how I stood up against them and honored you with that great office? If you do remember you know now why I now call you a rat for turning against me with Lundin!"[6]

The display of rhetoric, crude though it was, was effective. That is, Thompson apologized to the voters for having appointed an obvious incompetent as health commissioner; he recognized his debt to Lundin, but he also reminded his audience that Lundin had, in fact, been guilty of the fraudulent school purchasing practices with which he had been charged. In this outrageous performance, "Big Bill" proved that he had mastered the art of political showmanship and, more frighteningly, that he had also mastered the art of political demagoguery and so helped his political allies win nominations for nine out of ten major county offices. "Big Bill" Thompson, at age 60 and tipping the scales at almost 250 pounds, was once again a factor in Chicago politics.

America First

> "Big Bill the Builder, in person-n! See Bill Thompson, friend of the people!"
> Three thousand people hurry in. The meeting opens with the singing of the national anthem.
> The chairman shouts: "Our speaker, the Honorable William Hale Thompson is on the way."
> The audience cheers.
> Outside a bugle blares. Into the hall march two World War I veterans, one beating a drum, the other carrying an American flag. Then striding down the center aisle, on the veterans' heels comes a tall, pot-bellied man with a heavy-jowled, mottled face. In his right hand he carries a three-dented Western cowboy hat. It is "Big Bill the Builder."
> The audience rises. A piano begins "You're in the Army now." On the platform, Thompson and his honor guard right-face in infantry drill style. The piano player strikes up his campaign song, "America First." As the audience sings, Thompson sways from side to side in his chair, shouting, "Sing 'er out!"
> When the last line—"America first and last and always"—is ended, Thompson rises. Since every Chicago newspaper except William Randolph Hearst's *American* had denied him a "fair shake of the dice," he tells the crowd he is appealing to them — the people. He cries "Yes, they lie about Bill Thompson. But they rob you. They call you low-brow and hoodlums. They call me that, too. We low-brows have got to stick together. Look who's against us! ... the University of Chicago, the social workers, the reformers, the public utility and traction interests, and the rich."
> He "reveals" to them that his British Majesty had persuaded Chicago's superintendent of schools to have George Washington's picture removed from American history textbooks. He accuses Chicago's intellectuals of being royalist minded and denounces all aristocrats, both American and British.[7]

The demagogic nature of Bill Thompson's 1927 campaign is today self-evident. But in the brawling, still border "city of the big shoulders," in an age of ballyhoo and showmanship, the technique appealed to an important class of voters and was made-to-order for this cowboy/sportsman for whom the political campaign was the only game worth playing. Thus, "Big Bill" was a throwback to circus impresario P. T. Barnum and to the religious fundamentalist impresario Aimee Semple McPherson.

In the grand ballroom of the Hotel Sherman, Major Hamlet C. Ridgeway, a former prohibition agent, presided over a huge rally to obtain cards pledging support for Thompson's mayoral campaign. When the number totaled 430,000 pledge cards, Ridgeway strode over to Thompson, tossed the candidate's sombrero into the cards, and announced, "In behalf of the voters of Chicago I throw your hat into the ring."

"I accept with grateful thanks," Thompson assured the crowd.[8] A severe cold would not let him say more. But Thompson knew there would be lots of time to say more in a strenuous primary campaign that was about to unfold.

One would have thought that in the face of formidable opponents, and without the help of Lundin, "Big Bill" would falter in his attempt to become Chicago's mayor for a third time. But Thompson did not falter. Instead he drew upon his skills as a showman and did not disappoint a crowd who assembled to be entertained and to have the issues of the day personalized and simplified for them.

At yet another political rally, just as an enthusiastic crowd finished singing "America First Last and Always," Bill would be introduced as one of the greatest living Americans. He would then lumber forward, grinning his crooked-tooth grin, his brown eyes gleaming with pleasure. He drew his big hands from his pockets cracked them together over his ample paunch, and warmed up the crowd. With a sure hand he deflected criticism from himself and without skipping a beat, and with complete earnestness, announced that the real threat to Chicagoans came from none other than England's King George. "I wanta make the King of England keep his snoot out of America. I don't want the World Court! America first, and last and always! That's the issue of this campaign. That's what Big Bill Thompson wants! What's good enough for George Washington is good enough for Bill Thompson!"[9]

"Big Bill" won the Republican primary handily. Thus was the stage set for the 1927 election for mayor of Chicago with Democrat William Dever, the incumbent reform mayor, campaigning against his challenger, the demagogic William Hale Thompson. The latter won easily.

William E. Dever was a good man but a poor mayor. He had been an alderman for eight years, a superior court judge for six years, and an appellate judge for seven years. In 1927, after serving one term as mayor, he looked tired and drawn as if the office weighed too heavily upon him. It seemed that as mayor he could do nothing right. He opposed prohibition, yet felt that he had to enforce the constitutional amendment. He did so vigorously, thereby alienating Chicago's large ethnic population that loved their beer, wine, or whiskey. Strict enforcement of prohibition regulations appeared to make organized crime ever more aggressive, and Dever was blamed for failure to abate gang warfare in Chicago. He appointed William McAndrew, a highly qualified educator of Scottish ancestry who was recruited from New York, as superintendent of Chicago's schools, only to find that the superintendent's rigidity was such that he alienated his school teachers and thus kept Chicago's schools in turmoil. That Dever was a Catholic was not helpful. A picture, freely circulated among voters by the Thompson crowd, of Dever kissing the Cardinal's ring was a crude attempt to capitalize on religious bigotry. Thompson would resort to nativist appeals and religious bigotry in subsequent campaigns, as we shall see.

For Thompson, the campaign was seemingly its own reward. Vile and demagogic though his political tactics often were, Thompson was a better campaigner than civic administrator. He would berate the press of which all, except Hearst's *American*, were against him, and he would whip up the enthusiasm of his audience when he denounced rich tax dodgers who took their tax dollars to the suburbs. He vilified the "elitism" at the University of Chicago, another hotbed of anti–Thompsonism. He called William McAndrew a "stool pigeon of the King of England" because the superintendent was, allegedly, not teaching school children "America First." He chastised libraries for allowing readers to borrow books that seemingly criticized George Washington and the Founding Fathers.

In recognition that Chicago's African-American voters were overwhelmingly supporting William Hale Thompson, George E. Brennan, the Democratic boss of Chicago and the power behind the candidacy of William Dever, made an error of political judgment that inflicted a mortal wound upon Dever's candidacy. He decided to play the race card by asserting that the people of Chicago would not turn the city over to "the black belt." And, four weeks before the election, he had the Chicago police summarily jail one thousand innocent blacks on the skimpy allegation that since Thompson's victory in the primary, vice and bootlegging had grown dramatically in Chicago's African-American wards.

African-American business leaders and journalists insisted that the rounding up of black Chicagoans was but a veiled attempt at intimidating African-American voters either to stay away from the polls on election day or to vote for Dever. The imprisonment of African-Americans was likewise a grandstand play to Chicago's racist, white middle class, those whose property titles had clauses restricting home sales to whites only. Those imprisoned were detained for a weekend and were released without being charged. But "Big Bill" seized the opportunity to play on the fears of ethnic Chicagoans. "The Cossacks," he shrewdly responded, "were trying to bring about a reign of terror. If they do it to Negroes now, how soon before they do it to Jews, to Polacks, to Germans."[10]

Nor did the racism abate. During a meeting at which Thompson spoke to an African-American group, he leaned over and embraced the nephew of Oscar De Priest, one of Chicago's most prominent blacks and an enthusiastic supporter of Thompson. George Brennan again played to fears of whites: "Do you want Negroes or White Men to run Chicago. Bye, Bye, Blackbirds." Dever's campaign manager Colonel Sprague escalated racist sentiment by quoting the Louisville, Kentucky, police chief who declared that the "crap shooting, undesirable colored men ... would migrate to Chicago if Thompson were elected."[11]

Another tactic of Dever's campaign was to send shabbily dressed black men into white districts with pledge cards for Thompson. In an attempt to flood Chicago's downtown area, known as The Loop, with blacks, the Dever campaign sent out fake invitations to African-Americans to meet Thompson in person at The Loop Hotel. A yellow badge was to be worn for identification purposes. But Republicans learned of the deceit early enough and most blacks never went downtown. The Democratic tactic here was to frighten white voters with a racially charged depiction of what could happen to their city should Thompson win. Brennan, insensitive to the impact of the racist campaign he was mounting, went on to assert on the eve of the election, "Nature never makes a mistake. Mayor Dever will be reelected ... for the reason that this city [Chicago] is a white man's town."[12] Dever was uncomfortable with these methods but found himself unable to do anything about them. Thompson used them to his considerable advantage, especially during the critical last four weeks of his campaign.

When Brennan accused Thompson's friends and supporters as being nothing but hoodlums, "Big Bill" opened his remarks to a group of wealthy women by calling them "[m]y hoodlum friends." When the ladies looked astonished at thus being berated, "Big Bill" gave them one of his big smiles and explained, "Well, George Brennan calls my friends hoodlums and I hope you are all my friends. Well, my little hoodlum friends, just take one little hoodlum with you to the polls on election day." To his "hoodlums" Thompson talked beer and water in the same breath. He made it clear that he was "as wet as the Atlantic Ocean," and that he favored the free, unmetered flow of cheap and plentiful drinking water to Chicagoans. He promised that he would not allow his police to search Chicagoans for hip flasks of illicit whiskey or refrigerators for illicit beer. Then he segued to his favorite theme: "And remember what George Washington said. He said, 'Keep out of foreign wars and make the King of England keep his nose out of our affairs!'"[13]

Long before the 1927 election Chicagoans had become somewhat tired of reform. The campaign slogan "Dever and Decency" had little appeal for Chicagoans, and as a veteran of Chicago municipal politics wryly noted, "Who the hell is attracted by decency?"[14] And as raconteur and political humorist Will Rogers observed, "Dever tried to beat Bill Thompson with the 'better element' vote. The trouble with Chicago, there ain't a much better element."[15] Thompson defeated Dever by a respectable 83,000 votes.

A Third Term

Although he had a reputation for being gregarious, a "one of the boys" kind of guy, by the time he began his third term as mayor of Chicago in 1927, "Big Bill" Thompson was not an easy man to see. But if a reporter charmed his array of secretaries, and smooth talked the ex-policemen who guarded the entrance to his official office, he would have found "the Mayor sunk in an easy chair with his feet on another, chewing fifteen-cent cigars and letting them fall unlighted into the wastebasket. 'My election' he boasts, 'means that Chicago will be an example of patriotic devotion to American ideals— not a pesthole of anti–Americanism. My election, thank God, means that our boys will not be cannon fodder for Europe's battlefields. We will send these lackeys back to England where they can sing 'God Save the King.'"[16]

After a boisterous inauguration, Mayor Thompson went to work to choose his cabinet. His choices were not reassuring. As corporation counsel he chose yet again Samuel Ettelson, who was essentially in the pocket of Chicago's utility magnate and ultra-nationalist "Emperor," Samuel Insull. Because the latter shared Thompson's hostility to the World Court and the League of Nations, he had been an important financial supporter of the reelected mayor. With Ettelson at the mayor's elbow, Insull could rest assured that his utility holding companies would not be threatened. Insull also bludgeoned George Brennan, the Democratic boss and the man behind Dever, into getting the *News* to give up on a major exposé of Thompson. Insull threatened that unless the articles were suspended, he would buy up enough Democratic committeemen to swing the majority to Thompson. This may have been a bluff, but Brennan believed that it was not, and so the anti–Thompson editorials were never printed.

Thompson's campaign orator and wordsmith, Richard Wolfe, became commissioner of public works, and Michael Faherty became president of the board of local improvements. Charles Fitzmorris, Thompson's former police chief, became city comptroller, while George Harding remained county treasurer. To combat the crooks, Thompson chose as police commissioner Michael Hughes, who had been chief of detectives under Mayor Dever. Thompson made his impossible-to-keep promise that he would clear out the crooks "in ninety days." But would Hughes be able to live up to his reputation as Chicago's best thief-catcher if Thompson appointed as city sealer Daniel A. Serritella, an agent of "Scarface" Al Capone? To Serritella, once a newsboy and founder of Chicago's Newsboys' Union, went the charge of protecting Chicago's consumers against fraudulent weights from butchers, grocers, and ice and coal dealers. This was like inviting a fox to guard the chicken coop since Serritella's real job was to act as liaison between Al Capone and the city administration. He would pass along Capone's preferences in policies and appointments and extract favors and special treatment for his gangland boss. Serritella later became a state senator.

Thompson and Crime

"During the four years of Thompson's third term, organized crime obtained a grip on Chicago without parallel in American police annals."[17] With "Big Bill" as mayor, Chicago gained a deserved reputation as an "open" city with "Scarface Al," the all-powerful mobster, widely viewed as the "mayor" of the underworld. The tasteless showmanship of Mayor Thompson provided both the cover and the comic relief.

Crime seemed to grow with each year of the Thompson administration. While it is quite possible to demonstrate that under Thompson crime flourished in the windy and wide-open city of Chicago, what is less easily demonstrated is whether Mayor Thompson benefited politically or financially from organized crime in Chicago. "Prosecution of Thompson in Chicago," continues historian Douglas Bukowski, "would have shown [Herbert] Hoover capable of doing to a Republican as Franklin D. Roosevelt did to Tammany Hall and Jimmy Walker."[18] But the FBI appears to have been unaware of the Capone contribution to the Thompson campaign.

Reformers were also quite capable of exaggerating the extent of crime in Chicago and found crime nearly everywhere. To Chicago's captains of industry—including printing magnate Thomas E. Donnelley; Sewell L. Avery, head of U.S. Gypsum and later of Montgomery Ward; Samuel Insull of Commonwealth Edison; and Julius Rosenwald of Sears Roebuck—crime consisted not only of organized criminals, bootleggers running illegal whiskey, or pimps promoting prostitution, but also of organized labor accused of widespread labor racketeering as well as immigrants who were thought to be breeding juvenile delinquents, and Bolsheviks who were seeking to undermine a market economy. With such a broad definition of what constituted crime in Chicago, it was hard to find an institution crime free. But, concludes Bukowski, "in the 1920s Chicago worked well enough for millions. Blacks left behind the vestiges of Southern peonage as ethnic groups prepared to control political institutions and challenge WASP domination of business."[19] Considered in this light, "Thompson served an important function as a symbol of political discontent."[20]

"Big Bill" for President?

When, in 1927, President Calvin Coolidge announced that he would not run for another term as president of the United States, serious and frivolous candidates began to gauge their political potential as the Republican presidential nominee. It is hard to believe that "Big Bill" took his candidacy for the American presidency seriously, but his ego was such that he might have mused, "Why not?"

Toward this end he embarked on a ten thousand-mile journey to test his viability as presidential timber. "Big Bill" was careful to announce that his junket was merely about flood control and the Chicago to New Orleans waterway, but he could not really disguise that the purpose of the tour was to float his potential as a presidential nominee of the Republican Party. On the day before he departed on this self-imposed trek, he took part in the sixteenth annual Republican Labor Day picnic in Riverview Park. Here, sixteen thousand followers gave him a lusty send off. Presidential candidate "Big Bill" Thompson made stops in Omaha, Kansas City, Cheyenne, and Albuquerque before finally visiting William Randolph Hearst at his ranch near San Luis Obispo, California. His assertion at the Hearst ranch that he was not interested in the presidency did not square with a pamphlet he distributed which amounted to a set of principles upon which he would base his candidacy. These included America First, farm relief, inland waterways, and national flood control. After a reception in Los Angeles, "Big Bill" returned to Chicago, where he was greeted with an impressive parade of 750 cars that escorted him to the Hotel Sherman. At the hotel,

State's Attorney William Crowe announced, "He is a great American. He has done more for Chicago than anything that has happened in my lifetime."[21]

"Big Bill" Thompson may have been a flamboyant, emotional show-man who could fool his audience into believing that he was the candidate for them, but he rarely fooled himself. By the end of 1927 he was sure that presidential ambition was a goal too far and that, in effect, he had reached as high as he would go politically. What better time to torment others! With this in view, he went after William McAndrew, the distinguished Chicago superintendent of schools. McAndrew proved to be no match for the mayor, but he emerged from the confrontation with his soul intact. The same could not be said for his tormentor.

Chicago's Clowns, Act I: The Schools

When he campaigned for reelection as Chicago's mayor, "Big Bill" promised: "When I am mayor again I will see to it that McAndrew, imported from New York ... is sent back to his Tammany and Wall Street friends. That's where he belongs."[22] William McAndrew became the light-ning rod for Thompson's last term in office. As hope for higher level polit-ical opportunities faded, as further building of Chicago was curtailed by growing indebtedness, "Big Bill" took his political frustration out on a tar-get who could do little to defend himself and who could muster little in the way of outside support. Thompson and McAndrew could not be more different in mental capacity, political agility, and even in personal appear-ance. The Chicago superintendent of schools was a perfect foil for the Chicago mayor.

In 1927 "Big Bill" was described as "physically lethargic." McAndrew, by contrast, "at sixty-four, is sturdy, brisk, full of spirit and well set up."[23] If Thompson scaled Chicago's political ladder by buffoonery, McAndrew scaled the educational ladder by genuine achievement. After a career as a teacher and school administrator in Chicago and New York, he was appointed by Mayor Dever as superintendent of Chicago's schools with the mission to free the schools from political interference. The mission was made to order for the dour, no-nonsense Scotsman. Having been an edu-cator in Chicago years before, he should have known that cleaning out the Augean stable that the schools of Chicago had become would be a task that would require the velvet glove as well as the iron fist. Incorruptible and unbending, he could satisfy no one.

The public school system that Superintendent McAndrew adminis-tered served over 500,000 pupils who attended 301 elementary schools, 25 secondary schools and 1 normal school or teachers' college. With a budget of $70 million, and a payroll for 15,000, including elementary and secondary school teachers, school administrators, special supervisors as well as an array of clerical, custodial, and janitorial staff, the public schools employed a greater number of men and women than did all the other municipal agencies of that city combined and so was Chicago's largest municipal enterprise.

For a political buccaneer like Mayor "Big Bill" Thompson, Chicago's schools were not engines for learning and teaching but instead were sources of political patronage with which to feed the insatiable Thompson machine. The schools were there to be hijacked in the interests of partisan politics and political aggrandizement. Thompson used his power to appoint board members to unseat McAndrew and to make a political football out of what should have been an apolitical educational activity. Thompson would make the schools serve his political ends; McAndrew would make the schools serve the educational needs of Chicago. The two were on a collision course.

On April 27, 1927, barely three weeks after his victory, Thompson began his campaign to have Superintendent McAndrew removed from office. The superintendent was offered $15,000 by a private group of Thompson supporters if he would resign the superintendency and quietly fade away. The proud Scotsman refused as a matter of principle. If the school superintendent would not go quietly, then he would be roughly pried from the schools in an all-out political war. It would not be a pretty picture. Thompson would win a pyrrhic victory, but the attempt to make Chicago's schools a source of political patronage would become, in due course, a case study of what ought not to be in the relationship between the schools and local government.

To oust McAndrew, Mayor Thompson appointed J. Lewis Coath, "Iron-Handed Jack," as the president of the Chicago school board, with the Thompson-imposed mission of carrying out his campaign promise of ridding the Chicago schools of their "bunk shooting" superintendent. Coath relished the charge. McAndrew dug in his heels. Thus the curtain rose on the circus trial during which the clowns performed and the world howled at their antics.

McAndrew was represented by two distinguished attorneys: Francis X. Busch, who had been Mayor Dever's corporation counsel, and Angus Roy Shannon, a former school board attorney. They declared their client innocent and the charges preposterous. The first weeks of the trial were of little interest, and McAndrew seemed to defy the board by reading newspapers as minor witnesses complained of McAndrew's alleged anti–Americanism. Except for an occasional raised eyebrow, he seemed to concentrate on the reading he had brought with him to the trial. As if to add insult to injury, he occasionally fell asleep.

Chicago's teachers, under the influence of their union leader, Margaret Haley, testified to McAndrew's alleged indifference, insolence, high-handedness, and even flippancy. He was described as unkind, ungentlemanly, and a "stooge" of the Union League Club and the Chicago Association of Commerce. "Simon Legree, a faker and a cruel taskmaster."[24] The more they testified against their boss, the more Coath had occasion to gloat.

To get ethnic Chicago on his side, Mayor Thompson fanned the flames of anti-McAndrew sentiment by asserting that revolutionary heroes with foreign backgrounds had been slighted. Thus, he catered to Polish Chicago by chastising McAndrew for failing to teach about Casimir Pulaski and Thaddeus Kosciusko, and he coddled German-Americans by criticizing the superintendent for failing to teach about Barons Von Steuben and DeKalb.

Despite his seeming indifference, the proceedings were taking their toll on McAndrew. His bemusement with the charges faded, his insouciance vanished, and his anger mounted. Tired of the malicious charges being leveled against him, he demanded that he be tried on the one charge actually before the board, namely the charge of insubordination. Coath angrily refused. McAndrew walked out of the hearing room, took a brief vacation, and went on a speaking tour. Walter S. Raymer, one of the minority members of the board of education and a McAndrew supporter, echoed the latter's insistence that he be tried on the charges, not on allegations of lack of patriotism. The outburst between Raymer, Coath, and the board attorney, Frank Righeimer, the latter a drinking partner of the mayor, was grist for the circus-like atmosphere that increased as the seemingly purposeless trial went on. Without the defendant the trial took on an even greater comic-opera appearance. When the board president scolded an unruly audience with the comment that the trial was not a vaudeville show, *The New York Times* agreed:

> Technically he is right. It is a mixture of vaudeville, burlesque and broadest farce. The spectators appreciate it, but it is getting a little irritating to Americans who wish to believe that they live in a civilized country. The stupidities or drolleries of Cook County may become infectious.[25]

On March 14, 1928, the final hearing was held on the McAndrew case. Before a nearly empty spectator section Attorney Righeimer inveighed against McAndrew. A week later, the board voted eight to two to officially oust McAndrew as superintendent of Chicago's schools.

McAndrew filed a suit for $6,000 in back salary and a $250,000 libel suite against Thompson. He dropped both when, in 1929, Judge Hugo Pam officially overturned the board's ruling and declared that McAndrew had been neither insubordinate nor unpatriotic. Until he died, McAndrew lectured on educational matters in America and abroad but rarely alluded to his Chicago experiences. Yet, he often related an anecdote that Thompson, when asked if he opposed George III or George V, allegedly cried, "What? There are two of them?"[26]

Chicago's Clowns, Act II: The Libraries

Among those Thompson accused of spreading pro-British propaganda was the Carnegie Fund, whose $200 million capital was allegedly encouraging a British-American Union. Other Carnegie-supported organizations were likewise charged with being puppets of the British crown, including such international organizations as the Association for International Conciliation and the Foundation for the Advancement of Teaching. Thompson was particularly hostile to Rhodes scholarships, which he asserted was established to extend British rule throughout the world.[27] But his real target was the Chicago Public Library, and so, with the trial against McAndrew going his way, he opened a second front by threatening to burn the books he deemed as pro–British propaganda on the shores of Lake Michigan.

During the course of the trial of Superintendent McAndrew, Frederick Bausman, a former justice of the supreme court of Washington State, asserted that in his travels across the country he observed what he considered pro–British propaganda in many of the nation's public libraries. "England has chosen," he declaimed, "the easiest way to conquer a country. It is not by cannon but by propaganda! It is the first instance I have known in which a nation was so insidiously attacked!"[28] He charged the American Library Association with being the distributor of material he described as "tainted."

These spurious charges were just the bait "Big Bill" Thompson needed. He pompously declared that he would redouble his efforts until Chicago had been "purged ... of the pro–British poisons that's injected into the hearts of American youth."[29] To achieve these egregious ends, Thompson assigned Urbine J. "Sport" Hermann, one of his cronies on the library board, to launch an investigation of the Chicago Public Library and to get rid of any books that were not, in his view, 100 percent American. This member of the Masons, former billboard changer, and theater owner was scarcely the person with the erudition to act as library censor. But he pounced upon his assignment with enthusiasm. "I'm gonna burn every book in that there library that's pro–British. There must be thousands of propaganda books ... and when I find them I'll burn them on the lake shore."[30] That he couldn't conceivably carry out his pledge that "nothing'll be burned till I examine it personally," didn't seem to bother him.[31] Chicagoans would have plenty of fun with the bonfires along the lake.

The initial response of head librarian Carl Roden to "Sport" Hermann's threat was tepid. Roden assured the press and the library board that inasmuch as he was their employee he was obligated to carry out whatever mission was assigned to him. He assured the press, however, that he had no taste for bonfires of books, but he was also certain that very few books, would be found with objectionable historical interpretations. He proposed that if such books were found, they might be segregated in the library's "inferno," an area for books that were allowed to circulate only on a selective basis. "Sport" refused the compromise.

The Illinois chapter of the Ku Klux Klan enthusiastically supported "Big Bill's" efforts to sanitize the library collections by destroying books with a pro–British bias. The KKK urged "Big Bill" to go further and to attack reading materials that were pro–Catholic or pro–Jewish. Frederick Rex, the head of the Municipal Reference Library, quickly responded to the book burners by boasting that he had destroyed his pro–British books, letters, and pamphlets. Proudly he declared that now he had an American library. In addition, William Randolph Hearst called for an end to making books available that were critical of America. He applauded the efforts of Mayor Thompson in his attacks on Chicago schools and its libraries. He believed that other cities and states should follow "Big Bill's" valiant efforts.

However, there was a good deal of opposition to Mayor Thompson as well. In many ways, his exhortation to burn books that were objectionable on account of their pro–British bias, triggered a good deal more anti-mayor sentiment than his parallel attack on the schools. The distinguished attorney Clarence Darrow called the mayor's attack on the library "the most infinitely stupid thing ever suggested."[32] The *Chicago Daily News* added that the book censors were not in the habit of reading books nor were they aware of the functions of a great library. As for the library director, Carl Roden, while he had attempted to respond to the attacks upon the library with moderation, it appeared that his job was threatened with legal procedures not unlike those involving school superintendent McAndrew. That Roden did not lose his job was the result of some surprising resistance and resolve on the part of a number of library board members.

In a surprisingly spirited response, the Chicago library board published a pamphlet, *The Chicago Public Library and Its Claim upon Private Benefactors,* that reminded the mayor and other readers that the Chicago library had been the beneficiary of the largess of Britain's Queen Victoria, Benjamin Disraeli, William Gladstone, Alfred Lord Tennyson, and other distinguished Britons, as well as from Oxford and Cambridge Universities, after the library had burned down in 1871. The pamphlet was intended to embarrass "Big Bill," and it did. While the mayor promised he would continue to harass the Chicago library board and at a "proper time" would take further action against it, in fact, "Big Bill" gave up the battle against the library. A show called *The Scandals of 1927,* a political lampoon, depicted Thompson as a modern Nero who fiddled while library books went up in smoke.

In the case of the Chicago public schools, the board of education served as "Big Bill's" willing executioners of the freedom of the Chicago public schools from pernicious political influence. Its professional staff, including teachers and administrators, likewise could not see the forest for the trees, and in their insistence upon the status quo they conspired to oust their superintendent and with his ouster sacrifice important principles that would keep public education free of partisan politics.

In the case of Chicago's public libraries, the librarians and others of the professional staff were initially excessive in their timidity and appeared, for a time, literally ready to "burn" the books to which the mayor objected. It is to the credit of the library board that they stiffened the opposition of the professional librarians and successfully challenged the ludicrous assertions of the mayor and, thereby, demonstrated an understanding of the role of great libraries in enriching the lives of women and men. However, Mayor Thompson's having to give up the fight for eliminating books he considered objectionable may be viewed as evidence that in his struggle against the schools and the libraries his power was waning, his judgment flawed, and his political acuity dulled.

The Decline and Fall of "Big Bill"

"Big Bill" hoped his pandering to American patriotism would sweep him into higher office. It did not. When Thompson returned from the National Republican Convention in June, he realized more clearly than heretofore that no one at the Republican Convention even hinted at a possible run at the presidency. It was not his association with Capone, and not the scandal surrounding the expert's fees, that knocked the supports out from under Mayor Thompson but the humiliation brought to Chicago by the fiasco of McAndrew's spurious trial and the threat to burn pro–British books in the Chicago library that sounded the death knell for this political anachronism. In 1931, when he ran for reelection, he was widely regarded as a buffoon who had brought humiliation to the proud city of the "big shoulders."

If Thompson's reelection to a third term was the zenith of his career, his continuing substitution of ballyhoo for a sustained and reasonable approach to the problems of Chicago served as tragic and significant evidence of Thompson's frustration and failure. Why rant and rave about America First when the nation's second city seemed to some to be embarked on an uncertain course? Thompson's attempt to hide behind the American flag was symptomatic that he was clueless about Chicago's real ills. He had few ideas as to how he might make life better for the people of Chicago, but as he did in his other campaigns he continued to rely on pageantry, bluster, and ballyhoo.

On the fifty-ninth anniversary of the Great Fire, in October 1930, Thompson staged an elaborate celebration complete with fireworks, German and Swedish singers, and the police band and orchestras. Motorized floats depicted "patriotic" incidents in America's history. He was still introduced to the audience by Samuel A. Ettelson, his corporation counsel, as "the greatest mayor Chicago ever had." Graciously, Thompson introduced his guest, the newspaper tycoon William Randolph Hearst "as the greatest living American."[33]

Then, the mayor announced a scheme to combat the impact of the Great Depression on Chicago. His plan called for merchants to distribute one coupon for every twenty-five cent purchase. Lucky holders of numbered coupons, some 16,503 of them, would receive cash prizes totalling $975,000. Merchants did not warm to the proposal, and his new superintendent of schools refused to allow his teachers to distribute circulars publicizing the plan. But Thompson was undismayed.

Instead, dressed in a collegiate raccoon coat, one that prompted his New York colleague, Mayor Jimmy Walker, to quip, "freshman or sophomore?" Thompson traveled gaily through the city in an open red automobile and waved his now famous three-pointed cowboy hat. In the Hotel Sherman, in a speech that drew on the success of his "caged rat debate" supposedly between Lundin and Robertson (discussed previously in this chapter), he swung a horse's halter from the end of a rope. When he perceived his audience's curiosity was sufficiently piqued, he announced that the halter was intended for his opponents for the Republican nomination for mayor, thirty-year-old Arthur F. Albert and municipal judge John H.

Lyle. He asserted that if Lyle won, the halter would be manipulated by Colonel McCormick's *Tribune* and if Albert won, the halter would be controlled by the *Daily News.* Then he confided to his audience, "Tell me the name of a candidate who won't take orders from a newspaper?" The crowd raucously roared back, "Bill Thompson!"[34]

The ballyhoo continued. In one parade of animals, an elephant carried the legend, "Stamp Prohibition Out of the GOP. Vote for William Hale Thompson, February 24!" Then came a camel with a banner, "I can go eight days without a drink, but who wants to be a camel?" Two sickly mules bearing the effigies of Lyle and Albert, alongside a smiling and graceful "Big Bill" mounted on an elegant horse, followed.[35] Despite or because of these tactics, Chicago Republicans give Thompson a safe plurality. "I've tried to give the people something to laugh about," asserted Mayor Thompson.[36] And he did. But were they laughing with him or at him?

Thompson was congratulated for his victory in the primaries by Huey Long, the "Kingfish" of Louisiana, and by New York's mayor Jimmy Walker. With Walker still on the phone, Thompson called in the Chicago Police Quartet.

> "Jimmy, I wanna have you listen to the song I've written for my campaign against Tony Cermak. He's the winner for the Democrats. Just listen to this:
>
> > Tony, Tony, where's your pushcart at?
> > Can you picture a World's Fair mayor
> > With a name like that?
> > What job are you holding!
> > And now you're trying for two.
> > Better start thinking of one for me
> > Instead of two for you!"[37]

The Democratic candidate for mayor was Czech-born Anton Cermak, widely known as "Tony." By 1931, this militant wet had developed formidable control over Chicago's Democrats and proved to be more than a match for Thompson. The latter forgot his love for Chicago's immigrants and sought to poke fun at Cermak's name. He referred to "Tony the Jew-hater," and in another context "Tony the German-hater," then "Tony the Irish-hater." Thompson bellowed, "Tony Cermak is the biggest crook that ever ran for mayor." When Cermak referred to himself as a "master executive," Thompson warned his African-American constituency, "You Negroes know what a master is?"

These tactics failed Thompson this time, and Cermak was easily victorious with a 200,000-vote margin. Why did Thompson lose?

He lost because he faced a formidable opponent and a well-financed political machine. He lost also because Thompson's nativist appeals were seen to be inadequate to the challenges facing Chicagoans brought on by the Great Depression. That Thompson was too cozy with organized crime finally made an impression on the voters, especially when the Chicago city sealer, Daniel A. Serritella, was found conspiring with merchants by cheating American families of some $54 million in short weights.

The *Chicago Tribune* wrote his political epitaph as follows:

> For Chicago, Thompson has meant filth, corruption, obscenity, idiocy and bankruptcy. He has given the city an international reputation for moronic buffoonery, barbaric crime, triumphant hoodlumism, unchecked graft and a dejected citizenship. He made Chicago a byword of the collapse of American Civilization.[38]

But Bill Thompson was physically sick, politically dying, and a "sore loser." He was angry, sullen, filled with hate for those he deemed his enemies.[39] He suffered from mental depression and even for a time uncharacteristically sought comfort in religion. He became estranged from his wife but was fortunate to have the devoted support of Ethabelle Green, his stenographer, who remained loyally at Thompson's side until he died.

Despite failing health and a failing economy, "Big Bill" Thompson made plans to run for a fourth term as Chicago's mayor. But while Thompson continued to bluster, he could not retain his hold on Chicago's political machine. The more frustrated he became at his loss of control over the levers of political power the more irrational he likewise became. In the campaign for governor he, once again, supported Len Small and lashed out at his Democratic opponent, the distinguished Judge Henry Horner. Since the latter was Jewish, Thompson let his bigotry show for all to see when he declared, "Elect Henry Horner and the price of pork will go down to nothing." Judge Horner won with a plurality of 556,000 votes to become the first Jewish governor in America's history. The wide margin of Horner's victory demonstrated how little influence Thompson wielded with the Chicago voter, thereby thwarting Thompson's proposed run as Chicago's mayor.

In 1936, Bill Thompson continued to lust for office. Since he could no longer count on Republican support, he attempted to organize a third party, the Union Progressive Party, and had himself nominated for governor. In addition to some die-hard Thompsonites, the party was made up of professional haters, including Father Charles E. Coughlin's followers and Newton Jenkins' anti–Semitic Unionists. Senator William E. Borah was looked upon as the gray eminence of the party. The party opposed the

League of Nations and the World Court and supported the maverick Republican William Lemke of North Dakota for president. Borah assured, "We are all together. Lemkeites, Townsendites, Huey Longites, Thompsonites, Laborites, and the American people are going down the pike together!"[40]

However, few followed Thompson down the pike. He received but 108,614 votes. "Now he had no political friends—and no political enemies. He was ignored."[41] In 1937, he incorporated the William Hale Thompson Association to Keep America Out of Foreign Wars, with himself as president. This group sponsored a nonbinding public policy measure to be voted on in a special ballot:

> Shall the people of Illinois approve the William Hale Thompson public policy proposal which provides that all members in the Congress of the United State from the State of Illinois shall vote "No" on all legislation for the drafting of American boys to fight on foreign soil.

During the antiforeign cast in America's Midwest, the sentiment expressed in the proposal carried some interest, and in the November election his proposal won handily. It was a meaningless victory, but it was the only victory for Republicans anywhere in Cook County. Bill Thompson was gratified, "Bill Thompson's not counted out yet. He'll be heard from, wait and see!"[42]

What was heard were the ravings of an anti-Semite. He had, for example, frequently attacked the highly successful Jewish merchant Julius Rosenwald. Initially he had done so because Rosenwald was rich, a millionaire, and as such a useful target against whom public sentiment could be readily mounted. In Thompson's 1931 campaign, he denounced Rosenwald not as a millionaire but as a Jew. "Well, we got a great philanthropist in this town, and he's a Jew, and he's trying to edge his way out of hell by giving [away] part of the money he steals."[43] Five years later, Thompson addressed a meeting of the Chicago Nazi Clubs where he vilified "Reds and Jewish bankers."[44]

In 1939, buoyed by the vote on his resolution, Thompson declared himself a candidate for mayor of Chicago. Despite his best efforts, there were few Thompson supporters, and he was denied the Republican nomination. In one of his last public statements, he declared, "No more politics. What's the use? no one understands what you're trying to do. No one tries. They only want to get on the bandwagon if you look like a winner.... Maybe I was theatrical. I was trying to sell good ideas. The ideas were okay. But what has come of it all? Look at the Loop. Look at the local transportation service. Why all this stagnation? Taxes? Discouraging, isn't it?"[45]

On March 19, 1944, after a brief illness, "Cowboy Bill," "Big Bill the Builder," died. He was seventy-four.

While during his political life most of Chicago's newspapers had little good to say of him, at his death the comments were more balanced. The *Chicago Tribune* acknowledged: "He was a master of mass psychology."[46] *The News* was more critical: "Big Bill was not a great man.... To the extent that Big Bill was a political success, Chicago was a political failure."[47]

But near scandal followed him in death. Five days after his death, his attorney, Jim Breen, estimated Thompson's estate at only $150,000. For five more days a routine search was made through Thompson's desk and papers for a will. None was found. On March 30, Breen, Maysie Thompson, the former mayor's estranged wife, and officials from the probate court went to the safe-deposit vaults of the American National Bank and Trust Company in search of a will. They found no will in the two boxes Thompson had rented since 1931, but instead the boxes were filled with old-style gold certificates, currency, and bundles of stocks and bonds. They found $1,466,250 in cash, the certificates in denominations of $50, $100, $500, and $1,000, plus $20,000 in stocks. A week later another cache was found in the vaults of the First National Bank — $112,000 in stocks and bonds. Two additional safe-deposit boxes were found in the Boulevard National Bank which contained $220,000 in securities and $22,000 in bills. All of this, plus his real estate holdings, brought Bill Thompson's net worth at the time he died to $2,103,024. From where had this considerable sum come?

Some said that the source of most of this wealth came from Al Capone, who had made heavy contributions to Thompson's 1927 mayoralty campaign. Others believed that the money came from contractors and businessmen who had been favorably treated by the mayor by awarding them lucrative contracts. Thompson, others held, had kept a percentage of all campaign contributions and refused to return campaign contributions that had not been spent. His attorney insisted that none of this was true. After checking a substantial sampling of securities, the FBI concluded that nothing had been stolen. There the matter rested, and no one would ever know the truth about the source of these funds.

Nevertheless, the prize was great enough so that there were two hundred or more claimants to portions of the estate. Breen, working on behalf of Mrs. Thompson, rightfully refused to acknowledge these claims, but there was one that was strong enough to require attention. That claim was made by Ethabelle Green, who occupied suites with him at the Blackstone and Congress Hotels and had been a combination of secretary, nurse, housekeeper, and daughter. When her own health failed, Thompson had sent her to Florida to recuperate and promised that he would leave half of his estate to her. Now, at age thirty-six, she claimed that she had given Thompson the best years of her life and demanded half the estate. Breen was determined to fight Green's claims. Protracted legal proceedings seemed inevitable, but in the end, on January 10, 1945, Ethabelle Green accepted $25,000 in an out-of-court settlement. Maysie Thompson received the bulk of the estate, went on an extended vacation in Europe, and returned to live in comfort on Chicago's Lake Shore Drive.

If Boston-born William Hale Thompson had aspired to municipal politics in the city of his birth, it is interesting to conjecture how he, a Republican, would have competed for political power with formidable James Michael Curley, the astute leader of Boston's Democrats. Thompson and Curley were to the political hustings born, and to both gaining and holding office was the essence of their being. Both sought power, and both, for a time, achieved it. But, as we shall see, their political ascendancy, while sharing some similarities, was essentially different.

Part II

FRANK HAGUE: AMERICA'S SECOND WORST MAYOR

If you will keep clean and work hard and stay honest like your Mayor, you can grow up like him and be respected as the first citizen of your city.

Mayor Frank Hague to the youth of Jersey City

Thank you ladies and gentlemen for the privilege of listening to me.

Mayor Frank Hague in a radio address

5

Bad Boy or Momma's Boy

Frank Hague was from the beginning, as he often admitted, a "bad boy." His father had taken him to Public School 21 on Twelfth Street in Jersey City, but within minutes after he had been left in the care of the school's teachers he climbed out of the basement window and ran away. Running away from school was to be the essential story of his early life, until he was expelled from the seventh grade for incorrigible behavior at the age of thirteen. Hague's lack of education showed through in nearly all of his political career. While James Michael Curley of Boston would overcome the handicap of a poor education through self-study and the practice of oratory — taking pride in his intellectual accomplishments such as the ability to quote from Shakespeare and the Greek and Roman classics — Frank Hague would proudly abuse the English language and resort to the language of the gutter.

Jersey City's "bad boy" was born on January 17, 1876, in the slum area known as the "Horseshoe" to an impoverished Irish immigrant family, the third son and fourth child of what would become a brood of eight. The "Horseshoe," located in Jersey City's Second Ward, lies to the east of Bergen Hill where the Hudson Tube trains from New York to Newark stop. He grew up in this hard-scrabble environment among the stockyards, along the active and dangerous railroad crossings, and beside the canal. The house he lived in was shared by other equally hard-pressed families and was callously called "the Ark" because after a significant rainfall a large stagnant pool of rainwater would remain like a moat around it.

In Ireland, Frank's father had been charged with conspiring against the British government and was forced to make a speedy exit to Italy and thence to America, specifically to Jersey City where others from County Caven, Ireland, were likewise cloistered. Hague senior married Margaret Fagen, also from County Caven, but whom he met in America.

Serious and dignified in mien, mild in manner, but unskilled and uneducated, he went from one laboring job to another, but manual labor never did suit him. Instead, when he had an opportunity to don the uniform as a guard in a bank, he grabbed it. He looked the part, liked to wear the officer's uniform, and was glad to pass the time "schmoozing" with customers and colleagues. He died in 1899, well before he could see his son become mayor of Jersey City and a kind of role model for political bossism in America. His wife lived for twenty-three more years and would take pride in the political accomplishments of her son. She died in 1922.

Young Frank Hague's schooling was, for the most part, the schooling and discipline of such gangs of the Horseshoe as the "Lava Bedders" or "Red Tigers." Morality aside, Frank Hague and the boys of the gang were determined not to remain poor. Gang life lent a note of security, provided a sense of belonging, offered companionship, and seemed better than hawking newspapers at the rate of fourteen cents an hour. One had to be tough, quick on the feet, fast with the fists, and not too sensitive to the stealing, mayhem, and, sometimes, even murder that gangland discipline imposed. Frank Hague, as boy and man, had a pair of sturdy fists, which he used with some regularity, and boxing, as participant, manager, and fan, was his favorite form of relaxation.

Along with his brothers John and Hugh, Frank preyed on vulnerable pushcart vendors, small clothing merchants, and other small businesses whose owners were not much better off than were the gang members. But before long it dawned on young Frank that there must be a better way of getting rich. One night, after a narrow escape from the police, Frank Hague confessed to his pal who shared his hiding place:

> "This ain't for me Munk."
> "You got something that's goin' to make you rich, I guess?"
> "Hell, I got six grades o'school behind me, and that's enough.... You want to know where I'm heading? Politics, that's where."[1]

When Frank was growing up there was rarely a peaceful election in the Horseshoe. "The battles at the polls ranged from simple brass-knuckle affairs to full-fledged riots, in which bricks, knives, shillelaghs, and occasionally guns were brought into action."[2] Young Frank and his buddies joined the inevitable election-day frays with anticipation and relish. But political battles lured Frank Hague, and he never looked back.

Two Steps at a Time: Up the Political Ladder

In 1889, Frank Hague, at fourteen, was out of school, out of work, and hanging out with the youth gangs of the Horseshoe. A job his father managed to get for him as a blacksmith's helper working for the Erie Railroad had no appeal for him. Playing nursemaid to a locomotive, he said, was not a job to his liking. He began spending time at John McConville's gymnasium where he honed the art of boxing, becoming rather capable with his fists. But, inasmuch as he preferred to let others go into the ring, he chose to manage other fighters, and so he became a manager of Joe Craig, a light-weight pugilist from Brooklyn, New York. While Joe Craig was not a stellar performer, Hague, as his manager, accumulated a bit of money, began to wear nice clothes, and became a very presentable young man to members of athletic clubs on the one hand and to political clubs on the other.

In Hague's youth, political life in Jersey City centered on the forty or so saloons that framed the political canvas on which one minor political boss and then another competed for political power and the boodle such power made possible. With the backing of saloonkeeper Nat Kenny, who gave him $75 to "make friends" in the neighborhood, Hague in 1897, just twenty-one years old, ran for his first political office—constable in the Second Ward. It was his first step up the political ladder of the Democratic organization run by Robert Davis.

As constable, Hague received no salary but did get various fees, and he had the opportunity to mingle with people who took politics as their calling. In response to Davis's call, Constable Hague helped get out the vote in the 1897 mayoralty election in Jersey City. He rang doorbells, helped new voters to register properly, saw to it that a supporter's child received effective medical care, and collected clothing and furniture for those whose homes had been destroyed by fire. He arranged for political rallies, morale-building parades, and successful fund-raising functions. His efforts and, more importantly, his results were so impressive that in two years he was attached to the sheriff's office where, as a deputy, he earned $25 a week. In pursuing the duties of sheriff, he shortly became recognized as a leader of the Second Ward and could look to Davis for further advancement. Davis rewarded his rising political star with the position of sergeant-at-arms of the New Jersey House of Assembly assigned to Hudson County.

It took some courage for Hague to bolt the Davis machine and ally himself with H. Otto Wittpenn, the mayor of Jersey City and a reform opponent of the Davis organization. In 1908, Hague accepted from

Wittpenn the job of custodian at city hall at the munificent sum of $2,000 per year. The custodial job was both more or less than the title appeared to indicate. As custodian, Hague was nothing more than the chief janitor of city hall. On the other hand, the salary was more than Frank had earned in any position up to that time. Moreover, in Hague's hands, the job was more than merely being the chief building sweeper and general caretaker. He had at his disposal the opportunity to distribute patronage to some twenty-four deputy custodians who became a kind of nucleus for Hague's already emerging stature.

Among those who tied themselves to Hague's coattails as he climbed the political ladder in Jersey City was John A. Malone, who later became deputy mayor of Jersey City and Hague's alter ego, and, more importantly, A. Harry Moore, Wittpenn's secretary, who Frank Hague made New Jersey's governor for three terms. To understand the shrewdness of the man who would be Jersey City's "new boss," here's what Hague biographer Dayton David McKean had to say about A. Harry Moore:

> Moore was a handsome, charming young man of twenty-nine, full of anecdotes and pleasant banter. He was a Presbyterian and taught a Sunday School class; he was a Mason and a member of numerous other fraternal organizations. In short he was an ideal candidate, and Frank Hague recognized his qualities immediately. He was probably the first Protestant Hague had ever known intimately, but they struck up a friendship which, with only one little disagreement, lasted through Moore's three terms as governor.[3]

McKean described another friendship that developed during Hague's term as custodian. It was that of John Milton, a brilliant lawyer in the office of corporation counsel. "He was one of the shrewdest young lawyers who ever practiced in New Jersey."[4] Milton and Frank Hague bonded as the yin and yang of New Jersey politics with the former keeping the latter out of trouble most of the time. The two of them soon plotted the overthrow of Wittpenn.

In 1911, in a critical campaign, Hague was elected street and water commissioner, and for his services was assured a salary of $3,000 a year. Now, elected on his own, he declared his independence from Wittpenn, and when Bob Davis died in the same year, the coast was clear for another stage in the advancement of Frank Hague. Encouraged by Woodrow Wilson, New Jersey's new Democratic governor, the legislature of New Jersey passed the Walsh Act in 1911, which allowed the cities of New Jersey to choose the commission form of government. Hague, after initially opposing the commission, soon saw that he could control it and before long adopted the lingo of reform, got on the bandwagon of the commission form of government, and rode it all the way to become boss and mayor of Jersey City.

In the election for commission members that was called for on April 15, 1913, there was a roster of ninety-one candidates for the five vacancies on the commission. In the campaign Mayor Wittpenn was painted as a political "pol" of the old school, who preferred government by political machine rather than by an elected commission. Hague's popularity among Catholics won for him the endorsement of Monsignor John Shepard, vicar-general of the Newark diocese and a highly placed member of New Jersey's governing Catholic hierarchy.

Both Hague and Moore were candidates, and both were elected to the commission, but the latter made a better showing than the former. On the new commission Mark Fagan, a Republican Progressive and the only Republican commissioner, was named mayor; Moore was named commissioner of parks and public buildings, while Hague was made commissioner for public safety, a position that gave him control over both the police and fire departments, both of which were sorely in need of reform.

The departments Hague supervised were notorious for corruption, laxity, inefficiency, and general lack of professional training or discipline. Hague, undaunted, set out to correct whatever deficiencies he might find. Success in these departments would mark him as a man of ability and political promise. Hague would not disappoint. As a forerunner of what was to come when his political power bloomed, Hague first broke the affiliation of firefighters and police officers with the American Federation of Labor. He accused many police and firefighters of neglect of duty and drunkenness and in a single day put 125 men on trial for a violation of one departmental rule or another. Commissioner of Public Safety Hague asserted, "They're [firefighters and police officers] a lot of drunken bullies swaggering around with a pistol in their pocket and a nightstick in their hand."[5]

Hague dismissed hundreds of police officers and demoted captains and sergeants and made them walk a beat. He fined officers heavily for various infractions of sound police practices. He brought in new officers and established an elite group of undercover police to monitor the behavior of their peers and, not incidentally, developed a police presence that owed first loyalty to the public safety commissioner. When as Jersey City's mayor, Hague decided upon a show of force to win a political point or to undermine the opposition, he would have this personal police force available and devoted to him. The "Zeppelin Squad," as he called it, would hover over Jersey City with a watchful eye and report or arrest police officers who were sleeping or drinking on duty or who were otherwise slovenly in the way they wore their uniforms. The "Zepps" would later be compared with the SS forces available to Adolph Hitler.

In the 1917 Jersey City election for commissioners, held against the backdrop of America's entrance into World War I, there were forty-one candidates. Among the most important were those candidates who were Republican and led by Mayor Fagan, another group of Democrats led by Wittpenn, and a third group of Democrats calling themselves the "Unbossed," who were led by Commissioners Hague and Moore. Although Fagan had, by and large, served the people of Jersey City well enough, when the votes were counted, Moore was elected the first commissioner with the greatest number of votes, Hague was second, and the rest of the Hague supporters next in line. Wittpenn and Fagan were both politically wounded and never returned to the political fray in Jersey City. The commissioners met on May 15 and proceeded to identify one of their number as their mayor. Although Moore had received the greatest number of votes, the commissioners broke with tradition and, just ten years after he became the head janitor of Jersey City, unanimously named Frank Hague mayor of Jersey City, a post he would hold for thirty years.

Jersey City: Everything for Industry

Incorporated in 1820, Jersey City, the county seat of Hudson County, rests on the far side of the Holland Tunnel. Hudson County is a potpourri of local municipalities including Bayonne, Hoboken, Weehawken, North Bergen, Secaucus, Kearny, West New York, and Jersey City. Politically, whoever controls Jersey City controls Hudson County, and whoever controls Hudson County dominates politics in New Jersey and is not without influence in national politics as well.

While it was an unrealized ambition of Frank Hague to unite these communities into a "Greater Jersey City," that he failed to do so was a failure that worked to his advantage in many ways. That is, as mayor of Jersey City, the dominant city in Hudson County, Hague could control the county's other cities as well, and inasmuch as each city had its own police and fire departments, judicial systems, parks, schools, and hospitals, all created glorious opportunities for the distribution of patronage which the mayor of Jersey City lavishly allotted in such a way as to bolster his political power.

Two-thirds of Jersey City's population during the "reign" of Frank Hague was foreign born, with the Irish making up 23 percent while the

Italians and Polish numbered about 35 percent of the population. Although not an ethnic majority, the Irish dominated the city's politics. As a devoted son of the Catholic Church, Hague used the church to give his political activities a cover of integrity and respectability. Ethnic loyalties made it possible for their leaders to organize immigrants into political clubs whose leaders were to "deliver" the vote of the clubs' members by distributing jobs, doing small favors, and interceding in times of family crisis—and, when all else failed, to do so through threats and intimidation.

Hague learned early on to make good use of the legend that in Jersey City on election day the dead come to life and ask the "boss" how he wants their votes to be cast. As journalist John McCarten described, "To Hague, a registered voter is a registered voter, dead or alive, and somehow the registered dead of Hudson County continue to be politically active for years after their demise."[6]

Frank Hague: Momma's Boy

On Mother's Day, May 8, 1949, the flag-studded auditorium of Dickinson High School was filled with an audience full of anticipation. They were there to be entertained and to pay tribute to Jersey City's former mayor Frank Hague. He was there to urge the reelection of his nephew Frank Hague Eggers as mayor of Jersey City. There were vaudeville acts, acrobats, and swing music, and teen-agers from local political clubs sang and danced.

The band played "Hail! Hail! The Gang's All Here" as the peers of Jersey City's political realm entered the high school auditorium. Entertainers bowed in reverence and left the stage to Frank Hague, the elderly but unbowed, nattily dressed, still first citizen of the city but no longer mayor. Flanked by a huge entourage, the former mayor marched to the stage as the crowd gave a standing ovation which, condescendingly, he barely acknowledged.

Hague acolytes proceeded to warm up the crowd. There was the "pep" talk of Congressman Edward J. Hart, which Congresswoman Mary T. Norton, beaming with enthusiasm, appeared to second. The three-time governor of New Jersey, the Honorable A. Harry Moore, was called upon. Emotionally, Moore announced, "This is Mother's Day!" and told the story of a wounded Jersey City "kid" who carried the key to his mother's front door through the battlefields of Europe. Mayor Frank Hague Eggers, Frank Hague's nephew and heir apparent, proudly announced, "I learned the rule of honesty at my mother's knee."[7] With the crowd thus assured, it was Hague's turn.

Piously he asserted, "We must see that our wives and children are protected, that we live under a decent government. I built that hospital, the Medical center, for you, the people of Jersey City. It cost forty million dollars.... I conceived the thought of building a hospital to motherhood, the Margaret Hague Maternity Hospital, named after my mother.... I supervised the driving of every nail that went into those buildings." He then went on to denounce John V. Kenny, a former ward lieutenant who was now opposing Mayor Eggers in the upcoming election. He outlined his past battles against the railroads and appealed, "Don't surrender to the railroads! Don't surrender the Margaret Hague!" The crowd that left Dickinson High School was convinced that a vote against Eggers was a vote against motherhood.[8]

Frank Hague's mother, Margaret Hague, was an aggressive woman who was described by one old Jerseyite as "a bitch on wheels."[9] It was she who implanted a strong Catholic, puritanical streak in her son, a quality that proved invaluable as he scrambled up the political pyramid of this very Catholic city. He frequently accompanied his mother to church on Sunday, and it was she who made him a devout Catholic and Hague their lay leader. He led the Holy Name parades and allowed parishes to play bingo despite Hague-imposed prohibitions on gambling. He was received by two popes, made a $50,000 gift of an altar to St. Aedan's Roman Catholic Church in Jersey City, and contributed a stained glass image of Virgin Mary in the lobby of the Margaret Hague Maternity Hospital. He also served as honorary chairman of a citizens' committee of the Mount Carmel Guild, an umbrella charitable organization serving the twenty-eight Roman Catholic churches of Jersey City.

Frank Hague, even in his youth, was shy and cautious in his relations with women. As he grew older he dressed well, made a handsome impression, and appeared to be a young man who would be successful. He must have fluttered many a feminine heart, and mothers must surely have encouraged their daughters to make his acquaintance. To little avail. There were no romantic attachments as youth or adult, and even his marriage cannot be said to be one with a romantic element. In 1903, when he was already twenty-seven and still living at home, he married Jenny Warner, who also lived in the Horseshoe. They bought a house on Hamilton Square where Jenny gave birth to their first child, a daughter, who died in infancy. A second child, a boy named Frank Hague Jr., was their only other child, who, with considerable help from the Hague machine, was to be appointed to New Jersey's highest court. Little more can be said of Jenny as she seemed to play an ever-disappearing role in his personal and political life.

Hague did not fit the stereotype of a "city boss." By no means a glad-hander, he was not a gregarious man; on the contrary, he "is as cold as an Arctic ice-flow."[10] He believed that smoking irritated his throat and that alcohol was bad for a chronic stomach condition, and so he neither smoked nor drank. The pollution in the air of Jersey City aggravated his sinus condition, which he used as an excuse to escape the city as often as possible. Perhaps his hypochondria explains his devotion to building a medical center in Jersey City way out of proportion to the size of the city.

He was "thin-skinned" when it came to anything even remotely sounding like criticism and short-tempered when things did not get done according to his timetable. Like Mayor Curley of Boston, Hague disliked being called "boss" or by his first name, even by friends from boyhood. He preferred being addressed formally as "Mr. Mayor" or "Mayor Hague."

Getting to see the mayor could be a formidable, frustrating occasion. For one thing, he was rarely in his official office and, indeed, was often out of the city pursuing a lavish lifestyle in New York, Florida, or abroad. He maintained or leased several apartments in New York, Florida, and Deal, New Jersey, and lived in the fashionable Bergen Hill section of Jersey City. Few people knew where their mayor was at any moment, but among those who did were John Malone, the deputy mayor, and Frank Hague Eggers, his nephew and secretary. He used the phone obsessively as he was reluctant to set his thoughts or his orders in writing for perusal by future generations. The telephone left no fingerprints and thus was his chief method of communication.

As biographer David Dayton McKean observed, "He may look like a banker and dress like a floorwalker, but his language is the language of the horseshoe."[11] His speeches were rambling, incoherent, and needed to be polished before their release to the press. But even careful editing and scrupulous spinning of his remarks could not hide his limited vocabulary and grammatical skills. He denied having said in a public speech, "I am the law," but while impolitic and probably unintended, his denials rang hollow. He preferred to speak without notes, but when he did, his syntax and grammar became so confused that his sentences went nowhere and his speeches were long-winded and garbled. His entourage preferred that he write his speeches in advance, and he usually did. His off-the-cuff remarks, sometimes obscene and often profane, could not readily be controlled. McKean concluded, "The paucity of his general information is so well known to all his intimates that they do what they can to protect him from embarrassment."[12]

His booklearning may have been limited, but he knew his practical politics and possessed a keen sense of how his constituency would react to certain proposals. He proved wily in his dealings with other political leaders and maintained a sensitivity to what motivated them and to what their abilities and liabilities were. Despite shortcomings in erudition and elegance, there was a power to his oratory that seemed to be of a piece with his physical power and early aspirations to be a pugilist. Just as he boasted of the numerous times he physically pummeled a physician, firefighter, or police officer — "I hauled off and punched him in the face" — who did not respond as rapidly as the mayor had wished to an emergency, so he rammed his points home with little finesse and much stridency.[13] In his speeches, likewise, he appeared to punch his audience in the face. And, surprisingly, he remained humorless in doing so, despite an Irish tradition of wit and joviality.

He had a puritanical, if quirky, sense of morality. Hague did not allow street carnivals in Jersey City nor did he permit burlesque shows, night-clubs, or taxi dance halls to operate. He established the rule that if any-one other than a cop on a given beat reported the existence of a house of prostitution, the negligent cop would be removed from the force imme-diately. Police regularly inspected poolrooms so that they did not become a hangout for the derelict nor a breeding ground of crime. Hague deemed it inappropriate for women to sit at bars so that when they went into a saloon for a drink they were required to accept their drink at a table. To reduce the number of robberies in the city he furnished merchants and theater managers with armored cars free of charge to take their money to the bank or to pick up the payroll. Through these means Jersey City boasted a crime rate far below the average for cities of comparable size.

Mayor Hague never tired of reminding the people of Jersey City that he built for them the outsized medical center with its Margaret Hague maternity wing. When criticism arose, more than one resident of New Jersey would urge overlooking perceived shortcomings: "[W]hen I had my twins at the beautiful Margaret Hague Maternity Hospital they sure treated me swell."[14] The word was, "Have your baby on Frank Hague." Thus, "infants were figuratively born into the political machine and grew up in it."[15]

While not much concerned about the lacunae in his education, he believed he was unjustly labeled a juvenile delinquent and unfairly expelled from grammar school. Sensitive to what he believed was the shabbiness of his treatment as a youth, he established a Bureau of Special Services for troubled children, and he was successful in keeping juvenile delinquency at a minimum in Jersey City. Biographer McKean summed up his sub-ject's character with the following observation: "A ruthless, two-fisted, unscrupulous, unlettered Irishman ... rose from the slums of Jersey City to command his city and his state."[16]

On New Year's Day, Mayor Hague held a reception for the people of Jersey City. Each citizen and each politician could come up to him for a quick handshake and a brief word. Ambitious politicians viewed this as an opportunity to touch base with "the boss" in order to advance in Jersey City and New Jersey politics. Frank Hague held political office before he was old enough to vote. He was forty-one years old in 1917 when he first took the oath of office as mayor of Jersey City, and he would hold that office for thirty years. In 1947, he retired voluntarily from it. How did he get, keep, and lose power as mayor of Jersey City?

6

Mayor of an American City

Close to the retail shopping area of Newark Avenue was Jersey City's old city hall. Built in 1896, the green-domed building on Grove and Montgomery streets was "a cold, stone monument, an architectural hybrid that might best be described as American Ponderous."[1] If the building was monstrous, the mayor's high-ceilinged office in it was sumptuous. Luxuriously furnished with a huge mahogany desk and expensive modern furniture, the office was in sharp contrast with the grimy, dingy, tomb-like building in which it was located. That his city hall, a building in which he was once janitor, was an architectural monstrosity did not bother Frank Hague at all because "the last place he will be found is in his magnificent office in the dirty and ramshackle city hall; if he goes there at all he goes in a back door after the building has been closed for the day."[2]

An American Mayor of an American City

When accused of being corrupt as well as dictatorial, Hague asserted that his accusers "do not know what they are talking about. I'm only trying to be an American Mayor of an American city."[3] At the local level, in addition to traditional government institutions enshrined in the commission form of government, Hague's Jersey City had a primitive but effective invisible government, a kind of feudal system in which political vassals who pandered to the needs of Mayor Hague, the reigning monarch, enjoyed prestige, power, and even fortune. The journalist Joseph Alsop interviewed Mayor Hague in 1936 in the dining room of one of the local hotels. To demonstrate Hague's control over Jersey City, Alsop reported:

> He [Mayor Hague] took the squares on the tablecloth to illustrate the
> precincts and wards, tracing them with his finger, and he explained the
> feudal system of American politics, whereby the precinct captain is gov-
> erned by a ward lieutenant, the lieutenant by a ward leader, and each ward
> leader by the boss.[4]

In its more mature aspects Jersey City's political machine was a hierar-
chical structure which resembled a pyramid with Mayor Hague at its apex.
Unlike a pyramid, however, Hague's feudal political machine was more a
work in progress than an archaeological wonder.

Unlike New York's Tammany Hall, which was a system of political
checks and balances where political barons vied for power among themselves, Hague's machine, like feudalism of old, was based more on personal loyalty, obeisance to the monarch of Jersey City. Intimately involved
with every aspect of his political domain, Hague kept his political vassals
in line by a system of carrot-and-stick tactics. The carrot he held out was
the possibility to attain greater responsibilities and greater opportunity to
exert influence and reap substantial financial reward. The stick was demo-
tion, destruction of one's career, or even being punched, pummeled, and
bloodied. As he boasted, "Remember how Napoleon used to tell his soldiers that each one carried a marshal's baton in his knapsack? ... Well
that's my system too."[5] How did Hague know about this bit of Napoleonic
lore?

During Hague's tenure, there were 12 wards in Jersey City and 240
election precincts. Each ward and each district had a male and female
leader appointed as a reward for services already rendered and with the
potential ability to get out the vote. Hague's political vassals were on duty
twenty-four hours a day, every day of the year. Hague preferred that those
who took responsibility for ward leadership likewise be on the payroll of
Jersey City. In this way, he controlled their livelihood should they thwart
or challenge his decisions or otherwise joust with him over matters of policy or practice.

Ward leaders distributed thousands of food baskets to the poor; they
sponsored an annual boat ride and/or picnic during the summer. But
mainly it was the responsibility of the leader to get out the vote on primary day and election day, and woe to the leader who failed to do so.
Hague was convinced that many eligible voters failed to vote, mainly
Czech, Polish, Slovak, or Italian immigrants who knew little English and
had few clues as to the political issues involved in any election. "Hague
grimly decided that these people were going to vote. Whether they had to
be bullied or cajoled, bribed or frightened to the polls, they were his secret
weapon in Hudson County."[6]

David Dayton McKean, an early biographer and severe critic of Hague, described the Mayor's machine in action:

> The election-day performance of the Hague organization is perfection itself.... On the Sunday preceding an election the Mayor gathers the party workers into an auditorium in Jersey City called the Grotto, and there makes them a speech of final instructions. "Three hundred and sixty-four days a year," he often says, "you come to me wanting favors, wanting this thing and that thing. Now, one day in the year I come to you."[7]

Thus, the liege lord made his personal appeal to the loyalty of his political vassals, and they went forth to get out the vote. Cars and drivers took voters to the polls; women took care of others' children, while their mothers voted. Hour by hour headquarters kept tallies throughout election day. If an election district did not appear to measure up compared with a year ago or if there seemed to be some other anomaly in the vote count, Hague would find out why.

However, to be the mayor he wanted to be, Hague knew he would have to gain control over successive New Jersey governors as well, and this he set out to do. Because he could never get control of the overwhelming Republican legislature, in his approach to securing power over New Jersey's state government, he chose the velvet glove more than the boxing glove. Like the boxer Muhammad Ali, he showed that he could "float like a butterfly and sting like a bee."

Thus, Hague sought to place in the governor's mansion his Jersey City–born banker friend Edward I. Edwards. The fifty-five-year-old Edwards had been a state senator from Hudson County in 1919, but Hague saw in him a superb candidate for the governorship of New Jersey. Edwards, a Protestant, was also a prominent member of such fraternal organizations as the Moose, Eagles, Masons, and numerous others whose membership he could count on for support. Most of his career had been with the First National Bank, and he had risen gradually to its presidency. Parallel to learning the banking business he accumulated knowledge of state government and had become something of a power in it. In 1911, he had been elected state comptroller by the New Jersey state legislature. As comptroller, Edwards gained some notoriety for withholding Governor Woodrow Wilson's paychecks when the governor was campaigning for the presidency of the United States.

At Hague's urging, Edwards announced that he would seek the Democratic nomination for governor. His major opponent in the Democratic primaries was James R. Nugent, the political boss of Newark and a Hague rival. Although Edwards was the candidate, the real test was between Nugent and Hague, which the latter won handily by virtue of his ability to deliver the votes of Hudson County for Edwards. In the ensuing general election in which the Edward Edwards (Democrat) ran against Newton A. K. Bugbee (Republican), Edwards emerged the victor. The main issue in the campaign was prohibition, which Edwards opposed. He promised to make New Jersey wetter than the Atlantic Ocean. Bugbee favored prohibition since he felt he could not oppose an amendment to the United States Constitution without striking at the roots of that document altogether.

While Edwards's victory was a narrow one, it demonstrated to the opposition how a disciplined boss could garner the votes in Jersey City and in Hudson County and gain leverage in the state while the New Jersey State Legislature remained in Republican control. In a systematic way, Edwards appointed men who were acceptable to Hague to various state boards, commissions, and courts and to the very important offices of attorney general and the county prosecutors, and especially judgeships. Albeit with some bickering and bargaining, this practice continued into subsequent administrations, thereby, once again, strengthening Hague's stature as New Jersey's preeminent political boss. Hague's attitude toward appointing competent people to office may be seen in the 1940 exchange between Hague and Governor Charles Edison, an erstwhile ally. The latter asserted that he wanted a person of integrity for a judgeship. The former roared, "The hell with his integrity Charlie, what I want to know is, can you depend on the S.O.B in a pinch."[8]

George S. Silzer, a circuit judge from New Brunswick, followed Edwards into the gubernatorial mansion. But, the relations between Silzer and Hague remained distant as the governor was not as cooperative as Hague expected him to be. However, the Silzer administration was followed by that of A. Harry Moore, who won by 38,000 votes, a significant majority as Hague now delivered 103,000 votes from Hudson County. Hague's pal, first elected governor in 1925, would be elected for two consecutive three-year terms and one nonconsecutive term as New Jersey law required.

Moore was the son of a Scots-Irish housepainter who entered politics as secretary to Mayor H. Otto Wittpenn in 1908. Of A. Harry Moore, *The New York Times* had this to say: "A Harry Moore, whom Mayor Hague had been grooming for months ... can talk circles around any other politician in New Jersey. There is nothing of interest to the average citizen that he can't 'orate' about with the facility of a river flowing over a dam."[9] But, the journalist Clinton W. Gilbert was right on target when he wrote in the

Newark *Evening News*: "A. Harry Moore is Hague pure and simple, a creature of the master of Jersey City ... a baby-kissing, handshaking, clever-talking product of the Hague machine."[10] While the Hague-Moore axis would have its tensions, Moore essentially did as Hague directed. That Hague could reliably "deliver" a Hudson County plurality "became his club for bludgeoning the state party into submission, his instrument for substantially controlling the state, and his passport into the highest political society."[11]

On the national level, Hague likewise gained political power that he used mainly to fine-tune his machine in Jersey City. On the basis of Edwards's victory, Frank Hague became the New Jersey state leader of the Democratic Party and leader of the New Jersey delegation to every national convention. He became the vice-chairman of the Democratic National Committee and for over a decade, from 1920 to 1932, he was a friend, admirer, and political supporter of Alfred E. Smith's national ambitions. At the Chicago National Convention of the Democratic Party in 1932, when Smith's attempt to secure the nomination of his party failed, Hague realized his political mistake, and, friendship not withstanding, he made a hasty jump on the Roosevelt bandwagon (discussed later in this chapter).

Hague considered four groups as potential rivals to his authority: police, firefighters, teachers, and hospital workers. As commissioner for public safety, Hague had established his dictatorial authority over the police and firefighters and broke their ability to oppose him. As mayor he would see to it that Jersey City was well protected. There were in Hague's time more police in Jersey City than in any other American city with a population of 300,000 to 400,000. In 1940, it was also the most expensive police force of any city in the United States of comparable size.

With one policeman for about every three hundred people in Jersey City, there were enough police to tap telephones, open mail, and throw out would-be troublemakers and Hague critics. The $3,000 annual salary for patrolmen was the highest in America. Even though many patrolmen served as ambulance drivers, elevator operators, and drivers for important Jersey City officials, "The number of policemen to be seen on the streets of Jersey City is so great ... Jersey City always looks as if there were about to be a parade or a riot."[12]

The county jail likewise provided employment for law enforcement personnel. Where else but in Jersey City did a jail provide two organists to soothe the souls of often violent prisoners, where but in the Jersey City jail did one find a section which prisoners call "Palm Beach" named after the aristocratic Florida city? In "Palm Beach" the food was better, more visitors allowed; visitors could stay longer and the prison host could arrange to serve a cocktail from time to time.

Law enforcement and fire department employees were often the children or relatives of influential politicians. This arrangement served Hague well. If a politician fought the Hague machine, his relative may have quickly been out of a job; if law enforcement officials in Jersey City failed to kick back a portion of their salaries to the Hague machine, they could forget about promotions or preferred assignments.

As for the board of education, Hague had, as mayor, opportunity to fashion a board to his liking. Like Bill Thompson of Chicago, education was just another bastion of potential patronage in the appointment of teachers, custodians, health-care workers, clerks, and secretaries. It provided opportunity for kickbacks from contractors who furnished supplies, built new schools, made repairs, or sold textbooks. Neither Hague nor Thompson had any particular feel for public education as an important element in offering children and teenagers opportunity to develop skills of literacy, mathematics, or history. Moreover, the laws of New Jersey in effect gave mayors, not boards of education, control of school budgets, and Mayor Hague was not disposed to eviscerate that control by spending it on children. Under Hague, the docile leaders of the Jersey City Teachers Association were unlikely to oppose the mayoral will. Why should they? Sycophants, listless leaders, and lethargic teachers were those who were rewarded with administrative sinecures that owed allegiance only to the mayor.

Because of his preference for parochial schools, during his administration Mayor Hague reluctantly built only five elementary schools, three high schools, and the A. Harry Moore School for Crippled Children. In 1929, Hague used his political clout to secure the location of a state college in his city.

Yet if the Mayor lacked an interest in education, his hypochondria played to his interest in developing the Jersey City Medical Center, which can be studied to get some insight into the techniques of Jersey City's mayor as political boss.

The Medical Center Frank Built: A Case Study of Corruption and Compassion

On October 2, 1936, President Franklin Roosevelt laid the cornerstone of the new medical building at the Jersey City Medical Center. By proclamation Mayor Hague declared the day a public holiday and closed schools and public offices, allowing plenty of time for nearly a quarter of a million people to line the streets and cheer the president, the mayor, and other distinguished politicians as they made their way to the medical center. In the dedication ceremony, the mayor thanked the president for the $5 million grant by the Public Works Authority to enable the medical center to resume construction that had been stopped because of the Depression. When the president spoke, he declared: "The overwhelming majority of the doctors of the nation want medicine kept out of politics. On occasions in the past attempts have been made to put medicine into politics. Such attempts have always failed and always will fail."[13] How wrong the president was. For Hague, medicine was the centerpiece of his successful efforts to maintain a controlling influence over politics in Jersey City and Hudson County.

The idea for a medical center for the people of Jersey City appealed to Hague's political sense that this was how he could win the people to his side over the long term. He built a medical complex that would provide the people of Jersey City with the best medical care science and money made possible. When completed, the medical center at Baldwin Avenue and Montgomery Street would consist of seven skyscrapers that would dominate the landscape of the city, cost over $30 million, and stand as an ever-present reminder of Hague's beneficence. Because his hospitals reached every family in the city by providing cheap or free medical care Mayor Hague was sure that the hospital was an important way to get the voters of Jersey City to vote his way.

The first building of the medical complex was named after his mother, the Margaret Hague Maternity Hospital. The maternity hospital, the jewel of the medical complex, had an enviable record of handling 5,000 deliveries in a year with fewer than 15 deaths. In 1938, it was a record unequalled.[14] Its Mothers' Clinic, where the poor got the best available care for themselves and advice for keeping their children healthy, was the first institution of its kind to be fostered by an American city. Thus, Jersey City's newborns came squalling from the womb into the arms of its political boss and the organization he controlled. As they grew older they identified with the hospital that cared for them during illnesses in infancy, childhood, adolescence, and adulthood, and they repaid their benefactor by casting their vote the way he preferred. As Hague biographer David Dayton McKean commented, "They will no more vote against Hague than against life."[15]

The rounded total of running the medical center came to about $6 million, but Hague lost his temper when one asked about costs. By hospital standards this was about twice the cost that it was supposed to be. As McKean commented, "Public medicine as administered by the Hague organization costs approximately twice as much as private medicine in the same town, and if all the costs were opened to public inspection the proportion would very likely be greater.... There is every reason to suspect, moreover, that the payroll is padded with superfluous employees whose services are really needed only in their election districts."[16] The hospitals were so overstaffed that at times there were more employees than patients.

In one investigation it was disclosed that even those capable of paying all or even some of their medical bills were never asked to do so. Of 108 patients who paid nothing, some had moved away and were not entitled to the services of the hospital, 7 freely admitted they were able to pay, and 38 lived in circumstances that indicated an ability to pay. Only thirty appeared to need charity. Moreover, many of the politicians of the Hague organization just assumed that free medical care was a perk of office. "The word was out that you can, 'Have your baby on Frank Hague.'"[17]

To those who criticized Hague for allowing those who could pay to get low-cost or even free medical care, this is how he would respond: "If they say they cannot pay, that is good enough for me.... We do not argue with a sick person.... When you give me a sick man I will restore him to health at anyone's cost."[18]

The payroll was an important source of funds for the Hague organization as were the payrolls of the police and fire departments among others. "It is an open secret in Jersey City that 3 percent of every public salary is payable to the organization before every election and that failure to pay results in dismissal."[19]

The mayor took a personal interest in the hospital and ran it as if he had professional training in hospital administration. He worked in his office in the hospital more than in any other place and went around "his" hospital "in hushed and reverent fashion, as if he were in church" socializing with patients, doctors, nurses, and other employees.[20]

Hague did not hesitate to override the decisions of the hospital administrator. When Hague's son had the flu during an influenza epidemic, two nurses were requisitioned to pay exclusive attention to the boy. Years later, when Frank Hague Jr. totaled his car while attending Washington and Lee University in Virginia and suffered a fractured pelvis and serious internal injuries, the Mayor and Mrs. Hague were on a cruise to the West Indies. Deputy Mayor John Malone took Dr. Edgar Burke, the chief surgeon at the medical center, and set out for Lexington, Virginia. The young man recovered.

Despite care that was often of a high quality, many interns and physicians preferred not to work at Jersey City Medical Center because of the intrusive and self-evident political climate at the hospital. Physicians were readily aware that the hospital's ambulance drivers had an espionage assignment which required them to make sure that the interns in the ambulance did not mistreat or abuse patients and were considerate of them. This assignment often caused conflict between the policeman and the ambulance intern.

> "I have them watched," declared Mayor Hague, "because interns tend to look down on ambulance work and want to be up-front in the operating room with prominent doctors." On one occasion, while on one of his long evening walks accompanied, to be sure, by a bodyguard, Hague called for an ambulance to see how quickly it would respond. It took fifteen minutes, and Hague began excoriating the intern in charge. "It took me a while to wake up," the young man said insolently. Hague [had] belted him into the gutter.[21]

Most doctors were circumspect in what they said about the hospital as they needed its facilities for their patients and did not wish to appear to be troublemakers. The medical society had its offices at the medical center where Mayor Hague could keep an eye on its activities. The mayor often sent city detectives to annual meetings so that only those who had his confidence were elected officers. Young physicians, if they possibly could, sought internships elsewhere so as to escape the political control and outright espionage imposed by Hague's organization.

However, the Jersey City Medical Center was probably the only hospital in the nation that was not built primarily to provide medical services. Moreover, "no important piece of medical research has come from the medical center in the twenty years it has been in operation."[22] Instead, under Hague, it became a conduit to feed the needs of his political machine. The medical center was the largest hospital for any city of its size in the country. It was even bigger than those of Washington, D.C., or Newark, New Jersey, and twice as big as that of Indianapolis. And, its size had more to do with Hague's voracious need for political patronage and funds than with the health needs of Hudson County. It provided contracts to loyal business people. Its employees contributed 3 percent of their salary to Hague's political machine, while the free or nearly free service placed thousands of voters in Hague's debt.

When Hague left office, several floors of the medical center were found vacant. By 1977, however, the medical complex was in dire fiscal straits, and Jersey City could no longer afford it. The state could do no other than to try to operate it. Today, the complex is but a shadow of what it might have been.

The "Most Moralist City" in the Nation

Mayor Hague continued his holy war against pornography, hookers, and criminals, and thus could boast on radio that Jersey City was the "most moralist" in America. Fearful that somewhere in Jersey City someone might be having a good time, at Hague's insistence, a Jersey City ordinance prohibited dancing in an establishment that served either food or drink. Through aggressive measures, Hague reduced the crime rate in Jersey City from the average for cities of similar size. Unlike Bill Thompson, whose Chicago became a synonym for crime and for the likes of Al Capone, Frank Hague's Jersey City was essentially free of organized crime.

Priests and preachers were hugely supportive of the puritanical restraints Hague imposed upon the city. Enthralled with the morality of their mayor, priests heralded his virtues from the pulpit with such enthusiasm that Irish Catholics often treated their vote for Hague as a "religious obligation."[23] But Hague's moralistic stance was lopsided in that, hypocritically, the mayor and his clerical cheerleaders knew that would-be patrons of erotica could be accommodated just over the city line. And they were.

All was not as above-board as it seemed. To lay claim to being the "most moralist" city in America, Mayor Hague failed to acknowledge that bookmaking and gambling, including church bingo and betting on horse races, were crimes. Gambling on horses was a thrill of which Hague was especially fond, and he was determined that if he could gamble on the noble sport, should not all the good people of Jersey City likewise be able to do so? Jersey City poolrooms, protected from hoodlums, also often had sophisticated telephone equipment to relay information for would-be gamblers on horse races in a variety of cities. Under Hague, "betting on horses is a protected racket handling millions of dollars, and it would not exist for an hour if the local administration were not interested in its preservation."[24]

Gambling on such a scale required that the police look the other way and that telegraph and telephone companies, at the risk of losing the privilege of doing business in New Jersey, likewise overlook the fact that their facilities were being used for illegal activities. The journalist Westbrook Pegler, in a syndicated column written in 1938, asserted, "Jersey City is the Wall Street of the horse-gambling business, with many offices in daily operation ... and is able to make and control prices almost instantaneously at horse parks thousands of miles away."[25]

To Hague's credit, he also mounted a public safety campaign against litter, movie-house firetraps, and stores selling poisoned candy to children.

After twenty-three children died in a school fire in Massachusetts in 1915 because of insufficient emergency exits, Hague, then commissioner of public safety, sent inspectors to schools and other public buildings. When state and local education officials complained that the Department of Public Safety had no authority over school buildings, Hague gladly and ostentatiously shifted responsibility to the board of education.[26]

Although he was a teetotaler, Hague did not enforce prohibition measures rigorously. But he did prevent organized crime from siphoning off illicit income from bootlegging and gaining a substantial foothold in Jersey City. When a mob tried to divert a trainload of liquor through Jersey City to New York during the waning days of prohibition, Hague drove the Mafiosi off.

> As the hoods were busily unloading the booze in the rail yards ... searchlights clicked on from every direction and the place was suddenly transformed into high noon.... Hague's foghorn voice informed them that they were surrounded by 100 cops with machine guns. "Now start running. And don't stop until you're outa Jersey city," roared the mayor. The suggestion was instantly obeyed. Naturally, Hague appropriated the booze worth about a half a million dollars.[27]

The Odd Couple: Franklin Roosevelt and Frank Hague

Roosevelt, to the manor born, Hague, born in the "Horseshoe" slum of Jersey City, had little in common except a determination to seek and keep political power. As a result, the political patrician and the political boss found themselves traveling, for a time, on parallel trajectories to their mutual, if short-term, benefit. But initially the ordinarily politically sharp mayor would back the wrong candidate.

Frank Hague, a close friend and political supporter of Alfred E. Smith, the governor of the State of New York and the losing presidential candidate of the Democratic Party in 1928, supported Smith over Roosevelt as the Democratic presidential nominee in 1932. As vice-chairman of the National Democratic Committee since 1924, and Smith's floor leader at the convention, Frank Hague's clout in that party was not inconsiderable and his support of Smith not illogical. Both were politicians from Irish-Catholic backgrounds who had become friends. Smith, a man of great ability and soft heart, had been the Democratic presidential candidate four years earlier and felt that he had run a good enough campaign to deserve the support of his fellow delegates at the convention. Hague felt he was backing a candidate who had the potential to win, and on June 23, 1932, Hague announced that in his view, "Governor Franklin D. Roosevelt, if nominated, has no chance of winning at the election in November.... Why consider a man who is weakest in the eyes of the rank and file?"[28]

During the Democratic convention, Hague made strenuous efforts to turn the delegates to the "Happy Warrior," a title bestowed upon Smith by FDR in 1924, during the latter's first political foray on crutches. But Hague failed to turn the tide of the convention to his candidate. With this failure went Hague's own ambitions to be a political power behind a Smith presidency and probably a member of a Smith cabinet as well. Why did so brilliant a politician make such a whopping mistake as to support the wrong candidate?

When Huey Long, Louisiana's political boss, read Hague's statement in support of Smith, he shouted, "All Frank Hague knows is the road to Manhattan!"[29] Huey Long was right. Hague, the political boss of Jersey City, knew little about the temper of the country. He had neither studied the nation's history nor traveled widely about its continental expanse. He knew few cities beyond Jersey City and perhaps New York City, and he knew essentially nothing about the struggles and ambitions of the American farmer nor of the agricultural transformation that was taking place in rural America. His were provincial and ill-informed views, and they haunted him at the Democratic National Convention and limited his ability to play politics on the national level. In the end, provinciality more than corruption would bring him down.

Nevertheless, Hague knew that while he had supported Smith during the convention, he could do no other than to support Roosevelt in the general election. But how best to mend fences with James Aloysius Farley, who was managing the Roosevelt campaign, and with FDR himself?

Unabashedly, Hague publicly declared, "I have no apologies to make for the battle conducted at the Democratic Convention in Chicago." He urged his listeners, members of the Hudson County Democratic Committee, to disregard the words he uttered in the "white heat of political conflict" and support FDR in the November election. He promised Farley that if Roosevelt would come to New Jersey, Hague would stage a rally for the presidential candidate which would be second to none. He called Roosevelt and invited him to Sea Girt, New Jersey, where he likewise indicated that a "monster" rally would be held. Hague was as good as his word, and at Sea Girt one hundred thousand people showed up to listen to the Democratic presidential candidate. The outpouring of support for FDR in New Jersey was probably the biggest rally ever held for a presidential candidate up to that time.

When dealing with political, urban bosses, FDR chose to be selective.

He would deal only with those who were politically indispensable to him, with bosses who could turn out the vote at critical times. Thus, he held his nose when dealing with "Boss" Hague of Jersey City and did so only as a matter of necessity, not of preference. New Jersey, Roosevelt reasoned, was a populous state whose electoral vote could easily go Republican were it not for the Democrats Hague controlled in Hudson County. FDR sought and accepted Hague's support, yet he held Hague at arm's length so that Hague was rarely invited to Hyde Park and never became a stalwart among the "palace guard" that watched over the political moves of the president. Yet the boss gave the president exactly what the latter needed to reassure FDR's reelection. Until he retired in 1947, Mayor Hague supported FDR and was well-rewarded by him.

Hague never publicly criticized a New Deal policy and regularly referred to FDR as "that great humanitarian." He instructed the New Jersey congressional delegation to follow orders from Roosevelt's White House. Some months after the general election, Hague wrote to President Roosevelt: "Your recognition of our State Organization had been substantially manifested and in return I feel we owe you this pledge of loyalty. Should the occasion ever arise when New Jersey need be counted I am yours to command."[30] As a reward, the Hague machine was recognized as the sole vehicle through which federal patronage and federal largess would be cleared.

One theory of bossism has it that the coming of the New Deal would undermine political urban bosses since the federal government, not party machines, would come to the aid of the poor. No longer would the immigrant with limited English be subject to the disciplined voting required by the machine — a basket of food at Christmas in exchange for voting "right" in November.

However, what the New Deal did was to make the political machine more desperately needed than ever. In New Jersey, all patronage, state judicial appointments, and staffing of federal agencies in the state required approval from the Hague political machine. "The vast amount of patronage has provided them almost unlimited opportunities to reward the faithful. It has also given them complete control over city and county Democratic organizations."[31] In a speech he made in Jersey City on November 1, 1936, Hague declared. "You want to know what the President had done for Jersey City. We have had $500,000 a month to give food to our hungry and work for our idle."[32] As Hague scholar and critic David Dayton McKean asserts, "Without federal assistance the city would have been bankrupt long ago."[33] FDR, not Hague, saved Jersey City.

Hague: A Hitler on the Hudson?

Frank Hague's control over Jersey City and Hudson County was so complete that he was often compared to Stalin, Mussolini, and Hitler, European dictators whose years in power overlapped some of his. Huey Long, the "Kingfish" of Louisiana, and one who should have known about such things, declared that if Fascism came to America it would be imposed by one of its own — by disavowing democratic institutions even while playing lip service to them and by distorting them in the excuse that it was needed to fight a vile and immediate threat. To Frank Hague that threat was Communism, and he was determined to keep Communism out of Jersey City no matter how far he had to stoop.

Frank Hague's preference for dictatorship over democracy, for a controlled over a free press, for character assassination over fair debate, may be seen in the ruthlessness with which he sought and kept power. Because of its high taxes, Mayor Hague's Jersey City was one which industry would ordinarily avoid. However, what attracted industries to Jersey City was that it was a non-union town, where, so the claim went, workers were "contented," where strikes were few or nonexistent, where police favored strike-breakers not striking workers where health and safety regulations were nonexistent or carelessly enforced, where city officials turned away from the mushroom growth of sweat shops, and where wages were low enough so that business could afford the city's high tax levies. Little wonder then that Jersey City in Hague's day was widely known as "Scab City."

When the CIO sought to organize labor in Jersey City, its mayor literally saw "red." To Mayor Hague, the CIO was merely a front for "godless" Communism, and with the zealotry of a God-fearing, Irish Catholic he sought to banish it from his city. When, in 1937, organizers from the CIO launched a membership drive in Jersey City, the police under orders from their mayor, tapped their telephone calls, opened and read their mail, confiscated printed handouts, and searched homes, persons, and automobiles without warrants. "Boss" Hague denied them space in which to hold meetings and rallies, and he stationed his police at the entrance to the Holland Tunnel, at the railroad stations, and at entry and exit ramps to keep labor organizers, "Communist agitators," he called them, out. To curb this "invasion" of those he identified as Communists, his police arrested courageous organizers, put them on ferries and trains, and shipped them out of Jersey City. Some were severely beaten. He encouraged CIO audiences at outdoor rallies to throw rotten eggs and tomatoes at speakers and drive them off the platform. When the Socialist leader Norman

I AM THE LAW' by Ellis

NEWS ITEM: Mayor Hague's Jersey City police arrest CIO organizers attempting to distribute leaflets to workers and run others out of town. "I am the law": Mayor Hague of Jersey City lighting a cigar with the Constitution and the Bill of Rights, Daily Worker, December 1, 1937. Courtesy of the Library of Congress, Prints & Photographs Division, LC-USZ62-75123.

Thomas attempted to speak at a rally, he was seized by Jersey City police and "deported." As if in justification of his strong-arm tactics, Hague declared: "These strangers may as well understand that the Stars and Stripes will continue to fly over our city.... The red flag will never be hoisted here while we Americans live in Jersey City."[34]

The CIO, supported by the American Civil Liberties Union, brought a lawsuit against Hague that eventually reached the United States Supreme Court. The case, *Frank Hague et al. v. the Committee on Industrial Organization et al.* (1939), established the citizen's right to use public space for the expression of opinion. In denying labor unions the right to rent any meeting halls or use public places for rallies, the Supreme Court ruled that Hague had used the licensing and permit power of Jersey City as "an instrument of arbitrary suppression of free expression." At long last, the First Amendment included Jersey City.

The Supreme Court decision was a deep disappointment to the Hague machine and a source of elation to the CIO. William J. Carney, one of the leading organizers for the CIO, gloated triumphantly if somewhat prematurely, "The Hague machine is cracking."[35] A month after the decision, CIO organizers and members of the Hague machine reached an amicable settlement of their grievances. While this indicated that the Hague forces could be nimble and compromise when they must, it showed also that a retreat from power was also a real threat.

In butting heads with the CIO, Mayor Frank Hague met his match, and the beginning of his fall from grace may be traced to the arrogance of power, ignorance of the growing clout of labor, and lack of awareness that the world as he knew it was passing him by. Conflict with the CIO put Hague in publicity's glare, exposed the nature of Hagueism, forced the authoritarian mayor to explain again and again how he managed to live so well while drawing a modest salary, and exposed his organizational techniques and the means by which he exacted tribute from his political vassals. All these were matters that Hague would have preferred not to share with the American people in or outside of Jersey City.

7

To Make His Daddy Happy

Frank Hague Jr., unlike his father, was a convivial, apolitical young man who, at thirty-four, was still looking for a job. Like his father, however, Junior's formal schooling was wasted on him. While his father was expelled from a public school, Frank Hague Jr. had the most expensive education money could buy, but he learned little at schools with impressive reputations. In 1927, he managed to enter Princeton only to resign in the spring of 1930 when it became abundantly evident that despite repeated opportunities, Frank Jr. could not benefit from that distinguished university.

Carefree but persistent, these experiences did not deter Frank Jr. from trying to become a lawyer, and he entered the University of Virginia Law School, where he failed nine of the twenty courses he took. However, he married Mary Katherine Jordon, the daughter of a college dean. He left the University of Virginia and in 1932 entered law school at Washington and Lee University. He never graduated but continued some random study until 1936. He dropped out of Washington and Lee, and despite his failure to get a degree, he sat for the New Jersey bar examination, which two-thirds of the candidates normally fail in their first attempt. Frank Hague Jr. passed.

Frank Jr. served a required clerkship in the law office of John Milton, his father's attorney and long-time friend, and became secretary to State Supreme Court Justice Newton H. Porter, a Republican. Yet, Frank Hague Jr. had never tried a case. Governor A. Harry Moore nominated him to the New Jersey Court of Errors and Appeals, the highest court in the state of New Jersey, as a lay judge.

It was easy to get young Hague nominated, but confirmation faced

(Left to right) Frank Jr., Mrs. Hague, and Frank Hague in 1925. Courtesy of the Library of Congress, Prints & Photographs Division, LC-USZ62-119553.

three problems. In the first instance, there was no vacancy, and so one would have to be created. In the second, how to overcome the reluctance of a Republican-dominated state senate to confirm him? Last, how to overcome the opposition of the state bar associations who resented the appointment of an obviously ill-prepared lawyer? The nomination was, said a prominent member of the Essex County Bar Association, "a slap in the face of every bar association in New Jersey."[1]

In the controversy that followed, Frank Hague Jr., who was shrewdly advised and conveniently sheltered in Florida, made no comment. In an elegant triple play, a vacancy was deftly made for young Hague and his confirmation was expedited when six Republicans who owed Frank Hague Sr. a debt of gratitude for their jobs repaid their debt, thereby "making Daddy happy!" as Governor A. Harry Moore intended.

Her Honor: The Mayor of Washington

Among political bosses, power goes to those who can master the art of standing astride the horse of reform and the horse of corruption at the same time as they canter in the center ring of the political circus. Just as Hague transformed his medical center into a vote-getting and patronage-making machine, so he became aware, early on, of the voting potential of the Nineteenth Amendment that gave American women the right to vote. In anticipation that Tennessee on August 18, 1920, would be the thirty-sixth state to ratify the woman's suffrage amendment, Mayor Hague moved quickly to make Mrs. Mary T. Norton, a woman who came to his attention through her work with various Catholic charities, a member of the Democratic State Committee as Hudson County's woman representative.

Two days after the Nineteenth Amendment became law, Mayor Hague invited Mrs. Norton into his office and said, "The women now have the vote. It is your duty to organize the women of Jersey City. I have called a meeting for next week in Dickinson High School. You will make the principal address."[2] While she protested that she knew nothing about politics and less about making a public speech, the New Jersey boss recognized that she was no shrinking violet and that with a little encouragement, this formidable lady could be an important vote-getting cog in the political machine he was still building. As a member of the Hague machine, her task was largely to rally women voters for the mayor, and what she did was so effective that her political rise, greased by Hague, was rapid.

Mayor Hague initially appointed Mrs. Norton to an unpaid position as representative on the Hudson County Democratic State Committee. Three years later she got a paid job as a member of the Hudson County Board of Freeholders. She was a delegate to the Democratic convention in 1924 and was a delegate to every Democratic National Convention until 1948. In 1925, Mrs. Norton entered Congress to become the first woman representative of the Democratic Party and the first woman to be elected to the House of Representatives from a state east of the Mississippi. She remained in Congress for twenty-five years representing the interests of women. She was chairman of the House Committee on Labor, and chairman of the Committee on the District of Columbia. It was in this role that she was informally invested with the honorary title as "Mayor of Washington." From 1934 to 1944, she was chairman of the Democratic State Committee. In that capacity she was nominally the leader of the Democratic Party in New Jersey, and when Senator Smathers was defeated for reelection, she became Mayor Hague's dispenser of federal patronage for New Jersey.

Her Horatio Alger political rise shows the power of the Hague machine to keep useful people in office as long as they do exactly what he wants them to do. Her election was automatic. She did not need to campaign, and Hague's every thought became her command. It was she who made the judgeship of Frank Hague Jr. possible with her timely intervention directly with President Roosevelt.

However, neither Mary Norton nor her boss and mentor were women's rights advocates in the sense that the term is used today. Her theme was the unarguable and undebatable one of "womanhood." Who could be against it? But, what did it mean? It is inconceivable that Mrs. Norton would have supported legalized abortion, birth control, or women's rights to choose. She was a suffragist but not a feminist, and Mayor Hague was neither. Except for the fact that through Mary Norton he could enlist women voters as part of his machine, he was not especially interested in women's issues. Despite her sharp tongue, as congresswoman from Jersey City she was popular with her constituents and the ranks of organized labor. She made one of the early resolutions in Congress for the repeal of the Eighteenth (Prohibition) Amendment. She may not have been "the most important woman politician this country has ever known" as some writers have claimed, but she was a formidable woman and a source of strength to the Hague political machine.[3]

Politically, Frank Hague had a way with women. His technique was to discourage women from joining national organizations and so, for example, there was no League of Women's Voters in Jersey City. Instead, Hague encouraged the usual ward organizations to open their membership to women's auxiliaries so that a formidable structure of women's organizations grew parallel with those of men. This practice meant that Hague could keep tabs over what was happening at the ward level without worrying about whether a national organization in Washington, D.C., for example, could independently enlist the support of Jersey City's women perhaps in a reform direction Hague considered unhelpful to his political power.

The Decline and Fall of Mayor Hague

Because few political bosses rose so fast or fell so slowly, it is difficult to determine with any precision when Hague's decline began. However, when, in 1940, President Franklin Roosevelt sought to replace Acting Navy Secretary Charles Edison with Frank Knox, the president requested Hague, through Jim Farley, to run Charles Edison for governor of New Jersey. Jersey City's political boss was not at all sure that Edison was a man he could control, but Hague reluctantly felt he could not help but comply with the presidential request.

His doubts about Charles Edison as a player on Hague's team soon became evident. Hague had uncharacteristically erred in underestimating Edison's moral fiber and in overestimating his own political clout which, while still considerable, was beginning to wane. As he had done with other governors, Hague thought he could continue to pull the strings and so bend the mild-mannered, soft-spoken, and politically inexperienced, Edison to do his political bidding and make the governor another prop in the Hague puppet show.

Hague was not a little surprised when Edison turned down Hague's campaign money and not a little annoyed that Edison did not come to Jersey City's political boss for campaign advice. With Hague on the platform at a meeting held in Sea Girt, New Jersey, Edison announced that he would be his own boss, follow his own conscience, and be a yes-man to no one. Edison "was not used to being bossed, and his will was just as strong as Hague's."[4]

Edison was determined to be a governor, not a Hague puppet. Shortly after Edison became governor, in a symbolic gesture of independence, he pulled out the "hot line" telephone, which connected the governor of New Jersey directly with the mayor of Jersey City. He further infuriated Frank Hague by his appointment of Frederic R. Colie, a Newark Republican and no political clubhouse hack, to the New Jersey Supreme Court. Hague could not accuse the governor of appointing an incompetent, as Colie was a distinguished member of the New Jersey bar and eminently qualified for the position the governor intended for him. What irked Hague was that Colie had, with some vehemence, opposed the judicial appointment of Frank Hague Jr. From his vacation home in Florida, Hague thundered over the telephone: "Charley, you've turned out to be just the kind of governor I thought you'd be, you [expletive deleted] Benedict Arnold."[5] Thus began, historian Reinhard Luthin asserted, the so-called "Second Battle of Trenton."[6]

The "Second Battle of Trenton" took place over the complicated question of railroad taxation. High taxes levied on railroads by the Hague-bossed state, county, and city administrations were forcing many of them into bankruptcy. An Interstate Commerce Commission report stated that while the average tax per mile of track in the nation was $1,809, the tax in New Jersey was $10,395. In Pennsylvania the tax was $1,098, and in neighboring New York it was $3,276.

An expert committee on the subject of railroad taxation, appointed by Edison, proposed reform. Hague fought the plan every which way he could. He took out full-page newspaper advertisements at taxpayers' expense. He railed against what he called the railroad lobby. Edison, and those who agreed with him, Hague called "tools of the railroad lobby."

"The most palpably false charges were made, and the most weird arithmetic was used" to highlight the shortcomings of the reform proposal.[7] He lined up all the legislators he could and demanded that they vote against the railroad reform tax bill. They did their boss's bidding. But this time, "all the king's horses and all the king's men" were not enough. The Edison reform measure passed the legislature, and Hague's attempt to have the reform measure declared unconstitutional failed. The reform tax measure went into effect, and over the years, New Jersey's income from railroad tax reform increased substantially. Despite Hague's opposition, Jersey City's income rose significantly as well and, ironically, saved or at least postponed Jersey City's potential descent into bankruptcy.

A "Third Battle of Trenton" took place over revision of the state constitution. Edison, as did many gubernatorial candidates before him, included in his campaign rhetoric a commitment to constitutional reform. Nothing had ever come of it before, and so Hague blithely concluded that nothing would come of the Edison initiatives. But, to Hague's consternation, he found that Edison was serious. The governor dramatized the defects of New Jersey's constitution in every forum and at every opportunity. He took the initiative in helping form a nonpartisan group to push for constitutional reform. Hague was aghast that reform was gaining ground. Yet, neither he nor his Republican allies could halt a referendum authorizing the state legislature to form itself into a constitutional convention to revise the state constitution. Despite Hague's vocal opposition, the referendum carried by a substantial majority. The new state constitution, which went into effect in 1947, permitted a New Jersey governor to succeed himself. The constitution also made the governor of New Jersey one of the most powerful governors in the United States. Other provisions in the new constitution would make it more difficult for Hague, or any other county boss, to control the judiciary, as had heretofore been the case. "As the mayor has become a symbol of democracy at its worst, Edison has become to the people of his state a symbol of what democracy ought to be."[8]

Still, under the old constitution, Edison could not succeed himself as governor. As Edison's successor, Hague would have preferred to run the reliable and attractive A. Harry Moore yet again, but claiming fatigue, Moore turned the mayor down. Instead, Hague selected Mayor Vincent Murphy of Newark to be his gubernatorial candidate. But, despite Hague support in 1943, the Republican Walter E. Edge was elected governor. In 1944, Hague was unable to elect Elmer E. Wene, his preferred candidate for the United States Senate. Two years later, his candidate for governor, Lewis G. Hansen of Jersey City, was beaten by Alfred E. Driscoll, a Republican. Smelling political blood but not yet sure that the time was ripe for Hague's political denouement, Driscoll, to curry popular support, made a big show of going after Hague. In his hometown Hague's political machine, now old with arteries hardened and political hacks aging, was finding it ever more difficult to recruit promising young people. Funeral processions, not political campaigns, were the order of the day.

When on May 13, 1947, Mayor Bernard N. ("Barney") McFeely, the political boss of Hoboken and a Frank Hague political look-alike in his destruction of his city, was unexpectedly thrown out of office, Hague reached a decision. On June 4, 1947, he called newspaper reporters to his office and announced, "I am retiring." He went on to explain that he was resigning in favor of his nephew Frank H. Eggers. "My colleagues on the City Commission," he declared, "have agreed to accept by recommendation that Commissioner Frank. H. Eggers succeed me as mayor."[9]

On June 17, 1947, in a crowded auditorium at Dickenson High School, ten thousand die-hard Hague supporters reviewed his stewardship of Jersey City and applauded when the mayor concluded, "I am turning back the seal of the city, unblemished, with honor and dignity and with the knowledge that I have never betrayed the trust of the people."[10] The band played "Auld Lang Syne."

It was expected by the electorate that "the clown prince," as Eggers was promptly called, would continue to dance to the tune Frank Hague played.

In 1948, Hague's political acumen continued to betray him, and he supported Dwight D. Eisenhower for the presidency instead of working for the nomination of Harry Truman. The political rug was pulled out from under him when Eisenhower refused to run. He sought to elect Archibald Alexander as United States Senator from New Jersey. He failed.

Even in Jersey City Hague continued to lose ground. He had alienated union-oriented voters in his fight with the CIO. Sensing Hague's vulnerability, Polish and Italian Catholics resented Hague's preference for Irish Catholics and ever more boldly vied for a fairer share of political booty. American born, the new generation of Irish-Americans felt little solidarity with the Irish cohesiveness of their parents. In addition, the nepotism of the Eggers anointment did not go down well with them.

As if to support the doggerel that "what goes around comes around," among those who resented Eggers was John V. Kenny, son of the late Ed Kenny, the saloonkeeper who long ago had given Hague his start in politics. John Kenny was a forceful speaker and a rising star in the Hague machine. However, when Frank Hague felt the hot breath of rivalry getting too close, he ousted the young Kenny from the Hague organization.

In 1949, Kenny announced that he would run against Eggers. He carefully balanced the slate of candidates who would run with him as members of the new commission. These included opponents of Hague and reform Democrats. Irish Catholics were balanced with Italian and Polish candidates; others included a Republican, a Protestant, and even a Williams College classmate of Governor Driscoll. With such a balanced team, Kenny announced that he would put himself forward for mayor of Jersey City in direct opposition to Eggers. From his idyll in Florida, Hague rushed back to Jersey City, but his frantic efforts to save his leadership of the Democratic machine failed. On Tuesday, May 10, 1949, in an uncorrupted electoral count, which made use of new, almost tamper-proof voting machines, Kenny won with more than 80,000 votes while Eggers had fewer than 60,000 votes. Kenny's running mates were likewise successful. Frank Hague had been defeated in his hometown.

Hague was down but not out. Not yet. He said, "I stay in politics. It's in the blood."[11] He was still recognized as President Truman's chief dispenser of federal patronage in New Jersey, and he still held the rest of Hudson County. Hague sponsored Elmer E. Wene, whom he had once tried to get elected to the Senate, as candidate for governor against the Republican incumbent Driscoll. If Wene won, it would be a remarkable comeback in Hudson County for Hague. Inasmuch as the only way to assure Wene's defeat and prevent a Hague comeback was to reelect Driscoll, the word went out among Democrats to take a deep breath, hold the nose, and vote Republican. This they did, and Driscoll was reelected.

John V. Kenny, although anti–Hague, was no political reformer. Instead, corruption and labor racketeering continued apace as did gambling and graft, while thugs continued to control the waterfront and the longshoremen's union. Into this morass, an aging but determined Hague, now seventy-seven, once again, in May 1953, entered Eggers as a candidate to defeat Kenny.

The Kenny forces portrayed Hague as a crook and Eggers as his stooge. From a slow start, the momentum for Kenny grew. The Hague organization was mocked in a party newspaper; the Kenny people showed Hague's bills for expensive shirts and silk underwear, and they published the lofty telephone costs Hague incurred trying to run Jersey City from Florida. During the early stages of the increasingly tense and later violent campaign, Eggers was left to manage as best he could. However, Eggers's best was not good enough. Hague came to Jersey City from is home in Biscayne, Florida. He saw the Kenny campaign as a personal betrayal, "If now he betrays me, how can he be trusted not to betray you."[12]

However, Hague did not prevail, and surprisingly for a sophisticated politician, he could not believe what was happening. As he made his way to the speakers' platform in a Hague-Eggers rally, banana peels were thrown at him. The cowards in his entourage left him at once; the courageous, with some trepidation, mounted the stage of Jersey City's P.S. 37 with him. The Hague-Eggers party was pelted with rotten eggs. Eggers tried to speak and before long signaled to his followers to leave the stage with him, but Frank Hague would not move. He stood alone on the platform from which for so many years he had exhorted his followers to follow him once more. They would not do so today. A "Down with Hague" sign was provocatively thrust into his face. "G'wan back to Florida!" an aggressive protester shouted. "Hague almost choked with fury. Smashing aside the sign, he pointed down at the culprit. 'Arrest that man!'" Not a cop moved. Hague too walked off the platform.[13]

In the election that followed, however, three commissioners on Kenny's ticket were elected while but two of Eggers' were. This meant that Kenny had won another term as mayor.

Hague, now over seventy-eight, resigned as state and county leader of the Democratic Party. Few were sorry to see him go; few had a good or kind word to say for him. Like an old politician (or old soldier), Frank Hague faded away, but he left "the city of his birth bankrupt, and the life of the community corrupted beyond anything ever seen in the Republic."[14]

Hague's Paradise: The Worst American City

As Frank Hague waxed rich and powerful, Jersey City remained a ramshackle city of filthy streets, broken glass, offensive odors, ill-kempt housing, and decaying schools. Despite his access to federal funds, Hague did little during the Depression decade to modernize Jersey City's streets, sewers, or transportation. A plan to develop a modern waterfront was never addressed. Returning veterans were honored with speeches instead of jobs or other benefits. Not a single new school was built after 1931, and one still had an outhouse rather than indoor plumbing. Garbage was still collected in open wagons pulled by horses. Thirteen percent of all of Jersey City's buildings were "unfit for human habitation."[15]

Jersey City's numerous poor became even poorer and paid higher taxes for the privilege. During the reign of the Hague political machine, the tax rate in Jersey City climbed from $21 per $1,000 in assessed valuation in 1917 to the unbelievable sum of $76.80 in 1947. In the first decade of Hague's mayoralty, the cost of government in Jersey City rose 234 percent, from \$5,012,246 in 1918 to \$16,764,098 in 1927.[16] "The city spends more on itself on a per-capita basis than any other in the United States, by far."[17] An investigation conducted by the City Affairs Committee of Jersey City, disclosed that while most property owners were paying taxes on inflated property assessments, those of favored corporations, financial institutions, and newspapers were grossly under assessed. For example, the Prudential Life Insurance Company, represented by former State Senator Edward P. Stout, a Hague lieutenant, fared better than most of the other companies.[18]

David Dayton McKean, an expert and critic of Mayor Hague, made the following comparative observations:

It cost 15 times as much to govern Jersey City with 300,000 people as it did to govern Akron, Ohio, with 260,000.

It cost 4 times as much to govern Jersey City as it did Kansas City, which had a population of 400,000.

Cincinnati, Ohio, one-third larger than Jersey City, was governed for one-third as much.

The government of St. Louis, Missouri, twice as big as Jersey City, cost about half as much.[19]

McKean likewise noted that Hague's machine ran up the highest per-capita bonded debt for any city of it size in America. The average debt was \$108.85; Jersey City's was \$172.33.[20] Moody's Investment Service rated Jersey City bonds as "junk," a fourth-class risk. Because of the steady decline in the value of Jersey City's property, "the city has no further borrowing power. It has no cushion of credit against any catastrophe, and the exodus of any large taxpaying industry would push it into formal bankruptcy."[21]

The Depression years were especially unkind to Mayor Hague. Before the onset of the Depression, as a technique for getting and keeping political power, he had loaded up the city payroll with an excessive number of employees at fairly high salaries for the usually marginal work they performed. The municipal payroll more than doubled in size during the first decade and a half of Hague's rule. Yet, when the Depression coldly gripped Jersey City as it did every other city in America, Hague found it difficult to economize, to cut back on staff, to reduce salaries since every such reduction likewise meant some erosion of his political power and some falling away of political loyalties. Moreover, as World War II took its toll of human life and financial resources, some of the New Deal agencies upon which Jersey City had depended for relief were likewise reduced. The Works

Progress Administration, for example, was sharply curtailed in 1943. Local patronage and local control likewise vanished with the demise of the alphabet soup of New Deal relief efforts.

In the autumn of 1946, a reporter for Newark's *Sunday Call* succinctly explained Hague's loss of power: "His type of political machine is built around jobs and when a choice spot is denied him at the patronage counter, he is bound to suffer.... Without the key state bureau jobs, without the judgeships, and, most important, without the thousands of little jobs which keep a political machine functioning have hurt Hague and hurt him deeply."[22]

During World War II, many Jersey City youths were drafted for military service and were often sent to other parts of the country or abroad. It began to dawn on them that Frank Hague was not the be-all and end-all of political possibilities, nor was the kind of government he provided the kind of government they thought they deserved having served their country. They soured on Hague and laughed at his solemn admonitions that through study and hard work they could succeed as had their now-aging mayor. Hitler had been defeated in Europe, but Hague and Hagueism seemed to persist right in the American backyard. While bad things were happening in his city, Jersey City's mayor serenely spent his winters in Florida and summers at Deal. At one time he had tried to do something to shore up his city; now he threw up his hands in indifference.

Frank Hague died on January 1, 1956. He had held political office before he could legally vote and had served thirty turbulent years as mayor from 1917 to 1947. But, at his death, there were few who mourned. He died "unwept, unhonor'd and unsung."[23]

Part III

JIMMY WALKER: AMERICA'S THIRD WORST MAYOR

Will you love me in December as you do in May?
Will you love me in the same old-fashioned way?
When my hair has turned to gray,
Will you kiss me then and say,
That you love me in December as you did in May?

"Will You Love Me in December as You Do in May."
Jimmy Walker, 1905

8

Politician and Legislator

In his speeches, the future mayor of New York City would digress to inform his listeners that when his father came to America, Buchanan was president and there were but thirty-one stars in the flag. Jimmy Walker liked to tell of how his father arrived in New York penniless, hungry, and how, without shoes, he roamed the "sidewalks of New York." To be sure, William Walker had little money when he disembarked in America at Castle Garden from the paddle steamer *City of Paris* in 1857. He traveled steerage and was seasick much of the time, but when he arrived in America he was not without resources. He knew the carpenter's trade and had his carpenter's tool chest, a rosary, and a prayer book. He was young, just eighteen years old, and Irish. He also had a friend, William Brennan, a coal dealer, who met Bill Walker at the pier and brought him to Greenwich Village to join "a colony of Kilkenny folks." Through Brennan's introductions, Walker Sr. began getting carpentry jobs, and his customers liked his craftsmanship and his honesty. It did not take William Walker long to adapt to America, to build houses for a growing New York, and to prosper.

One James Roon ran the most respectable saloon in Manhattan at the foot of Little West Twelfth Street. There was no sawdust on the floor of this establishment, little profanity, and women could not come to a side door to fill their beer buckets for "the old man." Fist fights, loud arguments, and card games were forbidden. James Roon had a big family of five girls and four boys. Mr. Roon was as strict with his daughters as he was with his saloon. "After Sunday morning mass Mr. Roon saw to it that the window blinds of his front parlor were tightly drawn. Then he would snooze in the peaceful knowledge that his daughters could not peek out upon the Sunday parade of Village dudes."[1]

William Walker saw the Roon girls at Sunday services at St. Joseph's Church on Sixth Avenue, and he was determined to meet the attractive, brown-haired Ellen Ida Roon. From time to time, without knowledge of the elder Roon, the two would meet after Sunday mass for a brief talk. On New Year's Day, William Walker paid a formal call on Ellen Roon, but his overtures were not welcomed by the austere saloon keeper. Nevertheless, with Ellen's mother's help, the two continued to meet and talk from time to time, and before long they were married in another parish without the knowledge of Ellen's father.

Of the two, Ellen was more worldly, more sophisticated than the newly arrived immigrant. Ellen, the liveliest of the Roon daughters, loved parties, dances, and fancy dresses. Had she lived today, Ellen Roon might have been a feminist, but her fate was frequent pregnancies.

Of the many pregnancies, but four children survived into adulthood. The first-born was William Jr. The next was the future mayor, James John Walker, who was born on Sunday, June 19, 1881. He was named for Ellen's favorite brother and was baptized at St. Joseph's Church. Tragedy followed when twin brothers were stillborn; then came George, followed by a girl named Anna who lived but a few weeks, and then another baby girl, Nan, was born. All the children except Nan were born in a flat at 110 Leroy Street. The most quixotic of New York's mayors was born in Greenwich Village, the most quixotic of New York's neighborhoods.

In 1886, William Walker was prosperous enough to pay cash for a large, three-story brick house at 6 St. Luke's Place, around the corner from the apartment on Leroy Street. Jim called his father "the Boss" and his mother "Rosie." Home life was pleasant, and neither parent proved to be an extreme disciplinarian. His father, Jim said, "never scolded us or caused a storm in our house. But he would raise a brow or pull at his ear when annoyed."[2] Though built like a fighter, at home William was, said Jim's sister, Nan, a "passive and gentle" man.[3] Jim's father would live at No. 6 St. Luke's Place until he died in May 1916. The home at No. 6 would, in time, become the home of Mayor Jimmy Walker.

Father Knows Best

William Walker dabbled in local politics but took a lively interest in his children's education. The mayor-to-be was a happy child at St. Joseph's Parochial School and later at St. Francis Xavier, a Jesuit preparatory school on West Sixteenth Street. William Jr. was to be a doctor and Jim a lawyer. In 1898, when Jimmy was but seventeen, his father fell ill during an unsuccessful campaign for an alderman seat, and Jim was asked to make a speech in his father's behalf. Essentially, he was assigned to address local issues and describe how his father would deal with them. But Jim did not know the local issues, and so, with the aplomb of a seasoned actor and the self-assurance of the successful politician he would later become, Jim Walker tickled his Irish audience by painting an idyllic picture of what life could be like, "When you and I and every good Irishman can go back home to that green isle of ours and sit upon its shores and the blue ocean and sing 'Home Sweet Home.'"[4] His Irish audience had no intention of starving at home, but the picture he painted brought tears to their eyes and cheers to their throats. Had Jim found his true vocation? Not just yet.

It was William Walker's good luck that he could use his skills as a carpenter to build housing for the rapidly growing population of Manhattan and later become the proprietor of a lumberyard. Through his work and his political connections, he would lay the basis for his own upper-middle-class lifestyle. His son, Jim, not yet Jimmy, would be unable to boast of a rags-to-riches lifestyle as could his contemporary Alfred E. Smith, nor was his family one of the patricians of the city as was young Samuel Seabury, also a contemporary and later a nemesis. Yet, his father's political connections would give him some leverage in Tammany Hall, where his son could be noticed.

In 1902, after a brief stay at LaSalle Business College, Jimmy Walker began legal studies at New York Law School. While still at law school, Jimmy met the five-foot, ninety-five pound Chicagoan Janet Allen. Jimmy was trying to be a dutiful son by attending law school, but his heart was in the song-writing community of Tin Pan Alley. Janet was working as a chorus girl while waiting for her big chance as understudy for the leading lady in the George Broadhurst musical *The Duke of Duluth*. In 1905, when Jimmy left law school, Janet, whom Jim called "Allie," introduced him to the composer Ernest Ball, who wrote the music for Walker's most successful song: "Will You Love Me in December as You Do in May?" Its lyrics would become a kind of signature for the Jimmy Walker lifestyle and would be played *ad nauseam* at the most unlikely occasions.

A "hit" had been born, and several hundred thousand copies of sheet music were sold and produced royalties at one and a half cents per copy, in excess of $10,000, a huge sum in its day. A dudish dresser, Jim immediately went out and bought three custom-made suits, four pairs of shoes, a dozen silk shirts, three fedoras, and a walking stick. The latter he hid from his father because he knew it would not be well received. But Jim never did succeed in duplicating the success of his first hit, and, by 1909, it was clear that his talents as a songwriter were mediocre. Little wonder, then, that Jimmy's father tactfully pressed his son to resume the study of law.

To the Political Manor Born

If Jimmy Walker's musical talents were third rate, his political instincts were first rate. He was affable, smiled a lot, demonstrated a quick wit, and was an excellent speaker. With talents such as these, and with prodding from his father, young Jim came to the attention of one of Tammany's sachems, Charles W. Culkin, then head of Greenwich Village's Fifth Assembly District, which included the Ninth Ward, and at thirty-two the youngest district leader in the city. Culkin felt that perhaps Jimmy Walker would be the fresh face, the bright and likeable unknown who could unseat Assemblyman John Eagleton.

However, Culkin was initially put off by Jim's dandified wardrobe and thought that the voters might be disturbed by it as well. Nevertheless, he decided to back young Walker. "Jim, I've heard you speak," he said, "and if you really settle down to it I think you'll go places in politics."[5] With a thousand dollars of Culkin's money Walker campaigned vigorously against Eagleton. His strategy was two pronged. He would tour the saloons, announce that the drinks were on him, and in a spirit of much back-slapping, whiskey- and beer-induced camaraderie, "The Young Man's Candidate," as he was called, would make himself known and liked by those present. The second technique was to mount a street-corner platform, remove his hat and coat irrespective of the weather, and speak to the audience, some of whom came to cheer, others to jeer, and others to kill time. Jim captivated his audiences, and with another thousand dollars of Culkin's money thrown into the campaign, Jimmy Walker coasted to victory. He and Janet Allen marked the occasion by becoming formally engaged.

Allie gave up her Christian Science religion, Jimmy finally passed the New York State Bar Examination, and the two set the wedding date for April 11, 1912. For two hours, she waited nervously in the anteroom of St. Joseph's Church fearful that after so long an engagement perhaps she had lost her man after all. She had lost her singing voice, and to lose Jimmy as well would be too much. However, to the dismay of Monsignor Edwards, she marched down the aisle to the tune of Jimmy's "Will You Love Me in December as You Do in May," a not very traditional wedding march. After the ceremony and the reception at the Walker home, the couple left on their honeymoon to Atlantic City. Upon their return to New York, the Walkers lived on the third floor of his father's house at 6 St. Luke's Place.

In the Assembly

Before there was Ronald Reagan, there was Jimmy Walker. Both came to the world of politics from the world of entertainment. If President

Reagan viewed the presidency as a movie set from which he could move the nation, Jimmy Walker thought of the legislature as a stage from which he could secure the passage of legislation he favored through his wit, his disarming smile, and his geniality, rather than his mastery of issues. "A legislator," Jimmy Walker often said, "is like an actor thrown on the stage without any lines."[6] But Jimmy was never at a loss for words.

In 1910, when Jimmy Walker came to Albany to serve in the state legislature, Charles Evans Hughes was governor of New York and Robert Wagner was in the legislature well on his way toward becoming New York's distinguished United States Senator. "Paradise" Jimmy Oliver was there as was Marty McCue, the ex-prizefighter, who asserted, approvingly, that Jimmy Walker applied the Marquis of Queensbury Rules to the legislature. "Big" Tim Sullivan, one of the giants of the old and corrupt Tammany Hall, was there while Al Smith, reflecting Tammany's reform wing, was likewise in the assembly, where he served as Jimmy Walker's guide, mentor, and critic.

When Jimmy was elected to the state assembly, Smith urged Jimmy Walker's father to "let me take that young fellow and tip him off at Albany."[7] The elder Walker needed no urging and was glad to have his son mentored by so promising a politician. In Walker, Smith was to find an apt and ready pupil. The new assemblyman quickly mastered the often arcane aspects of parliamentary procedure and proceeded to introduce a spate of legislative proposals. Over the five years he served in the assembly, he introduced 152 bills, many of which were merely proposals in which one or more members of Tammany were interested, but most came from his own interests. So impressed was Smith with his protégé's progress that he said of him, "This boy is a greater strategist than General Sheridan, and he rides twice as fast."[8]

However, even in these early days in his political career, Jimmy Walker was up late making the most of the limited nightlife Albany had to offer. Weekends he would head for New York, where he was a regular at nightclubs and where he met his friends at Toots Shor's famous restaurant, an informal meeting place for people from Tin Pan Alley and show business. Yet, his energy did not flag. He showed up in the assembly, often late, but always sparkling, clean-shaven, and immaculately attired.

Over the years Jimmy Walker's lateness became legendary, and he once kept President Calvin Coolidge waiting. "One evening at a Jewish fund-raising dinner, he arrived hours late where the guests had already dined and wined well. The crowd became almost hysterical when they saw their Irish mayor prancing in wearing a *yarmulke*. One buxom matron shouted: "Jimmy, circumcision next?" "Madam, I prefer to wear it off,"

Mayor Jimmy Walker (seated on the left) with his mentor Alfred E. Smith in 1929.
Courtesy of the Library of Congress, Prints & Photographs Division, LC-USZ62-
1117854.

was the mayor's instantaneous reply. In those days the press was more judicious in what they printed, and at the time the public never read about it. It was not reported until fifty years later, in 1976, when the distinguished journalist Warren Moscow reported it in a piece reminiscing about the 1926 election of Jimmy Walker as "playboy" mayor of the city of New York.[9]

Yet, his fast-paced nightlife was jarring to the staid Al Smith who warned him again and again that flouting conventions would, in time, bring him down. As time went by, Al Smith turned hostile. While he was in the assembly, however, Smith conceded that Walker was an effective legislator.

As an assemblyman, Jimmy Walker received $1,500 a year and he would get $2,600 as state senator. But few legislators could, even in those days when a dollar went a long way, maintain themselves on salaries such as these. Most required two residences, and to maintain themselves in decent style was no easy matter. Given the expensive tastes of Jimmy

Walker, his financial situation was often precarious. He fell behind in paying his bill at the Ten Eyck Hotel, where he lived when the legislature was in session in Albany, and he incurred even larger debts because of his liberal tipping and generous use of room service. Of some help in meeting these expenses was when, at age thirty-one, he passed the bar and was able to practice law in New York. Never motivated by money, Jimmy grudgingly engaged in law as a means to an end.

Forced into law by his father, Jimmy Walker found in politics a better outlet for the showmanship he enjoyed than in the law at which he labored. Law was his livelihood, politics was his vocation, but show business was his mistress. Perhaps because he wandered between the worlds of Albany and Broadway, he clung to a flamboyant lifestyle against the advice of more statesmanlike, more serious-minded political figures.

In the Senate

Among the well connected in New York during the early twentieth century, there were only two addressed as "Mr." One was John J. McGraw, manager of the New York Giants; the other was Charles Francis Murphy, the laconic sachem of Tammany Hall. When the latter asked Jimmy Walker to stop by his home at East Seventeenth Street, the former knew something important was up.

> Murphy entered the library where Jimmy Walker was waiting and without fanfare: "Keep your seat, young man. And how would you like a seat in the Albany Senate?"
> "I hadn't thought of that," Walker replied.
> "Well," Mr. Murphy said, "suppose you say nothing about it right now, but start thinking about it."
> "I am greatly flattered," Walker said.
> "I flatter nobody," said Mr. Murphy. "And I advise you to treat flattery as you would treat abuse. Pay no attention to either."[10]

What did "Mr." Murphy see in Jimmy Walker?

He saw a young man with a gifted tongue and a quick wit who had some connections on Broadway, which might be useful to Tammany Hall. Perhaps also, he saw in Assemblyman Walker a man who had not yet been corrupted who, along with Al Smith and Robert Wagner, could become part of a still-powerful Tammany but now a political machine genuinely devoted to reforming its image and putting the needs of the people of the city ahead of its own. Charles Francis Murphy was aware of Walker's love for the nightlife, but he may well have felt that under his tutelage Jimmy Walker's high spirits could be redirected toward an enlarged career in public service. But "Mr." Murphy died from a heart attack while shaving on April 25, 1924, at the age of sixty-five. Ten years later, as if wondering what his political life might have been had his mentor lived, Jimmy Walker stood beside "Mr." Murphy's grave and declared, "There lies all that is left of the brains of Tammany Hall."[11]

On May 16, 1916, at age sixty-seven, with his wife and family around his bed, William Walker died at home of a heart condition. But the son in whom he took so much pride was not there. He was trying a case in Mineola, and although he excused himself the moment he heard of his father's terminal illness and hurried home, he was too late. "Your good father has gone," Mrs. Walker softly told her son.[12] Her husband's death was too much for Mrs. Walker, and following a stroke, she died in a coma fifteen months later. From his mother Jimmy Walker inherited a zest for life, from his father a sentimental loyalty to friends.[13]

However, in Jimmy, both characteristics, because he carried them to excess, would cost him dearly. His zest for life was often at the expense of his work as a political leader, and his loyalty to friends of often-questionable character was frequently at the expense of his better judgment. Jimmy found the restraints of married life uncongenial and stifling. He preferred living at the edge, late nights, nightclubs, and mingling equally with the conventional and the libidinous, with the law-abiding and the criminal, with the serious and the fun-loving and sharing dalliances with beautiful women while often ignoring Allie, who had lost her voice and was rapidly losing her figure and her looks. During the senate years, none of this seemed to matter. His late nights and his night clubbing seemed to recharge his batteries, and for a time he was the man to watch.

In Senator Walker's day, the state legislature met in formal session from January to the middle of April. On Monday nights, it became the custom for senators to come to their chambers in white tie and tailcoats with the women wearing long evening dress. "They came by train from Park Avenue and Fifth Avenue and Broadway to see and hear James J. Walker, perhaps the greatest actor of all the political men of the century. David Belasco often sent his actors to Albany 'to learn something from the little master.'"[14]

Walker remained in the senate for eleven years, the last six of which he served as Democratic floor leader. There were fifty-one senators in Walker's time, almost equally divided between Democrats and Republicans. The difference between the minority and the majority was most often one seat. Walker sponsored a bill to legalize boxing and to permit Sunday baseball games; he supported and put through a bill to allow motion pictures to operate on Sunday. He sponsored a bill to unmask the Ku Klux Klan by compelling publication of its membership roll. As Democratic whip, he managed the repeal of the Mullan-Gage Act, a New York version of prohibition. Biographer Gene Fowler discovered among Jim's private papers memoranda having to do with the welfare of neglected children and the rights of the underpaid and the underprivileged. "Finding this envelope," Fowler declared, "was like coming upon the man's real nature and looking into his secret heart."[15]

When Al Smith became a candidate for governor for the first time, "Mr." Murphy gave a dinner for fifty prominent politicians and others from sports and entertainment who were influential but only peripherally involved in politics. But the seating arrangement around the dinner table were not to his liking. He went around the table and made sure that Smith sat on his right and Walker on his left. To anyone who cared about symbolism, it readily became apparent that the troika in New York's politics would be Murphy, Smith, and Walker.

Initially Smith and Walker worked effectively together. As a legislator, Walker often knew more about the bill under discussion than anyone else on the floor, though it was said that "he had probably barely glanced at the measure until a half hour before the debate began."[16] Assemblyman Smith together with Senator Walker worked for and obtained passage of New York State's first Workman's Compensation Act, despite important opposition from corporate lawyers and lobbyists. The new legislation made employers largely responsible for occupational accidents. When Al Smith became governor and Jimmy Walker was majority leader of the Senate, it was the latter who disciplined his members by requiring their attendance and their vote so that he could pass the governor's pet projects. The Smith/Walker team was a legislative duo made in heaven, but it could not last.

The Walker lifestyle grated on Smith's nerves and clashed with his sense of morality and public decency. For Al Smith it was, after all, the nostalgic lyrics of the "Sidewalks of New York" while for Jimmy Walker it was the racier sentiments of "Will You Love Me in December as You Do in May." Smith reluctantly agreed to support Jimmy Walker for mayor, but even during the height of their cooperation their relationship was an uneasy one.

Tales of Senator Walker's wheeling and dealing with friend and foe, with Democrats and Republicans, with senate prima donnas and less-assertive types, are legion. One well-known, but worth-repeating story is of a group of upstate Republican senators who supported John S. Sumner's

Clean Books bill. As an example of the kind of books the bill would censor were those of D.H. Lawrence, some of whose passages from *Women in Love* were read to a rapt audience of senators all of whom were men. Many were sure that such salacious material must be eliminated by way of protecting home, hearth, children, and womanhood. While Walker was opposed to smut, he was also, after all, an actor, a songwriter, and a man of creative talents and opposed any limitation on the originality of creative artists inasmuch as he thought of himself as one.

Walker addressed his senatorial colleagues on the matter. "I have heard with great interest the address of the gentlemen on the other side, and I have utmost respect for what they have said. But I submit, gentlemen, that they are either naive or confused. Why all this talk about womanhood? I have never yet heard of a girl being ruined by a book."[17] The Clean Books bill was lost.

In assessing Jimmy Walker's effectiveness in the New York State Senate, historian Henry F. Pringle grudgingly admitted that Walker brought startling changes to the legislature:

> He brought laughter, good humor, tolerance and a high measure of talent to his work. He was at his best during the Winters of '22 and '23, when he was the majority leader with the microscopic advantage of a single member more than the Republicans had. Having all of his men in their seats when a vote was due, making certain that none of them had been incapacitated by alcohol or other poisons— this was a job that would have driven most politicians to an untimely grave. But Jimmy liked it, and was good at it. Always he gave a great show.[18]

The Mayor-Elect

By 1925, Jimmy Walker was nearing his forty-fifth birthday, but looked younger, and was serving his sixteenth year as a *solon* in the legislature of the state of New York. But popular and effective in the legislature as he was, did Jimmy Walker have a future in politics? George Washington Olvany, the 6-feet 2-inches tall, 210-pound new leader of Tammany, thought so.

George Olvany was born on June 20, 1876, at One Pike Street; he attended Public School No. 3 at Grove and Hudson streets. He was the first Tammany leader to graduate from college having been awarded the baccalaureate from New York University. As a boy he played in the streets with Jimmy Walker and attended mass at St. James with Al Smith. Olvany began working for Tammany at age twenty-one and was elected alderman from the Fifth District at age twenty-nine. As one of a group of "Polar Bears," Olvany, in the dead of winter, would lead his companions in a hasty dip in the frigid Atlantic Ocean off Coney Island. As legend has it, when a practical joker pushed his head into the aldermanic chamber and shouted, "Alderman, your saloon's on fire," he was the only alderman to remain seated. His rise in Tammany was rapid as "Mr." Murphy thought highly of him. And, in 1924, with little opposition, he became Tammany's leader upon Murphy's death. In this position he joined Al Smith in a hard fight to throw Mayor John F. "Red Mike" Hylan into the "ashcan," as Hylan himself inelegantly put it.[19]

However, Broadway, not city hall, became Jimmy Walker's springboard for higher office.

At the Cafe de Paris on West Fifty-Fourth Street, comedian George Jessel was having a hard time as master of ceremonies. The star of the evening, Bea Palmer, the singer who originated the "shimmy," failed to appear, and so Jessel called on a variety of performers who were in the audience to help him out. Eddie Cantor gave him a fifteen-minute monologue, and Nora Bayes sang "Shine on, Harvest Moon." When Jessel noticed Walker at a corner table, he ordered fanfare from the trumpet player and a cymbal crash from the drummer and announced Jimmy Walker as "a young man who may be the next mayor of the great city of New York." Walker, always at his best when least prepared, did not disappoint. For a half-hour he entertained an appreciative audience and a much-relieved Jessel was eternally grateful. Thus, it was that a delegation from Broadway petitioned Olvany on Walker's behalf.

Olvany and Flynn, the latter a graduate of Fordham College and Fordham Law School, were supportive. In their view Walker would "deliver" the patronage Tammany needed to live; his sunny personality would be a refreshing change from the dour Hylan, and his connections to Broadway would not be insignificant. But, to overcome the opposition of the political leadership of Brooklyn, Queens, and Richmond, Walker would need the support of Governor Smith. Smith wavered.

The latter had offered the nomination first to "Mr." Murphy's son-in-law, Surrogate Court Judge James A. Foley, and then to Supreme Court Justice Robert Wagner. Only when his preferred candidates turned him down did Al Smith accept Jimmy Walker as the Tammany nominee. Running with Walker were Charles W. Berry, a staunch friend of Al Smith, for controller, and from the Bronx, Joseph V. McKee for aldermanic presidency.

The New York Times regarded the group approvingly as progressive, and in the primary and the election that followed, Smith effectively stumped for Walker and his running mates. He told his audiences repeatedly how Walker had supported improved housing, rent control, penal reform, minimum wages, soldier bonuses, and child welfare. He did not tell his audience that these were all bills Governor Smith had proposed but which Walker steered through the legislature.

Endorsements came from the Interboro Baseball Association, representing 200 of the better-known amateur baseball teams; from music lovers, who thanked Walker for free concerts in Central Park; and the Anti-Fanatic League, who saw in Jimmy Walker an enemy of intolerance. George M. Cohan declared that every member of the theatrical profession "owed" it to Jimmy Walker to support him. In the mayoral campaign, George Jessel made fifty speeches on behalf of Walker.

Walker was likewise an impressive speaker and in several serious speeches demonstrated a grasp of the city's problems. He promised to keep the nickel subway fare, build a number of needed highways, and add to the city's subway network. Grover Whalen, who had once been Hylan's private secretary and Hylan's commissioner of plants and structures, defected to Walker.

In the Democratic primary, Mayor Hylan, looking for an opening to attack Walker, warned that if Walker were to become mayor of New York, the city would be rife with thieves, gangsters, dope peddlers, and prostitutes. He attacked Walker for his wanton ways, for the allegedly many women in his life, and for his contacts with the world of Broadway and the denizens of the speakeasy. Nevertheless, Governor Smith was on Walker's side. He responded to attacks on Walker that appeared in the Hearst-owned *American* and referred to the powerful newspaper publisher as a "liar" and a "debaser of journalism," and of making "wicked and insidious appeals to race hatred." The Governor went on to say that Hearst had the nerve of a Bengal tiger "to be loafing in the splendor and grandeur of his palatial estate on the Pacific Coast, and attempting to dictate the politics of the greatest city in the world."[20]

On September 15, 1925, as Walker relaxed at the Commodore Hotel, the votes came in. Out of the approximately 400,000 votes cast, Walker won the primary by 100,000 votes. Thus, the way was cleared for Walker to make a run for mayor of New York in the general election. But, to paraphrase Jimmy's song, "would the voters love him in November as they did in September?" Of course, they would.

Compared to the raucous primary fight, the mayoral campaign that followed was relatively staid and gentlemanly. Frank D. Waterman, the fountain pen manufacturer and the Republican candidate, was endorsed by the reform-minded Citizens Union. Waterman sought to appeal to the electorate as a prudent but savvy administrator in contrast to the flamboyant Walker. He presented himself as a shrewd and thrifty businessman who would save the city money. Waterman promised the voters that his administration would "say it with shovels," that is, that it would speed the development of lagging public improvements. When the Republican candidate declared, "I tell you this, Mr. Walker, that every woman in New York knows that the underworld will vote for you to the last stickup man," Eleanor Roosevelt wrote a letter to *The New York Times* reprimanding him as a slanderer.[21]

In New York City, the Socialist Party still had enough members and vitality to nominate their standard-bearer, Norman Thomas, as their candidate for mayor. Although he never had a chance of being elected, his stature on the national scene, commanding presence, and oratorical skills, lent a note of *gravitas* to the mayoral campaign of 1925. Thomas ran on a platform that showed an appreciation of the needs of poorer New Yorkers. He called for public ownership of subways and buses and municipally owned housing to attempt to rid the city of crime and disease-infested slums. Jimmy Walker took Thomas's platform seriously but contrived, when jointly occupying a speakers' platform, to encourage the Socialist candidate to speak first. When Thomas was through, Jimmy Walker would get to the lectern and say, "I enjoy listening to Mr. Thomas. I want you to know that all the things he wants for New York, I want too. But *I* can get them for you."[22]

And, the campaign was not without its dirty tricks.

Without Walker's knowledge, a reporter for the *Morning Telegraph* wrote a letter asking for a reservation to the manager of the Fountain Inn, a hotel in Eustis, Florida, owned by Waterman. He signed the fictitious name "Miss Esther Robinowitz." Mr. Waterman's hotel manager in Florida replied to a Bronx address, "Our clientele is such that the patronage of persons of Hebrew persuasion is not solicited." On October 30, the *Telegraph* carried the letter on its front page. Although Waterman tried to disown the implication that he was anti-Semitic and fired his hotel manager, the damage had been done. Jimmy Walker, rather than deplore the demagogic electoral tactic, roared with laughter.[23]

Mayor Hylan grumpily supported the "the Democratic candidates" but did not mention Walker by name. The Civil Service employees supported Walker with enthusiasm. Even William Randolph Hearst offered his last-minute support. The support came also from the glitterati of Broadway. The bandleader Vincent Lopez and the songwriter Irving Berlin backed Walker as one of their own. Members of the cast of *Gay Paree* gave a block party in Schubert Alley on Walker's behalf.

Thus, it was on a mild fall Tuesday in November, a day conducive to a high voter turnout, Walker easily defeated the Republican nominee Frank D. Waterman. Norman Thomas polled just under 40,000 votes. Jimmy Walker carried all five boroughs with a plurality of 400,000 votes to become New York City's mayor. His running mates, Berry and McKee, were swept into victory with him.

At 10:15 P.M. Walker and his party arrived at the Tammany Hall Wigwam with police clearing the way for the mayor-elect. Olvany, Smith, and Walker made up the triumphant triumvirate, and they all made gracious speeches and were roundly cheered by an audience of Tammany loyalists, well-wishers, and job-seekers. Then Walker went off to celebrate his victory first at other rallies and then, in true Walker fashion, with his Broadway friends. His wife, Allie, remained alone in her suite in the Commodore Hotel.

A few days after his victory, the mayor-elect took the first of what would be a number of extended vacations. Without Allie, he took a four week vacation in the South with a stop in Atlanta, where he tried to show Georgians that they need not fear Tammany and that Governor Al Smith was worthy of the 1928 presidential nomination of the Democratic Party. After Atlanta, Walker went to Miami, where he assured Southern women that they and their children were safe in the streets of New York. He visited Cuba as a guest of the president, who had sent a warship to bring Walker and his party to Havana. When Walker returned to New York on December 8, 1925, he assured Tammany that patronage opportunities would be legion and that he would be guided by Tammany's leadership.

On January 1, 1926, Jimmy Walker briskly mounted the stairs to be sworn in as New York City's one hundredth mayor. But, in 1926, America was hitting its stride, and New York was in the forefront. What kind of man had been elected, and what kind of city would he govern?

9

Mayor of a City
That Never Sleeps

When he emerged from his stately town car to mount the steps of city hall to be sworn in as mayor on January 1, 1926, Jimmy Walker seemed nervous and uncharacteristically serious. His support among New Yorkers was deep and genuine, and the press, with few exceptions, idolized him. Yet, the new mayor did not appear to hear the hosannas or acknowledge the cheers of the crowds. Instead, seemingly oblivious to their accolades, Jimmy Walker "touched his silk hat three or four times but did not raise it from his head. He walked along, nervously it seemed, his shoulders hunched forward, his eyes fixed ahead. Nor did he smile or offer any word to the bystanders."[1]

The inauguration brought to city hall "the largest collection of silk hats ever seen in that edifice."[2] More than 700 guests overflowed the Board of Estimate chamber, a space with a seating capacity of no more than 400. Standing uncomfortably hip-to-hip, the elite of New York's political and business communities watched Walker take his oath of office. The new mayor bowed to Allie and the surviving Roons and Walkers who had come to the ceremony. He acknowledged the presence of the leaders of Tammany by whose grace he had been brought to this exalted position. Before a radio microphone, the first one ever used for an inauguration ceremony, Jimmy Walker took the oath of office administered by Justice Robert F. Wagner.

In his inaugural address, Mayor Walker acknowledged feeling "deep responsibility" upon assuming the office of the mayor of the city of New York. But, he said, "the mayor alone cannot run the whole city government…. This administration," he went on, "will endeavor to make the city better in every respect." He then made a frank appeal for cooperation and called upon all citizens and all civic organizations to work with him in governing the city.[3]

The New York Times noted approvingly Walker's initial appointments to the important posts of police and health commissioners and his promise to take police, health, and education out of politics. Those three departments he would free from the suspicion that they were to be made a happy hunting ground for Tammany dispensers of patronage. "All told," the editorial concluded, "in the matter of filling the important offices, Mayor Walker has fulfilled the prediction that he would name the best men he could find for the three departments which are most conspicuous in the eyes of the people."[4]

With Walker's election, Tammany reigned as well as ruled. As inaugural festivities continued, Tammany patted itself on its back for its victory, prepared to enjoy the feast of patronage, and crowned Jimmy Walker "King of City Hall." As the *Times* observed, New York City's government had been "thoroughly Tammanyized."[5] In 1926, the journalist Douglas Gilbert of the *World-Telegram* wrote, "New York wore James J. Walker in its lapel, and he returned the compliment."[6]

The Man

Mayor Walker was forty-five when he took the office of mayor but looked as if he were in his early thirties. "His hair is black, thick and unruly. His eyes are dark and restless. He has the slim build of a cabaret dancer of a *gigolo* of the Montmartre.... He looks, in brief, to be slightly wicked."[7] But there were little-known contradictions in his character.

Jimmy Walker feared driving more than twenty miles an hour in an automobile; he forbade his driver from sounding the siren in his official car and constantly admonished his driver to "go slow" and obey every traffic signal. His claustrophobia was such that he disliked elevators. Friend and journalist Gene Fowler observed that Jimmy Walker actually feared crowds even though he spent a lifetime in the midst of them and seemed to need them for nourishment as others do food. He cringed when supporters would crowd around him. Fowler quoted Jimmy's wife, Allie, "He couldn't stand being mauled, and very much disliked being slapped on the back or having anyone grab hold of his lapels."[8]

Generally, Jimmy Walker was healthy, but, like Frank Hague of Jersey City, Walker was something of a hypochondriac. Whenever a dear friend got sick or died of some disease, Jimmy would appear to experience sympathy pains or symptoms such as coughing, sneezing, or sniffling.

While in the senate, he was operated on for a hernia that was surgically corrected, and his appendix was removed at the same time. Impatient with the speed of his recovery, he left the hospital a week earlier than his doctors advised. On one occasion, not long after assuming office, he was being taught the Charleston, the new dance craze that was sweeping the city and the country, when he struck his knee against a table and for two weeks thereafter hobbled into his office aided by a cane. But the press was kind and reported that he had hurt himself at home while hurrying to take a telephone call.

He did have a sensitive stomach, partially brought about by the rich food he ate and by an occasional over-indulgence in alcohol. But many of his stomach complaints were symptoms of a nervous tension as of a man who is always functioning at the margins of his body's ability to sustain itself. Fowler reported that in one of his last interviews with Mayor Walker, the latter confided: "The excitement of politics got into my veins. I had happy years in the senate, but always my heart was in the theatre and in songs. I really was moving against my own desires most of the time, and the inner conflicts were great."[9]

Jimmy Walker was a better legislator than a city administrator. He preferred the give-and-take of legislative debate where he was a quick, if often superficial, study of the issue being debated. In the legislature he could get by on his geniality, rapier-like wit, mastery of parliamentary detail, and loyal supporters. As mayor he would find life behind the big desk confining, and attention to administrative details was not his forte. Little wonder, then, that he rarely arrived at his office at city hall before noon and took all-too-frequent vacations. His many absences from his duties often rankled more-disciplined administrators such as Governor Al Smith. When investigations into Walker's administrations began during his second term, his frequent absences were held against him, created a hostile climate in which the investigation would be pursued, and eroded the support of formerly loyal colleagues who distanced themselves when he came under fire.

Walker's tailor, Jeann Friedman, who had a shop near the Ritz-Carlton, dressed the mayor in the florid fashion of Broadway rather than in the staid ways of Wall Street. Jimmy preferred sharp, form-fitting clothes, which he changed three to five times a day depending on the weather and the occasion. His morning coats were braided; his dinner suits had shiny lapels. When he took office there was no dressing room for the mayor, and so Walker saw to it that this defect would be shortly corrected. At the beginning of his political career, Tammany politicians often appeared in top hats for state occasions. Jimmy Walker favored a derby he had designed himself even when that style was giving way to the homburg. Walker detested whiskers and was always clean-shaven. His barber since 1906 was Philip Scallato who "shaved Jim six thousand times and cut his hair nine hundred times." His barber recalled that the mayor said little and could stand the hottest towels, and he insisted that the mayor did not need to dye his hair.[10]

His Women

In an oral history of Manhattan, the author-interviewer wheedled the following reminiscence from a former speakeasy employee:

> "When I was working for my uncle, I delivered booze to Jimmy Walker. Betty Compton, his girlfriend, used to open the door sometimes. Wasn't she some good-looking broad. I was sixteen, seventeen years old, and once she opens the door wearing a negligee and lace and nothing down there. I just stood there stuttering, "I-I-I-I-I." The first time I ever saw a woman's pussy.
> Once, she gives me a hundred dollars. I say I got no change.
> She says, "You always say you got no change. That's okay, keep it."
> Boy, she was a gorgeous broad."[11]

In 1985, some fifty years after the Seabury investigation brought Jimmy Walker's administration to a dismal end, Warren Moscow, then a young and promising journalist, remembered what he could not print in 1929.

Jimmy Walker's steady girlfriend was the star of a new musical, *Fifty Million Frenchmen,* which was opening in Boston and was to open later on in New York. He and Betty occupied a suite at the Boston Statler for the opening of the show. At about 3:00 A.M. Jimmy and Betty got into one of their fights during the course of which she chased him around the hotel suite with her favorite weapon, a slipper. Jimmy sought safety by running for the nearest door and retreated to the corridor. The door slammed behind him, but Betty wrenched it open and ran after him with the slipper still menacing. The door closed and clicked shut behind them.

> And there they were, the mayor of New York and his current mistress, locked out and stark naked except for Betty's slipper, in a 14th floor hotel corridor, in the wee hours of the morning. How they were rescued was never told, but for the rescuer it was too good a story not to be repeated. It circulated on Broadway, and eventually on Park Row, but never got into print.[12]

Warren Moscow observed that in those days the press was kind to public officials and refrained from printing many of the self-incriminating things they said or did. Reporters knew, but did not print, "that at the Mayor's private home (and birthplace) at 6 St. Luke's Place there lived only the first Mrs. Walker, eating bonbons and growing stouter, while her husband lived, loved and slept in a succession of posh uptown-hotel suites."[13]

Jimmy Walker revered his parents but did not follow their saintly example. Jim's wife, Allie, lost her voice and her looks; she became stout and dull and no match for Jimmy's vitality and gregariousness. If Allie was no longer the pert showgirl that he had married, his long-term liaisons were relatively few, and Allie often overlooked what she called his "passing fancies."

More than a passing fancy, however, was Yvonne Shelton, "Vonnie," a singer-dancer whom he met in 1917 well before being elected mayor. They were introduced at a cocktail party by none other than Mayor John Purroy Mitchel, who was not above being attracted to lovely, long-legged young women of screen, stage, and song. French Canadian, Vonnie was appearing in the *Ziegfield Follies of 1917,* which featured such stars as W. C. Fields, Fannie Brice, and Will Rogers, and marked the debut of Eddie Cantor. The impulsive, 5-foot, 85-pound Vonnie and the *bon vivant* Jimmy were an item for several years. But the relationship ended tragically for Vonnie inasmuch as the Tammany powers behind Jimmy's candidacy for mayor viewed her as an obstacle and insisted that she disappear from his heart, sight, and mind. To the voter Jimmy was to be seen only as a model husband devoted to Allie.

On November 8, 1926, Jimmy Walker met Betty Compton, who became the love of his life and his second wife. Betty kept Jimmy at arm's length for about a year before agreeing to be alone with him and then only for a short ride in an automobile. A day or so later she agreed to have dinner with the mayor, and Jimmy was jubilant. Allie, now accustomed to traveling alone without her husband, took two trips to Europe, and during those intervals Jimmy's passion for Betty grew.

English-born Betty Compton, sometimes called "Monk," was twenty-three when Jimmy, exactly twice her age, met her. She had been married in her teens, but the marriage had been dissolved. Betty was slow to respond to Jimmy's overtures, and in 1927 he left for a grand tour of Europe. In 1928, after sixteen years of marriage, Jimmy Walker left Allie and moved into the Ritz. Newspapermen knew of the rift between the mayor and Allie, and Jimmy made little effort to conceal his way of living from them. Reporters were more protective of his personal life than the mayor was. In those days reporters would not report marital discord between celebrities until the couple appeared in divorce court. Perhaps Jimmy's assertion of separation from Allie triggered a latent interest in Betty Compton in that she acknowledged that she was interested in him. But, she wanted no transient thing. Her aim was nothing less than marriage.

When Al Smith learned that Jimmy had left Allie he was not pleased, to say the least. Smith was preparing to be nominated by the Democratic Party for the presidency of the United States and did not want an important campaigner like Jimmy Walker to be tainted by scandal. What followed was a long but bittersweet romance. Jimmy did not want to give up Betty as Tammany urged, and he could not marry her until he got a divorce from Allie. In retrospect, one writer noted, "[Walker's] passion for Miss Compton was as genuine and as profound as any of the tragic love stories of history. It was totally monogamous, totally dedicated attachment and in the end had not a little to do with destroying his political career. If he had been able to keep his mind off her and his eyes on the fantastic political poker game for control of New York, he might have been one of the winners."[14]

His City

"The city seen from the Queensboro Bridge is always the city seen for the first time, in its first wild promise of all the mystery and the beauty in the world." Thus did F. Scott Fitzgerald describe Jimmy Walker's New York.[15] As mayor, Walker entertained six million people who came from nearly every country of the globe and every section of America. The Irish, the Jews, the Germans, and the Italians were the four main immigrant groups; the former two groups, with more than a million each, were the most numerous. "Political leaders attend the functions of all. Goldfogle marches in the St. Patrick's Day parade, Walker and McCooey attend the Purim ball. Smith issues a message of greeting at Rosh Hashannah."[16]

Two hundred and fifty thousand African-Americans lived in New York, mostly in Harlem, and were not yet well integrated into the political fabric of the city. Yet, there were fifty-four African-American policemen, a fire lieutenant, an assistant district attorney, and a hundred schoolteachers. The highest position was held by F. Q. Morton, of the Civil Service Commission at a salary of $7,500. Although by Walker's day women had already won the right to vote, their participation in the government of New York City or in the councils of Tammany remained minimal.

Jimmy Walker's New York was the cultural and financial capital of the world. It was a magnate for people with or without money, for those who came to admire and leave, and for those who came to admire and stay. It was a magnate for the wicked and the righteous, for the aspiring or accomplished artist and the writer, the dancer and the actor, the celebrity, and the "wannabe." Its skyscrapers seemed to confirm that New York was a fantasyland where everything was possible and success was just around the corner. Indeed, "If you can make it in New York, you can make it anywhere."

New Yorkers could see any number of Broadway plays and scintillating musicals including *Ziegfeld Follies, Show Boat,* and *A Connecticut Yankee.* More plebeian tastes could be accommodated in the opulent movie house the Roxy, which cost $12 million to build and could seat 6,200 moviegoers. In 1925, a new Madison Square Garden was built on Eighth Avenue and Fiftieth streets to replace the one on Twentieth Street which was torn down.

In 1923, Henry R. Luce introduced the hard-hitting news magazine *Time,* and in 1925, under the brilliant leadership of Harold Ross, *The New Yorker* magazine began publishing to cater to the tastes of sophisticated New Yorkers as opposed to those of the "little old ladies of Peoria."

Far uptown in Harlem there was another cultural center in the two hundred thousand-person black community of Harlem. Harlem became a magnate for white jazz enthusiasts who would arrive in limos to enjoy the music of Duke Ellington or Cab Calloway. Harlem, too, was the home of such gifted writers of the Harlem Renaissance as James Weldon Johnson, Countee Cullen, and Langston Hughes. Singers like Paul Robeson were gaining recognition. But, important as these developments were, they could not entirely mask the overcrowding, grinding poverty, crime, and drug use to which rampant and generally accepted racial discrimination contributed.

In maybe a hundred thousand speakeasies, the otherwise law-abiding citizens broke the law and enjoyed themselves. Among the more notorious of these was one hosted by Mary Louise Cedilia Guinan, "Texas Guinan," who greeted guests to her establishment with "Hello, sucker." Suckers they were inasmuch as they were willing to pay a $20 cover charge for illicit booze. Mayor Walker would be one of her patrons.

Yet, the New York City to which Mayor Walker had been elected did not live up to its reputation as a Babylon on the Hudson, let alone to the wilder imaginings of Americans in the hinterlands. Instead, "vice conditions in New York are better than they have ever been and superior to those of any other large city in the country. Street-walking simply does not exist. Brothels are equally unknown. There is no organized or obtrusive prostitution.... Gambling has been checked.... The burlesque shows, though not exactly elevating, are on almost the same moral plane as the Broadway revues. Speakeasys abound, but responsibility for them must be laid at the door of the Republicans."[17] For these reforms Professor Joseph McGoldrick of Columbia University gave credit to the "new" Tammany as led by Mr. Murphy.

Yet the new mayor was worried that the beatings and fights and occasional murders commonly associated with speakeasies would give the city a bad reputation. Walker urged a three o'clock curfew in an attempt to curb the wilder proclivities of the nightclub crowd. Such an ordinance was passed, but it did little good. Under Walker's police commissioner, Edward P. Mulrooney, some degree of control of nightclubs and dance halls was wrested from the criminal element. But with the onset of the Depression of the 1930s, nightlife lost much of its vitality and glamor.

Jimmy Walker's New York had an army of 120,000 permanent employees, an annual budget of $550 million, an annual payroll of $250 million and $375 million worth of contracts to be awarded each year. Seventeen thousand police tried to patrol its 5,000 miles of streets and its 585-mile waterfront. In complexity, the government of New York City was second only to that of the government of the United States. Yet, at the beginning of Mayor Walker's administration city hall moved at a snail's pace. On even the busiest of days, there were but two dozen or so cars in the parking lot as most employees arrived by public transportation and few citizens had any business at all with city hall. There were no unions of city workers. There was no sales tax. The city received no federal money and just a little money from the state for education. There were no central departments of highways or public works. The city street cleaning department did not extend to Queens and Richmond, where the borough presidents made their own arrangements. There was no department of hospitals until Walker created one in 1929, and no housing authority. "The Mayor's presence, apart from Board of Estimate calendar days, was a sometime thing. He would arrive around 3 P.M. a couple of days a week and other days not at all. And that was enough."[18] Yet the "city hall circus" over which Walker was about to preside was generally a "well governed city ... any competent observer must admit."[19]

Few could present a better mirror image of New York as it existed in the mid–1920s than its newly elected mayor, Jimmy Walker. Between his first election in 1925 until he was driven from office in 1932, Walker was New York's undisputed master of ceremonies. As mayor of New York he would not so much govern the city as preside over it as a host might, seeing to it that insofar as possible everyone was having a good time.

Hitting the Ground Running

There was dancing in the streets when Jimmy Walker took office. Few mayors came into office with more good will. He had a popular mandate and a supportive press. His reputation as a gregarious, good-natured politician preceded him, and New Yorkers were anticipating with relish a more-vigorous leadership than that provided by the heavy-handed Hylan. Newspaper editorials representing all shades of the political spectrum were unanimous in wishing the new mayor well. The Citizens Union, which had endorsed Walker's main opponent, Frank D. Waterman, noted, "No new Mayor ever faced his responsibilities with a clearer mandate or a more hopeful and confident volume of public sentiment behind him than did James J. Walker. He had been emphatically commissioned to lift forthwith that humiliating smoke screen of bluff, bluster and hollow sham, behind which his predecessor had been playing at discharging his public duties."[20]

With Walker's election, Tammany's victory was complete. That his erstwhile rival, Norman Thomas, disparagingly described Mayor Walker as "machine made," did not diminish the reforms New Yorkers expected him to carry out with the help of an allegedly more enlightened Tammany Hall. There was general optimism in journals of opinion that despite of or because of the mayor's intimate association with Tammany, his administration would be a successful one. Joseph McGoldrick, a political scientist and sometime critic of Walker declared, "New York is a well-governed city. In spite of the close domination which the Tammany machine and its allies have maintained, any competent observer must admit that it shines by comparison with the other huge cities of the country.... Tammany is merely the biggest, certainly not the blackest of political machines."[21]

As revealed in headlines culled from *The New York Times* of 1926, the new Mayor was perceived as having "hit the ground running":

> January 4: *"Walker Takes up City Duties Today."*
> January 5: *"Walker Orders End of Transit Clashes."*
> January 6: *"Walker Lays Down Rules of Conduct for all His Aids."*
> January 7: *"Walker Will Stop Board Logrolling."*
> January 8: *"Walker Outlines $400,000,000 Plan for New Subways."*

At the suggestion of Governor Alfred E. Smith the new mayor chose as his police commissioner George V. McLaughlin, the former state superintendent of banking — a tough, decisive, and incorruptible administrator. Dr. Louis I. Harris, an eighteen-year veteran of the Department of

Health, was appointed the new health commissioner. And John H. Delaney, chairman of the board of transportation, a protégé of the late Tammany leader Charles Murphy and not a Walker appointee, nevertheless, was a jewel among New York City's administrators. Duncan McInnes in the controller's office "had the city's financial books memorized."[22]

The *Times* commented favorably on Walker's choice of administrators, and the Citizens Union was astonished but pleased to find "new spirit of honest effort among the rank and file of the [police] force has been developed."[23]

Mayor-at-Large

Following eight dull years with Hylan, New Yorkers were ready for a good time with Walker. They would not be disappointed. The new mayor of the city of New York, for good or ill, would become more widely known worldwide, more frequently photographed, and more often reported on in the media in all parts of the country than any other occupant of New York's city hall.

In late summer and early fall of 1927, Mayor Jimmy Walker, his wife, Allie, and a supportive entourage, made an extended tour of Europe with the alleged purpose of learning how the great cities of that continent dealt with such perennial problems as building low-cost housing, disposing of garbage, making vehicular traffic flow smoothly, developing cheap public transportation by bus or subway, or otherwise making city government more efficient in providing the services it offers its citizens. But inasmuch as the nine-week tour of Europe was given over more to receptions, luncheons, dinners, speeches, and sightseeing, rather than study as such, how much the Mayor actually learned cannot be assessed.

The mayor, however, proved to be a natural ambassador of goodwill. The Houston *Post-Dispatch* observed, "With the exception of Colonel Lindbergh, no American who has visited Europe since war days has been received with such enthusiasm as that accorded the young Gotham executive."[24] In each of the stops in his triumphal tour of Europe — London, Paris, Dublin, Munich, Berlin, Rome, and Venice — he was viewed as the lovable rather than the ugly American. The dapper mayor of New York was, perhaps, not taken seriously and so seemed no threat. His somewhat roughish appearance was such a radical departure from what Europeans would expect of their own political leaders that the masses of Europeans who followed him in every city he visited warmed to his charm and delighted in his quips, wise cracks, and repartee. Europeans, perhaps more broad-minded than puritanical Americans, appeared attracted to Walker's slightly naughty appearance and reputation. Whether visiting his ancestors in Ireland or Benito Mussolini in Rome, he made an irresistible impression, one that evoked a smile rather than a frown.

He endeared himself to the French, even though he could not understand a single word, when he said, "It isn't hard to understand the French people if you have an ear for music."[25] In Italy, after a 46-minute interview with Mussolini, the mayor and the dictator mutually admired each other. The mayor declared that he found Mussolini "a man of superior attainments" while Mussolini was sure his smartly clad visitor was "a man of great talent, an idealist, and a practical man at the same time."[26] In Rome, Pope Pius XI gave Walker a gold medal bearing the Pope's likeness and Allie a gold rosary.

In Ireland he visited Castlecomer, the village in County Kilkenny from which his father left for America in 1857. Several of Walker's cousins still lived there, and they, together with country people from miles around, hailed him as he stepped from his limousine, "Three cheers for William Henry Walker's boy!"

The London press commented favorably on their visitor from New York: "He is a rare Mayor, a Mayor of the type not often seen in this country.... He takes his work seriously, but he does not take himself too seriously. Some of our English Mayors do!"[27] Little wonder that to one historian he was America's "Mayor-at-Large."[28]

Although the mayor had expressed a wish that his welcome home be a modest one, Grover Whalen, chairman of the Mayor's Reception Committee, saw to it that he received a hero's welcome. When the new luxury liner *Ile de France* made fast to her pier, a red plush carpet was laid from the gangplank to the waiting room at the head of the pier where relatives, friends, and colleagues waited to welcome the mayor. As he was escorted off the ship by Grover Whalen, the band played the pompous "Hail the Conquering Hero." To those who came to the pier to meet him, he had a kind word for the cities that had offered him their hospitality. He declared, "I feel myself enormously benefited by the insight into foreign municipal processes. London with its fine old traditions and courtesy; Dublin with its progressive spirit; Berlin with its spick-and span cleanliness; Rome with its modern vitality and ancient loveliness; Paris with its cultural eminence — to visit these cities has been a privilege and a pleasure."[29]

But the mayor was tired. He suffered from indigestion from eating too much and perhaps drinking too much in a Europe not bound by prohibition during his nine-week, comic-opera trip. Nevertheless, with the music and the plaudits from his well-wishers still ringing in his ears, Jimmy

Walker plunged into his mayoral duties. As a headline in the *New York Evening Post* reported:

> Amazing Mayor Early at Work on First Day Home.
> Walker Runs Nimbly Up Steps at 10 A.M as Scrubwomen
> Rub Unbelieving Eyes.[30]

But those who knew him well had no illusions. The prediction, "He'll make a lousy mayor. But what a candidate,"[31] was borne out by any objective evaluation of his administration. Nevertheless, New Yorkers would love him for his faults and enthusiastically reelect him.

Reelection

On July 18, 1929, millionaire philanthropist August Heckscher led a group of 682 public-spirited New Yorkers who put their names to a petition begging Mayor Walker to run for reelection. The petition was no spontaneous demonstration of support. Instead, it had been carefully crafted by Grover Whalen at the urging of the mayor.

In his private office at city hall, to which Grover Whalen had been summoned, the mayor said,

> "Grover, it is the custom of reluctant candidates to be drafted. They always hear the call of the people, even if it is but a whisper. Will you see to it that I receive this call? And will you manage it with your usual David Belasco skill, plus a bit of Phineas T. Barnum?"
> "You will hear the call," said Whalen smiling.[32]

The committee of 682 crowded into the cramped board room to hear the distinguished chairman Heckscher read the petition. Allie Walker, sharing the platform with the mayor, did her duty by playing the role of the loving wife by smiling as though Jim was still her devoted husband. Radio microphones picked up the voice of Heckscher as he read the mayor's forty accomplishments as Grover Whalen had prepared them.

Walker responded, as if surprised by this "spontaneous" outburst of support, with a long speech which he concluded with the rhetorical question, "Who can say no?"[33]

Because New York City's Republicans could find no one else to run against the seemingly unbeatable Jimmy Walker, the party, on August 1, 1929, meeting at the Mecca Temple on West Fifty-fifth Street, reluctantly nominated the colorful Fiorello H. La Guardia as its mayoral candidate.

The "Little Flower," as he was called, could not have been more unlike his opponent. While Walker dressed to "the nines," La Guardia cared little about his appearance. The mayor could not or would not concentrate on the issues before him; his opponent, as a United States congressman since 1916 and for a short time president of the board of aldermen, was a tireless worker who read the details of every bill and knew the nuances of every issue on which he was called to speak or vote. In his speeches Jimmy Walker sought to charm his audience with wit if not always with wisdom. La Guardia's flamboyant speeches, during which he gesticulated wildly, his voice rising to a harsh falsetto when he sought to be particularly sarcastic about his opponent, often masked his real grasp of complicated issues. Although La Guardia knew he was not his party's favorite candidate, he fought the good fight and promised victory in the November elections.

La Guardia spared no effort to win. If Walker represented those who flourished in the jazzy days of the twenties, La Guardia was a symbol of New York's minorities, its ghettoes and ethnic enclaves. He promised honesty in government, low-cost housing, lower food prices, an end to tax breaks for business, urban planning, parks, and more recreational opportunities. But neither his promises nor the criticisms of the Walker administration could jar the electorate out of its complacency and their confidence in Jimmy Walker.

Even critics of Tammany could not see in Fiorello La Guardia the person who could restore efficiency and propriety to the office of mayor of the city of New York. The Citizens Union, which was at first enthusiastic about Walker's seemingly effective start during his first term and later a severe critic, declared, "It is difficult to find in Mr. La Guardia's record anything tangible upon which to base hopes that as Mayor he could formulate and adhere to a constructive program of administration."[34] The liberal journal *The Nation* likewise could not bring itself to endorse the La Guardia candidacy. After identifying the many times it had agreed with La Guardia's policies as congressman, the journal continued, "Why, then, can *The Nation* not endorse his candidacy? Because … it is quite aware of the fact that the Republican machine, despite its fringe of respectables, is not one whit better and is far less able than Tammany Hall."[35] *The New York Times* expressed its confidence in Jimmy Walker, urged his reelection, and asserted: "Everybody who knows Mr. Walker well is confident that he has in him the makings of a remarkable chief magistrate of this city. The mayor that he has been gives only a hint of the mayor that he might be."[36]

Although the stock market had crashed the week before and snow was falling, neither could keep New Yorkers away on that first Tuesday in

November when voters flocked jubilantly to the polls to reelect their beloved Jimmy Walker. La Guardia lost by almost five hundred thousand voters and failed to carry a single assembly district. The voters did not yet realize that the good times were ending, that Walker, the mayor of their choice, was the wrong mayor for the times, while La Guardia, the candidate they spurned, would have had been the right man for times that were coming.

Shortly after the polls closed and reelection was assured, the forty-eight-year-old Jimmy raced uptown to his twenty-five-year-old Betty Compton who was rehearsing her routines for the new play *Fifty Million Frenchmen*, which was about to open in New York. "I wanted you to be the first to congratulate me ... I've been reelected," he exalted. "Well, it's no surprise, or is it?" Compton remarked coolly. "I believe you would be better off and happier if you quit politics."[37] She was right.

Walker's reelection was to be his undoing. He should have listened to the inner voices which urged caution and recognized that he could not ride the magic carpet of popularity indefinitely. There were omens that, had he listened to them, might have warned him that times were changing and that his leadership style would no longer fit a less prosperous New York, much less one mired in deep depression. He would preside over a city for which the easy times of the twenties were over. According to historian Thomas Kessner, columnist Henry McLemore correctly observed that Jimmy Walker was "not fitted for hard times."[38]

10

The Mayor
and the Inquisitor

"Hizzoner," the mayor, was doing what he did best, namely meeting and greeting dignitaries to "his" great city. The occasion was the arrival of Queen Marie of Rumania to New York City to begin an extensive tour of America. Mayor Walker was waiting for her on the steps of city hall where he presented her with a hand-illuminated scroll of the city's charter and a special medal from the city of New York. He was about to pin the medal on her coat in the vicinity of her ample bosom when he remarked:

> "Your Majesty, I've never stuck a Queen before, and I hesitate to do so now."
> "Proceed, Your Honor," she replied graciously. "The risk is mine."
> "And such a beautiful risk it is, Your Majesty," replied Jimmy Walker."[1]

Taking Her Majesty by the arm, he escorted her into the great Aldermanic Chamber. There, Walker proceeded to charm Her Majesty and the official audience who had come to see, to be seen, and to be entertained.

The steps of city hall were made an open-air theater by Jimmy Walker. Here, this frustrated actor gave almost three hundred performances as he welcomed dignitaries with extemporaneous speeches, scrolls of the city charter, medals, and keys to the city. According to Grover Whalen, the high-water mark of these receptions was 1926–1927, when in a space of a few months the mayor greeted, in addition to Queen Marie, Charles A. Lindbergh whose solo flight across the Atlantic thrilled the world, Gertrude Ederle who swam the English Channel, Sweden's Crown Prince Gustavus Adolphus and Princess Louise, Guglielmo Marconi, and Prime Minister

Ramsay MacDonald of England. Whalen described, with understandable pride, the thrill of greeting heroes and celebrities, the famous and the notorious, the glitterati and the literati, stars of stage and screen, dancers, crooners, and song writers from Tin Pan Alley as they disembarked from stately trans-Atlantic ships in the great harbor of a great city.

But these official welcomes cost money. Limousines to meet the dignitaries, gilt chairs suitable for royal derrières, four horses from the Ben Hur Company, and four Hussar uniforms had to be rented. Cleaning up after a parade was by no means cheap. Streamers of ticker tape, blizzards of shredded newspapers and telephone books, floated down from the office buildings of lower Manhattan and had to be swept up. The welcome for Lindbergh, for example, cost $71,850. Did the city get its money's worth? Most New Yorkers thought so.

Few mayors bore their official duties more lightly than Jimmy Walker. He was propped up on every hand. Grover Whalen was the city's official greeter, and Tammany Hall recommended patronage appointments. Thus, the mayor could shirk his duties, and he did so. Of his first 30 months as mayor, Walker spent 149 days on vacation.

Yet, Walker's six years as mayor would not be without accomplishments. These included the first citywide sanitation system, new docks for superliners, and the city's first hospitals department. He started the West Side Highway and worked out a deal with the railroad which put some of the New York Central freight trains underground. He laid the groundwork for the Triborough Bridge and the Queens-Midtown Tunnel. Some progress was made in adding to the parkland of the city by acquiring, at a reasonable price, 600 acres on Staten Island and 260 acres in Queens. Widely commended also were the plans for restoration and rehabilitation of Central Park. In his first term, the Walker administration spent $316 million on building new subways and extending old ones. More than 100 miles of subways were laid out in Manhattan, the Bronx, Brooklyn, and Queens, the ultimate cost to be $500 million.

Although a "quick study" Mayor Walker was guided more by expediency than by an overarching ambition for the city. As *The New York Times* expressed it after he retired, "The best characterization of his administration was one of gay and cheerful muddling through."[2]

The Mayor

THE POLICE: "DON'T MESS WITH TAMMANY"

Commissioner George V. McLaughlin, ably aided by police captain Lewis Valentine, went after the illegal gambling of "Nigger" Nate Raymond,

Nick "the Greek," and the notorious and well-connected Arnold Rothstein. Under McLaughlin, the police department broke up the then illegal but lucrative Park Avenue abortion practice of Dr. Robert Thompson and closed down many fake auction houses, gyp joints, gambling dens, and bordellos that clustered in Times Square and entrapped innocent New Yorkers and gullible tourists. The reenergized police department initially seemed a match for the ever-creative scams. Gambling floated from one hotel location to another to escape being caught by aggressive policing. Behind steel doors gambling continued, but police, equipped with sledgehammers, broke them down. But, most often, not soon enough. Before the police could break through, the gambling equipment disappeared, and the gamblers vanished.

Tammany sachems grew grouchy when McLaughlin's cops broke down the doors of their clubhouses, and the police commissioner grew frustrated as convictions appeared all but impossible. In 1927, after only little more than a year, Commissioner McLaughlin resigned his $10,000 police commissionership to accept the vice-presidency of the Mackay Telegraph and Cable Companies at an annual salary of $75,000.[3]

Joseph A. Warren, a former law colleague and a Tammany comrade of Walker, who had been serving as commissioner of accounts, was appointed the new police commissioner. But Warren did not grasp the mayor's broad hints that McLaughlin's aggressive policing style should be moderated. Instead, he informed the press, "I shall endeavor to continue the policies of Commissioner McLaughlin."[4] Contrary to Walker's expectation, Warren instructed his police officers to "carry on" as usual. Because they did, it was not long before the new commissioner got on Walker's and Tammany's nerves. Warren, who was not a strong man to begin with, was torn between the desire to be an honest and aggressive cop yet aware that Tammany was unhappy with stringent enforcement of the law, and he resigned in 1928. Sick and weary, he died eight months after Walker forced his resignation allegedly for his failure to apprehend the murderers of the notorious gangster and gambler Arnold Rothstein.

Walker signaled his retreat from strict law enforcement when he appointed the dandified Grover Whalen to be his new police commissioner. With a prominent gardenia in his lapel and a carefully trimmed mustache under his nose, Whalen banished the able policeman Captain Lewis J. Valentine to an obscure post in Queens. To get the citizens to think about something other than the unsolved Rothstein murder, Commissioner Whalen was a torrent of energy as he reshuffled and reassigned staff, and the Black Maria paddy wagons brought in hundreds of derelicts, panhandlers, and vagrants, few of whom had committed any crime and had to be discharged before the day was over for lack of evidence. A new system of traffic control in midtown made it possible for theatergoers to get to the theater before the curtain went up. New Yorkers were grateful, and no one cared that the Rothstein case had not been solved. Grover Whalen's foot-dragging in an interminable investigation of Arnold Rothstein and a series of unsolved crimes delivered the message machine politicians wanted to hear: "Do not mess with Tammany."[5]

Parks: "This Will Be Our Place, Monk."

At his inauguration on January 1, 1926, Mayor Walker made clear his intention to lead a campaign on behalf of the need for additional parkland in New York City. The city's Park Association, with the help of Robert Moses, prepared the mayor's commitment to a vast program of city parkland acquisitions. By making the acquisition of more open space for parks a high priority of his administration, Jimmy Walker climbed aboard a popular theme and widely acknowledged awareness that New York City lacked sufficient recreational and park spaces and that existing parks were in desperate need of repair. The City of New York set aside a smaller percentage of land for park and recreation than did any of the other ten largest cities in America. Moreover, according to distinguished journalist Robert Caro, New York's parks "were scabs on the face of the city" and were to remain that way through the Walker administration.[6]

In Walker's day the management of the city's parks was in the hands of the president of each borough. As a result, borough presidents often used the parks to derive illicit revenue by leasing public property for private gain. A politically well-connected brick manufacturer in Brooklyn, for example, leased ten acres of parkland as storage space for $2.50 a year. Some of the most desirable beach property was removed from public use and rented to political insiders for a fee of $15 upon which those thus favored could build a private bungalow.[7]

Most park vehicles were still horse drawn and most park personnel unskilled. Children's wading pools were stagnant, smelly, and a threat to health. "One survey found that not a single structure in any of the city's parks that did not require repair. Central Park ... had deteriorated into an unattractive patchwork of rutted walks, broken benches, and untended fields, its zoo filled with elderly and diseased animals."[8]

In his campaign Jimmy Walker promised to make substantial and much-needed improvements to Central Park. But the jewel of his accomplishment, the Central Park Casino, became a watering hole for the city's political and social elite, a restaurant built with public money to massage private egos.

The restaurateur Sidney Solomon proposed to Mayor Walker that he take over the low rambling building that had been built in 1864 as a "Ladies Refreshment Salon" and was shabbily run as a casino by Carl F. Zittel, a small-time theatrical publisher whose lease would expire in mid-1928. The mayor ousted Zittel and turned the lease over to Sidney Solomon for a modest annual rental. Zittel sued the mayor, alleging that the lavish new Casino restaurant was contrary to the recreational goals of Central Park, but Zittel's claim would not prevail.

Located just off Fifth Avenue in the posh Seventies just within the boundaries of Central Park, the Casino was more than a restaurant with Walker carefully devoting his attention to the details of the lavish $400,000 Casino. When reopened, it was the swankiest restaurant in New York.

On opening night applicants sought reservations, but only six hundred could be accommodated. Among the celebrities on opening night were socialite Charles M. Amory, Hollywood producer Adolph Zukor, and Broadway producer Florenz Ziegfeld. So great was the demand for opening night admission that two opening nights were held, with Mayor Walker and Betty Compton attending the second one. Prepared by the finest chefs, guests dined on Caviar des Grands Ducs, Frivolités Éscoffier, Cardinale de Mer a l'Américaine, and Pousin désosse Armenonville. They digested their meal to the tunes of "Sweet Sue–Just You," "You're the Cream in My Coffee," and "Ain't Misbehavin'."[9] But, of course, they were.

In a lavishly detailed upstairs backroom the mayor would hold court for those seeking favors. In an adjoining room, equally hidden from public view, was a room where the rulers of Tammany could be entertained by bevies of chorus girls brought to the Casino under motorcycle escort for the occasion. On the main floor, to the strains of the most popular dance bands of the day, Leo Reisman, Emil Coleman, and the young Eddie Duchin, who would become the most popular and expensive band leader of the decade, the privileged guests would dance into the early hours of the morning. To get around prohibition, chauffeurs would arrive with their well-heeled clients in expensive cars well-filled with illicit alcohol and champagne. When an observant maitre d' would notice that a table was running out of booze, a quick signal to a chauffeur brought prompt relief.

This pleasure palace became "Jimmy Walker's Versailles," where he spent more time than at city hall. To his mistress, Betty Compton, he said, "The Casino will be our place, Monk."[10] And indeed it was.

CRIME: "THE KING OF EASY MONEY IS DEAD"

On the night of November 4, 1928, after dinner at the Casino, Jimmy Walker and Betty Compton were driven to Joe Pani's Woodmansten Inn in Westchester to dance to the music of Vincent Lopez. Betty was having a great time, and the bandleader was about to autograph "Cinderella's" slipper when an acquaintance of the mayor strolled over to his table and whispered the news that the gambler Arnold Rothstein, "the king of easy money," had been shot. The mayor knew that there would be trouble immediately ahead. "His instinct was on target; there would be even more trouble that he could possibly have imagined."[11]

Rothstein was found wounded at the side entrance of the Park Central Hotel on Seventh Avenue. He would die of his wounds at Polyclinic Hospital on election day when American voters chose Herbert Hoover over Alfred E. Smith. But he would not reveal the names of his assassins, although it was clear that he knew who they were. Failure to find Rothstein's killers, despite significant clues which were not followed up on, is explained less by the ineptitude of the police and more by the close connections between Tammany leaders and the underworld of crime which politicians understandably sought to hide from public view. Walker would make a great show of his effort to solve the Rothstein murder while, with a wink, nod, or shrug, he supported foot-dragging by his police department, but first he needed to find a foot-dragger.

Alleging that he was dissatisfied with the progress being made in apprehending Rothstein's assassins, the mayor, in a rare move, fired Police Commissioner Joseph Warren and appointed the more-compliant Grover Whalen in his stead. Warren knew he had been set up and was taking a "bad rap" inasmuch as none of the politicians were eager to find Rothstein's assassins and were not helpful in his investigation. Whalen, for his part, could make Jimmy Walker look good. As a new broom he boasted that he would sweep criminals out into the open. That never happened. Failure to solve the Rothstein crime may be considered the start of the slippery trail that led to Walker's political disgrace.

In the fall of 1929, a serio-comic escapade worthy of a Hollywood screenwriter, dull-witted, pistol-toting bandits raided a lavish party at the Roman Gardens sponsored by the Tepecano Democratic Club in honor of Justice Albert A. Vitale. To the gathering were invited politicians and celebrities from Hollywood, Broadway, and organized crime. Among those who came in a bullet-proof limousine was one Ciro Terranova, the "artichoke king," whose gangland connections made it possible for him to maintain control over the importing and marketing of exotic vegetables.

Others of similar ilk were likewise present, when all at once the mobsters, at gun point, stripped the guests of their jewelry, watches, and cash while a city detective, who was an invited guest, meekly turned over his revolver to the thieves. But who would dare embarrass such a distinguished jurist, mar a testimonial dinner in honor of a leader of Tammany Hall, and steal from his guests? The guest of honor hastened to find out. It did not seem to be much of an effort for the magistrate to track down the perpetrators of this madcap crime and to have the swag and the detective's pistol restored at once to their proper owners.

However, New Yorkers began to wonder at the underworld connections of this well-wired judge. Was this the kind of man who should be sitting in judgment over others? In four years on an accumulated salary of $48,000, Judge Vitale had managed to save over $165,000. How had he done so? The embarrassment was too great even for Tammany to bear, and so, shortly after the spectacle in his honor, the judge was out of his job and disbarred. His political connections, however, were such that he continued to develop a lucrative business as a middleman between the world of politics and crime.

SUBWAYS: "FIVE CENTS IS ENOUGH"

During the late nineteenth century, a number of elevated rail lines were constructed, and in 1904 the first section of the Manhattan Interboro Rapid Transit subway system was placed in operation. In later years the system was extended into Brooklyn, Queens, and the Bronx. The IRT was built and owned by the city and leased to a private firm that operated the subway. In 1913, the Brooklyn Rapid Transit Company, later Brooklyn-Manhattan Transit (BMT), was added to New York City's subway system.

In return for the franchise and city financing, the BMT and the IRT agreed that the transit system would charge "the sum of five (5) cents for a single fare, but not more."[12] The nickel fare was enough to bring substantial profits to IRT stockholders who initially realized a 187 percent return on their investment. But over the years inflation eroded the subways' profitability, and the "traction interests," as they were collectively called, sought relief from their commitment to the nickel subway ride.

Clifton Hood, who wrote a history of the New York City rapid transit system, called inflexibility on the five-cent fare "the San Francisco earthquake of municipal fiscal calamities."[13] Nevertheless, support of the five-cent fare became a litmus test for those who aspired to elective position in the City of New York. When "good-government" advocates urged greater efficiency, the populace took this as code words for attacks on the nickel subway fare. Walker had an instinctive awareness of what the nickel fare meant to working-class New Yorkers. By fighting for the five-cent fare, Walker further enhanced his popularity as a champion of the "little guy."

In 1928, traction interests were putting renewed pressure on Governor Smith for legislation that would provide them with relief from the five-cent fare. When a day was set for a hearing in Albany on the matter, Walker, who had been urged to testify, was late as usual. He had missed his train and thus kept the governor, the legislative committee, and the group of prominent traction attorneys, headed by the distinguished De Lancey Nicoll, waiting. As they waited, they heard once again from Jimmy, who announced that he had missed yet another train to Albany and was en route by automobile.

By four o'clock in the afternoon, a tired Jimmy arrived and was chastised by an irate Smith who berated him for wasting the time of the governor. To the discomfort of Governor Smith, however, the crowd cheered Walker when he entered the executive chamber to listen to the finely honed arguments for a seven-cent fare offered by the lawyers for the elevated and subway lines. Nicoll discoursed for over an hour on the need for a fare increase. Governor Smith, who presided over the hearings, then sourly announced, "The mayor of the City of New York will now reply." "Jim rose, as jaunty as you please, did his usual handkerchief trick, and then said in reference to the lawyer's lengthy speech; 'Gentlemen, that was the longest ride I ever had on a Nicoll.'"[14] The mayor went on to explain that since the traction interests could not guarantee every passenger a seat, they were not entitled to be guaranteed a fare of more than five cents. Attorney Nicoll left Albany defeated.

But the traction interests continued their fight for a fare increase in the courts. When a decision in Federal District Court on behalf of the Interboro Rapid Transit Company allowed it to raise the subway fare to seven cents, Mayor Walker, with much fanfare, announced that the city would appeal all the way to the United States Supreme Court.

An accident on the IRT line at Times Square Station at the height of the 5:00 P.M. rush hour in August 1928 killed sixteen riders and injured more than a hundred others. The incident gave the mayor further opportunity to berate the subway and blame it for heartlessness, inefficiency, and indifference to human lives. He was down at the scene of the wreck within fifteen minutes, and when he was told by the police that a switch known to be faulty was the cause of the accident, an enraged mayor took the tragedy as a means of expressing the grief for the entire city.

The mayor was extraordinarily lucky when on April 8, 1929, by a vote of six to three the United States Supreme Court denied the Interboro Rapid Transit Company the seven-cent-fare increase it sought. The stock of the IRT had risen to 55 on the New York Stock Exchange in anticipation of a favorable decision, it fell to 33½ when the court's decision was announced. Jimmy's personal rating, however, soared; his renomination and reelection as mayor was assured. He became "the hero of the hour ... the savior of the strap-hanger."[15]

Recognizing that he was the beneficiary of a political windfall, Walker gloated: "Personally, I am very happy in this vindication, but not as happy for myself as I am for the millions of people who must of necessity use the rapid-transit lines. This is a great day for the people of the city of New York."[16]

THE MERIT SYSTEM: "GET YOURSELF A RABBI"

This was the advice given to rookie Irish cops as they embarked upon a career of law enforcement with New York's finest. In New York City, political influence was more important than merit in getting and securing advancement in the New York Police Department and in every other department. In every department, with the possible exception of teaching, a political intermediary was more important than was securing a high grade on civil service examinations for career advancement. Indeed, the merit system of municipal appointments was distinctly at odds with Tammany's needs for patronage in exchange for votes and resources. As a result, the city was slow to bring in office machinery that would reduce the number of clerks needed in municipal offices or in introducing labor-saving equipment that would reduce the number of firefighters or lower the number of sanitation workers. It was more in the interests of Tammany to pad the payroll than to find reasons to be more efficient in the deployment of municipal personnel. According to Robert A. Caro, "Between the day Hylan entered office and the day Walker left it, the number of city employees almost doubled, and their salaries, paid as political rewards at levels far above those paid for similar work in private industry, almost tripled."[17]

While reformers could get legislation adopted requiring competitive civil service examinations for appointment to a municipal department, Tammany found creative ways for getting around the civil service laws. One example was that of the mayor's brother, Dr. William H. Walker, who was hired as a medical examiner and health consultant by the New York City Board of Education without the required civil service examination. The Walker administration took advantage of the exemption in the civil service requirement that allowed the appointment of scientific experts on an "as needed" basis without requiring an examination.

Exempt positions, that is, municipal jobs that required no examination, grew rapidly, as did the number of municipal employees who were hired in haste in one alleged emergency or another. Without reference to examinations were 6,000 employees working on the new subway and 12,000 in the sanitation department. "The Civil Service Reform Association in 1932 found ninety Democratic district leaders and their relatives, together with sixteen Republican district leaders on the payroll. Not one of these individuals had passed a civil service examination."[18] In 1933, shortly after Walker resigned his office, no more than 55 percent of municipal employees were appointed on the basis of competitive examinations. Little wonder that Norman Thomas, the Socialist candidate for mayor, concluded that New York City was losing its fight for civil service reform to Tammany Hall.[19]

During the Walker administration the number of "no-show" jobs likewise dramatically increased. Despite the fact that the city's 4,225 voting machines were stored in bonded warehouses and were regularly guarded by police, the city hired a crew of 20 custodians at $2,810 a year to provide additional protection. But a *World-Telegram* reporter, curious about the work done by these custodians, visited the warehouse and discovered that the custodians showed up for "work" merely between the hours of 10 to 12 — sometimes.[20]

In the parks, female toilet attendants, widows of Tammany Hall faithfuls, would curtain off most the stalls so that they could meet, picnic, and socialize with one another. In one such comfort station the aged attendant in charge built a cozy sitting room complete with grand piano. "*Never go near the first aid stations,*" admonished parents, lest their children come into contact with prostitutes who gathered there.[21] Lifeguards at public beaches were often over-weight, over-age, and could not swim. As one park patron wryly observed, "You couldn't tell the difference between a park employee and the bums hanging out in the parks."[22]

Engineers in the very departments that required their services had little or no training in engineering much less an engineering degree. Some even lacked a high school diploma. Little wonder then that "[n]o fewer than forty public schools constructed during Walker's administration had to be closed for major repairs—for ceilings that fell, roofs that leaked, stairways that collapsed and plumbing that didn't work at all — within a year of opening."[23]

The End of Easy Times

During the summer of 1929, workers in New York were tearing down the Waldorf-Astoria Hotel at Fifth Avenue and Thirty-fourth Street to make way for the Empire State Building. The Chrysler Building was rising at Forty-second Street, and John D. Rockefeller was planning what would become Radio City. The stock market continued its seemingly inexorable upward trajectory; the skyscrapers which rose ever higher appeared a manifestation in concrete and steel of a soaring economy and rising spirits. But the euphoria would abruptly end.

On October 21, 1929, prices on the New York Stock Exchange began to sag, and on October 24 the stock market fell even further when 12 million shares changed hands. On Tuesday, October 29, investors experienced the single worst day when 16,410,000 shares were traded, and prices virtually collapsed.

Despite a precipitously falling market, on Friday, October 25, 1929, Mayor Walker participated in ceremonies marking the start of construction of the Triborough Bridge that, upon completion, would connect Manhattan, the Bronx, and Queens. Despite growing evidence that the end of easy times was at hand, the multitude of New Yorkers still loved him and did not yet recognize that "good-time" Jimmy was not the man for the difficult years ahead. Jimmy Walker mirrored the Jazz Age, and when that age abruptly died, the oxygen he needed to survive likewise appeared to be depleted as were his energy, wit, luck, and judgment. His continuing popularity dulled his political instincts.

In launching his first administration, Walker struck just the right notes and made just the right appointments. But as his first term waned and even as he prepared for his second campaign, he sounded a number of sour notes. An example of this was the salary increase from $25,000 to $40,000 the Board of Estimate voted for the mayor in late 1929. Other salary increases included that of controller from $25,000 to $35,000, aldermanic president from $15,000 to $25,000, and the salaries of the borough presidents from $15,000 to $20,000. Seemingly oblivious about how this might look to a citizenry hit hard by the stock market panic of October and the imminence of a depression of indeterminate duration, growing unemployment, and even rapidly spreading hunger, Mayor Walker, on January 1, 1930, as the first act of his second administration, signed the bill providing for salary increases for himself and his seven colleagues. Insensitively, he joked that the increase would make little personal difference, "I shall have nothing left at the end of the year."[24]

Aware that there was substantial criticism of the salary increases, the mayor asserted at a meeting of the Chamber of Commerce of the State of New York that he would donate the pay raise to charitable organizations that were doing important work among the city's poor. "You don't have to worry about immorality any more."[25]

He was wrong. As pressures from good-government "goo-goos" mounted, Governor Franklin Roosevelt reluctantly urged Judge Samuel Seabury to investigate an ever-widening assortment of questionable practices in the Walker administration.

The Inquisitor

They were both Democrats and born in close proximity of one another — James Walker in Greenwich Village and Samuel Seabury (1873–1958) in the Church of the Annunciation on West Fourteenth Street. The mayor and his inquisitor could not have been more different. When, in 1908, Jimmy Walker wrote "Will You Love Me in December as You Do in May?" and was haunting Tin Pan Alley in search of a career in the uncertain world of show business, Samuel Seabury was already well established as a young judge in the New York State Supreme Court.

The mayor was a son of recent Irish Catholic immigrants; his father was a carpenter and a member in good standing of Tammany Hall. The inquisitor was the ninth of the American Seaburys and the fifth of their Samuels. The first Samuel, a physician, arrived from England with the Puritans in 1639. Samuel Seabury's father, a professor of canon law at the General Theological Seminary, was a descendant of the first Episcopal bishop of New York and a long-time foe of Tammany. If America had nobility, the Seaburys would surely be among them.

If Walker's modish dress mirrored Broadway's glitter and Hollywood's excesses, Seabury's attire of clerical black or gray, white shirts, and somber tie, all of which seemed to frame a mammoth emerald ring on his left hand, reflected the staid world of law and finance. If Walker was the master of the quip, the repartee, the wisecrack, Seabury never used slang or indulged in a joke. "[H]is presence was such that he could invest the blowing of his nose with theological overtones."[26] Where Walker flaunted his infidelities, Samuel Seabury and his wife, Maude, were a childless but devoted couple. On the Seabury's family crest was the exhortation in Latin "Supra Alta Tenere"—"Hold to the Most High." Had the Walker's a family crest it might have read, "Hold to the Most Expedient." The Seaburys and the Walkers were natural opposites and natural enemies.

Around midnight on August 26, 1930, while affectionately perusing a newly acquired, rare, first edition of a 1631 legal book entitled, *The Just Lawyer*, Seabury in his suite at London's Carlton Hotel received a call from a journalist requesting a comment from him concerning his appointment to investigate the Magistrates' Courts in New York. This was the first inkling the fifty-seven-year-old, well-connected attorney had of a new assignment which would return him to public life after an absence of fourteen years.

Samuel Seabury left his prosperous law practice in the hands of others and devoted himself almost exclusively investigating three aspects of the government of the City of New York. The first had to do with alleged corruption in the magistrates' courts, which dealt with crimes ranging from traffic violations to gambling and prostitution. The second dealt with the office of the district attorney and the third into all the departments of the government presided over by Jimmy Walker. Before his assignment ended Seabury would change the political climate of New York and Mayor Walker would be forced to resign.

"They're Not Going to Find Anything"

Had he been a less popular mayor, Walker might have seen trouble coming, and he might have drawn on his political capital to urge those in his political debt to vote against the legislation leading to an investigation of his performance in office. He had, after all, spent sixteen years in Albany and could count many political friends among Republicans as well as Democrats. Reportedly one Republican senator from Westchester let Walker know that he was ready to vote against the inquiry if the mayor would but signal him to do so. "The hell with it," said Jimmy. "They're not going find anything."[27] But they did.

When, in 1929, the fifty-six-year-old John F. Curry became leader of Tammany Hall, he haughtily announced that there is no such thing as a "new" Tammany, that is, a reform Tammany, and that there never had been. "I will carry out the policies in which I grew up."[28] With Walker as puppet and Curry pulling the strings, the Walker/Curry policies of giving lucrative political jobs to party loyalists, favoring certain contractors over others, and by-passing civil service examinations so as to build party loyalty seemed to be a challenge to the Republican majority in the state legislature to do their worst. They did. The Walker/Curry policy of politics as usual despite a mounting depression, triggered a rising tide of public indignation against incompetent civic officials and corrupt practices. Thus was the stage set for the Republican majority in the legislature to shift the discussion from Republican responsibility for the onset of the Depression to the Democrats' blatant involvement in corrupt government practices and political scandal.

Moreover, so went Republican wisdom, with Franklin D. Roosevelt, a man who had a clear shot at the Democratic nomination for the United States presidency, as governor, what could be more cunning than to put this seemingly sure-footed political operator on the spot by seeing how he would handle scandal in his own party?

During the time that Seabury was investigating the magistrates' courts and the district attorney's office, Jimmy Walker still had time to deflect a direct examination into his own administration. But his continuing popularity with New Yorkers dulled his political instincts, and he could not see the seriousness of the scandals he knew were growing under his administration. He knew, but he did nothing about them, believing that Tammany's political style, despite its shortcomings, was essentially immutable. He should have recognized that support was slowly but steadily eroding.

The influential Patrick Cardinal Hayes of New York was a man with sufficient political judgment and practical temperament so that he could, if he chose, overlook "honest" graft, political scandal, a bit of fiscal irregularity, and other departures from the saintly pursuit of good government. But he could not forgive that this mayor, this son of his church, was living in sin. The cardinal called the mayor into his office for a dressing down which even the latter's legendary charm could not deflect. The mayor left after making vague and not very believable promises to mend his moral behavior. He never did. Had he done so or made some concession to the cardinal, mainly by leaving Betty, it is conceivable that the cardinal's influence might have been effective in calling off the worst aspects of Samuel Seabury's investigation.

Nor was the cardinal alone in withdrawing support for the mayor. Late in the evening of March 17, 1931, Rabbi Stephen Wise and the Reverend John Haynes Holmes joined in an attack on the Walker administration. When Governor Roosevelt returned to his New York townhouse from giving a speech at a dinner for the Friendly Sons of St. Patrick at the Hotel Astor, the religious leaders presented Governor Roosevelt with a four-thousand-word commentary accusing the mayor of general negligence and incompetence. The mayor, as usual, was on a holiday, this time in Palm Springs, when the charges were filed, but they were potent enough so that he thought it prudent to return to New York and respond as best he could.

Governor Roosevelt accepted this polemic without comment and thought it somewhat unfair to make such charges while the mayor was not in the city to respond. Yet, these and more serious charges would be uncovered during Seabury's investigation of the mayor's office. The Reverend Holmes, at an open meeting of the City Affairs Committee, vigorously attacked Walker, "How much longer shall we be amused by this little man?"[29]

As in a drama in three acts, the Seabury investigations pursued allegations of impropriety in the magistrates' courts, the office of the Manhattan district attorney, and, finally, in the city administration itself. Like the Starr investigation of President Bill Clinton in 1999, the Seabury investigation took on a life of its own. Walker jauntily refused to accept the seriousness of the investigations swirling around him. By seemingly thumbing his nose at the proceedings, he became a thorn in the side of the committee, and in a way most unusual for Jimmy, the evidence against him was presented with a special venom and became a very personal attack. Mayor Walker was viewed as the lightning rod for political corruption in New York and symbolic of municipal corruption among American cities.

"OLD HEADS FOR COUNSEL YOUNG HEADS FOR WAR"

In assembling his team of investigators, Samuel Seabury drew on the best and the brightest of his day. His chief counsel was pint-sized Isidor Jacob Kressel, a self-made lawyer from the Lower East Side of New York. It was said of him that he could run under a table wearing a high hat, but no matter, he could bring the biggest witness to tears as he zeroed in with incisive questions which were based on detailed studies of reams of seemingly dull evidence: bank accounts, cancelled checks, income tax returns, brokerage accounts, expense accounts, leases, mortgages, and contracts. Based on these documents Kressel could build an accurate picture of what had taken place and what was rotten in the witness or the office. In six months of service to Judge Seabury in the investigation of the magistrates' courts, Kressel established the techniques that Seabury and the young lawyers surrounding him adapted in investigating the Walker administration.

At the first full staff meeting, Seabury uttered a slogan that would be his strategy for the next two years, "Old heads for counsel — young heads for war." He told his legal foot soldiers:

> The public will not be aroused to an awareness of conditions in the magistrates' courts through a series of graphs, charts and reports. We must divorce this investigation, as far as is possible, from legalistic machinery. There is more eloquence in the testimony of an illiterate witness telling of oppression suffered from legal processes than in the greatest sermon, editorial, or address ever written. Where preachers, editors, and lawyers have

Cartoon of Jimmy Walker elegantly dressed and acting as if he had not a care in the world, despite the ongoing investigation by Samuel Seabury into widespread graft and corruption in his administration in 1932. Courtesy of the Library of Congress. Prints & Photographs Division, LC-USZ62-35860.

failed in arousing the public to a consciousness of unjust conditions these simple, unlearned witnesses will succeed.[30]

ACT I: INVESTIGATING THE MAGISTRATES' COURTS

A friend of Mayor Walker remembers that when he went over a list of the men he had appointed to judgeships in the magistrates' courts the mayor would come to a name and comment with disgust and anger, "That thief!" "That thug!" When he finished, Walker shrugged, "God knows they can never accuse me of not being loyal to the organization, Lord, what a gang."[31]

Walker should not have been surprised at the shady practices of some of the judges, many of whom, with the blessing of Tammany, he had appointed. He should not have been astonished by the testimony of stool pigeons who, for a fee, went bottom fishing among the low-lifes of New York — pickpockets, prostitutes, gamblers — so that they might be shaken down still further by the police, district attorneys, and the magistrates themselves. One such stool pigeon upon whom the magistrates relied was the colorful but despicable "Chile" Mapocha Acuna — the "Human Spittoona."

Acuna "was a man of about thirty-one, of slight build, beady brown eyes, curly hair, about five feet and weighing about one hundred and twenty-five pounds."[32] He came to America in 1919 from Chile with $2,500 in his pocket, a sum that did not last long in America. Under Kressel's detailed questioning, Acuna, in 1929, testified that his job of framing women in vice raids paid him $150 a week. He received a share of the take from raids on brothels whose addresses he furnished.

Police Commissioner Mulrooney used Acuna to identify those policemen who had participated in framing innocent women. With nearly perfect recall, Acuna identified twenty-eight policemen, and before the day was over a furious police commissioner was drawing up departmental charges against these men.

Exposure of widespread police corruption during the Walker administration put the mayor on the defensive as he admitted, "We believed conditions were pretty good in New York in comparison with the past until the findings of this investigation."[33] Before the investigation of the magistrates' courts was completed, every magistrate was investigated. Some chose to resign on the eve of their date in court. Two magistrates had been removed by a unanimous vote of the court; one left the state in a hurry.

Seabury made recommendations to divorce justice from politics, such as placing clerks under civil service and making fines payable to a central

office. He called for the immediate arraignment of arrested persons before
a magistrate instead of at the police stations. "There can be no remedy"
for the conditions he found in the magistrates' courts, "unless the court
can be entirely free of political control." Some of Seabury's reforms were
adopted, but, as Seabury biographer Herbert Mitgang noted, "The idea of
removing judgeships from politics remained a reformer's dream."[35]

ACT II: INVESTIGATING THE DISTRICT ATTORNEY

At the behest of Richard S. Childs, president of the City Club of New
York, Governor Roosevelt was petitioned to seek the removal of Thomas
C. T. Crain, district attorney for New York County, for alleged incompetence in pursuing crime and criminals. He was charged with being
ineffective in prosecuting stock frauds, racketeering, and graft. The City
Club was joined in its complaint by the City Affairs Committee, whose
leading lights were Professor John Dewey of Columbia, Bishop Francis J.
McConnell, and Rabbi Stephen S. Wise. The charges against Crain were
vague and included words such as "timidity," "inertia," "ineffective," and
"inadequate." But were these crimes?

The investigation into seventy-year-old District Attorney Crain's conduct was conducted at 80 Centre Street, with seventy-four-year-old Samuel
Untermyer serving as his attorney. John Kirkland Clark acted for Seabury,
who was continuing his investigation of the magistrates' courts. Many witnesses were examined at both private and public hearings between April
8 and May 29, 1931.

Among the sordid aspects of the investigation were questions about
why Crain had failed to investigate the Fulton Fish Market, where one
Joseph "Socks" Lanza, a labor delegate of Local 16975 of the United Seafood
Workers, was allowed to get away with a shakedown racket in which, for
a substantial payoff, he "negotiated" a sweetheart contract favoring employers, not workers, at the market. Parallel racketeering also took place in the
millinery trade where manufacturers of ladies' hats made payoffs to hardened criminals like "Little Augie" and "Tough Jake" Kurzman in exchange
for "protecting" manufacturers against labor-union violence. In the cloth-
shrinking business, Joseph Mezzcapo dissolved the Cloth Shrinkers Union
and replaced it with a union of his own. Only a paid member of his union
could work as a cloth shrinker. Little wonder then that Mezzcapo could
deposit some $332,000 in a single account.

To Seabury, however, the evidence against Crain was short of con-
vincing:

Truth compels the conclusion, declared Seabury, that in many instances he [Crain] busied himself ineffectively, and that he did not grasp or act upon opportunities for high public service which some of the matters referred to presented him. I am satisfied that wherever he failed, and I do think he did fail in many cases to do all that he should have done, his failure was not due to any lack of personal effort or any ignoble motive.[36]

Seabury then graciously recommended that Crain not be removed as district attorney.

In his book *The Man Who Rode the Tiger,* Mitgang poses a number of reasons for Seabury's generosity in the matter of District Attorney Crain. Perhaps Seabury did not wish to embarrass a distinguished layman of the Episcopal Church, of which Seabury was likewise a member. Or, he felt he could not recommend removal of an officer of the judicial system who had been elected by the people rather than appointed by the mayor. Seabury may also have been reluctant to punish Crain out of respect for the aging district attorney because of his prior satisfactory record as a judge. However, it was more than likely that Crain escaped with the mildest or reprimands because Seabury's group felt that once dismissed, Crain would be nominated for district attorney once again by Tammany and would probably win, thereby undercutting the prestige of the Seabury investigations. And, indeed, Seabury was eager to get on with the investigation of the entire city administration under Mayor Walker.

ACT III: INVESTIGATING JIMMY WALKER

On March 23, 1931, the New York State Assembly and Senate adopted a joint resolution for the appointment of a committee for "the investigation of the departments of the Government of the City of New York." Governor Roosevelt signed the legislation, approved a $250,000 appropriation, and designated Judge Samuel Seabury as counsel to the committee. With State Senator Samuel Hofstadter serving as chairman of the joint committee, "[t]he most far-reaching investigation in New York City history was under way."[37]

The mayor had been served with a subpoena on May 23, 1932, and ordered to appear at the county courthouse on Foley Square on May 25, 1932, with all personal financial records since January 1, 1926. Although advance notice had been short, thousands thronged the Manhattan County Courthouse, and some seven hundred managed to squeeze their way into a hearing room that ordinarily seated half that number. Each side had its adherents, with Seabury supported by good-government types such as the

Committee of One Thousand and the League of Women Voters. But, more numerous, or at least more noisy, were Jimmy Walker's fans. There was the theater magnate A. C. Blumenthal, attorney Dudley Field Malone, and labor leader Joseph Ryan. Tammany Irish and swanky types from Park Avenue elbowed each other to secure a perch at the hearings and to cheer for their mayor. As a contemporary journalist described it, each group emerged "with a new respect for each other's elbows ... they had met there where the race went to the strong, in the narrow doorway [to the chamber]."[38]

Samuel Hofstadter, chairman of the Senate Legislative Committee and nominally in charge of the investigation, entered the courthouse unnoticed. Seabury's reception was polite but cool. But cries of "Good luck, Jimmy," "Atta Boy," and "You tell him, Jimmy," were warmly received by a smiling mayor, who was moved to clasp his hands over his head in the manner of a prize-fighter about to enter the ring.[39]

Both Walker and Seabury came to the hearings thoroughly prepared, but they had prepared in strikingly different ways. Walker's entire political life had been shaped by patronage, back scratching, favoritism, nepotism, and papering over critical issues rather than meeting them forthrightly. Those who in public testimony sought to criticize the mayor for malfeasance or misfeasance were invariably thrown off their stride by the legendary Jimmy Walker charm, flair, wit, and repartee served up in the height of fashion — if not always good taste. Walker continued to believe that he could charm Seabury out of the worst of the charges that would be leveled against him. Jimmy watchers advised Seabury, "Don't look Walker straight in the eye when he is on the witness stand. He has an uncanny ability to stare you down. Once he's eyed you, you're liable to be stunned and confused, like a deer caught in a car's headlights."[40]

Judge Seabury was armed with the facts. Mayor Walker was a sartorial symphony in his blue, one button, double-breasted suit, matching blue socks, pocket handkerchief, blue shirt, and tie. "Little Boy Blue is about to blow his horn — or his top," he remarked to his valet.[41]

Among the major incriminating charges against Mayor Walker were the following:

1. That he had used Russell T. Sherwood, a modestly paid accountant who disappeared rather than testify, to open a joint safe-deposit box in which he held a number of bank deposits and checks accumulated with the aid of a mysterious brokerage account. Since 1926, some $1 million had accumulated.

2. That he had conspired with State Senator John A. Hastings, who may

have made millions, to push the Equitable bus franchise through the Board of Estimate.

3. That taxi entrepreneur J. A. Sisto had, through an intermediary and in a sealed envelope, sent him some $26,500 in bonds which the mayor pocketed in exchange for the mayor's cooperation in setting up a taxi control board that would protect his taxi interests.

The confrontation was to be high drama.

During his first line of questioning, Seabury sought an explanation as to why Mayor Walker favored giving a franchise to the Equitable Bus Company despite the fact that Equitable owned no buses and despite better contracts from several other companies, most notably the Service Bus Company, a company that had many buses.

Walker's answers were often vague and hardly forthright. He resorted frequently to:

> "I cannot remember the details."
> "I wouldn't attempt to say ... which franchise was the better."
> "I don't remember."
> "Yes, I think so."

But Seabury was getting to the mayor, who was getting uncharacteristically prickly.

> Seabury: "The question I am interested in is why, as Mayor of this city, you urged the passage of the Equitable bus franchise."
> Walker: "Mr. Chairman," [addressing committee chairman Hofstadter,] "I don't believe that your counsel or you have any legal right to inquire into the operations of an Executive's mind or cross-examine him about how he reaches his conclusions.... But notwithstanding that, let me tell you why...."
> Seabury: "I will be most happy to have you do so."
> Walker: "Upon the recommendation of the Board of Transportation — based upon their analysis — [the Equitable] was the best independent company, because it not only offered the initial five-cent fare but something that I had advocated — namely, new blood into the traction interests of this city."

Seabury continued to probe well into the afternoon and Walker weakly countered:

> I don't remember what I said at a meeting two years ago.
> I don't know that ... I have no recollection of it in any event.

Late in the afternoon of May 25, 1932, Seabury adopted a new line of inquiry having to do with Walker's "benefactor"— the wealthy newspaper publisher Paul Block, who had given the mayor about $246,692 from which Block had systematically deducted income-tax payments between February 1927 and August 1929. During this time, Block had an interest in a firm selling tiles for the subway then under construction. The money, Walker testified, was his share of the profits from a joint brokerage account in which Block had put up all the money and had done all the investing. Under sharp questioning Walker asserted that the money from the Block account was kept in a safe in the mayor's home to be drawn upon as needed by the mayor and Mrs. Walker. Seabury sought to find out how the money was spent, but Walker was evasive in as much as he did not wish it to become a matter of public knowledge that $7,500 had gone to Betty Compton. Seabury, however, was gallant enough not to mention the lady by name. On this note, the hearing adjourned for the day.[42]

Walker left the hearing room as he had arrived, smiling, affable, and to the cheers of the applauding crowd made his way to his limousine. That night "an enthusiastic audience of 18,000 gathered at Madison Square Garden for the Police College graduation exercises" to hear Mayor Walker's speech.[43] From the cheering crowd it would appear that the Seabury interrogation had not dented the armor of popularity the mayor still so easily wore. In his speech the mayor advanced the questionable notion that the Seabury investigation was eroding police morale and had turned New York into a lawless city. "Criticism based on individual ambition, criticism arising out of political jealousy, criticism emanating from vindictiveness," he asserted, "have brought back to the streets of New York something that had not existed for the past twenty years."[44] Self-serving and specious though the charge was, Walker's remarks were greeted with thunderous applause. So armed with seemingly limitless popular support, Walker returned jauntily to testify for a second day on May 26. The testimony continued with the mayor's relationship with publisher Block, with the taxicab entrepreneur J. A. Sisto, and with his accountant, Russell T. Sherwood, who had fled to Mexico.

> Seabury: "Would you be good enough to state the reason for Mr. Block's donation to you?"
> Walker: "...Mr. Block for several years had manifested a very generous friendship for me. It is not an unusual thing. Mr. Block's life has been characterized by generosity...."
> Seabury: "Do you not recall that Mr. McKeon called on you at City Hall, and rode uptown with you at the end of the day, and that on the way

uptown he took a sealed envelope and handed it to you and said it was from Sisto and you put it in your pocket?"
Walker: "*No* is the answer to every element in that [question]."
Seabury: "That is my recollection of Mr. McKeon's testimony."
Walker: "That did not happen."

As a justification for having accepted the bonds from Sisto, Walker established the fact that he had in fact vetoed a taxi-fare increase in April 1930, which Sisto of the Parmalee Taxicab Company would have been the beneficiary.

After a lunch recess, Seabury plunged into Walker's relationship with Sherwood.

Seabury: "Mr. Mayor, do you know whether after that safe-deposit box was opened in the joint names of yourself and Mr. Sherwood another box, a larger box was subsequently obtained?"
Walker: "I do not."
Seabury: "There were never any bonds, securities, stock, or cash placed in either of these boxes?"
Walker: "I don't know, but there were never any of mine."

The questioning of Walker continued relentlessly until the Democratic committee members expressed offense that Sherwood's character had been questioned and, by indirection, other members associated with the mayor. But Seabury plowed ahead and before the day was over showed that Sherwood had, on August 9, 1927, withdrawn $263,836 from an investment trustee brokerage account that he had opened only four and a half months before with $100,000 that he admitted was not his money. At Sherwood's request the brokerage house officer converted the $263,000 into $1,000 bills. The accountant left the Federal Reserve Bank heavily laden with bags of money.

Thus the Mayor's two days of testimony ended. He expressed satisfaction that "I have had my day in court."[45] But, as he made his way out of the courthouse, less enthusiastic cheering pointed to the fact that on the second day of testimony Walker had clearly been hurt.

On Memorial Day 1932, when Jimmy went to Yankee Stadium to unveil a memorial tablet to the late Miller Huggins, the first great manager of the Yankees, Walker heard the boos. Shocked though he was, he left his box in the grandstand and deliberately walked across the baseball diamond to the Huggins memorial in centerfield. He stood before the microphone for a long moment, regained his composure, and went on.

Politics is like baseball…. In baseball the greatest star may be cheered for a home run today and then, on the very next day, be booed if he strikes out…. That's the way it is, and that's the way it should be. "Freedom of Speech," [and he pointed to the flag flying overhead,] is guaranteed by that emblem up there. It also guarantees us the right to criticize, or even to boo. If a politician pops out, fouls out, or strikes out, he must expect adverse criticism. If he cannot withstand the boos—and I mean *b-o-o-s* and not *b-o-o-z-e* [roar of laughter from the fans] then he also should not pay attention to the praise.

The great little fellow to whom this memorial tablet has been placed upon the scene of his many triumphs, Miller Huggins, sometimes heard his mighty team booed. Fame is a comet that chases its own tail in the sky. Huggins is now well beyond the reach of criticism or praise, but we still remember him as a wonderful man. It is so important to be a man first, and regard whatever else that comes to you or is denied you in the way of laurels as a secondary consideration. It is much more important, when all else is over, and one has gone through the narrow door from which there is no returning, to have been loved than to have been exalted.[46]

The mayor, hatless, stood at attention. The crowd rose. The band played the national anthem. As Jim marched back across the field there was a tremendous ovation that lasted until he reentered his box and sat down. "Play ball," the umpire called.[47]

But Seabury would continue to play hardball.

11

Scandal:
The Decline and Fall

In a tersely worded letter to the city clerk, Jimmy Walker, on September 1, 1932, resigned the office of mayor of the city of New York to take effect immediately. Later that night, a more detailed and bitter explanation was issued by the mayor. "I was," he complained, "being subject to an extraordinary inquisition." He complained that in the course of the proceedings before Governor Roosevelt he was being "denied even the elementary rights guaranteed to any defendant in a court of law." He concluded, "Why then continue before him [Roosevelt] when there is another forum open in the spirit of true democracy, conscious of the rectitude of my official acts and with a faith in the fair judgment of my fellow citizens. I am … submitting my case to the people who made me mayor, the people of the city of New York."[1]

On September 10, 1932, just eight days after his resignation, the former mayor was off to Europe on board the Italian ship *Conte Grande*. Betty Compton was eagerly waiting for him in Paris, and Jimmy promised to be back in New York and seek reelection as mayor as a means of reasserting his integrity. But, out of sight, out of mind. Support, even among Tammany loyalists, proved not even skin deep. As a British newspaper, *The Guardian*, observed, "Tammany doesn't like backing losers."[2]

Hot Coal

Governor Roosevelt flew from Albany to Chicago to accept the nomination of the Democratic Party as its candidate for the presidency of the United States. Since his small plane had been buffeted by high winds, he

161

arrived late, but on July 2, 1932, to the tune of "Happy Days Are Here Again," the nominee cheerfully accepted the nomination and declared, "I pledge to you, I pledge myself, to a new deal for America."

On August 11, 1932, the man who faced Walker in the Executive Chambers in the Hall of Governors in Albany was not merely the governor of the state of New York, but a candidate for the highest office of the land. The result was that the hearings on Walker's competence to continue in office became part of a campaign during which voters could take the measure of a future president. According to the Schenectady *Union-Star,* "'there is political dynamite' in how the governor dealt with the Mayor. No matter what he does with it, the Governor is bound to be embarrassed between suspicion of 'whitewashing Jimmy Walker,' to gain Tammany support and removing him, and thereby losing New York State. This is a test for Mr. Roosevelt. His decision will influence the votes of thousands of persons."[3] The Walker case is "hot coal in Roosevelt's hands."[4] While Roosevelt and Walker were thus both on trial, the latter, not the former, was the one who got burned.

In his capacity as New York's chief executive, Roosevelt had called for a trial to hear Seabury's charges and Walker's response. Seabury asserted that the mayor "failed properly to execute the duties which, as mayor of the City of New York, it was incumbent upon him to discharge; that he has so acted in his official capacity so as to prejudice the best interests of the people of the City of New York; ... and that his explanations of circumstances seriously reflecting upon the manner in which, as its chief executive, he has conducted the affairs of the City of New York, have been so incomplete or so unworthy of credence as not to constitute acceptable explanations."[5] Judge Seabury continued to document his charges and concluded: "...since he assumed office, the Mayor's conduct has been characterized by such malfeasance and nonfeasance in disregard of the duties of his office as mayor, and he has conducted himself, to the prejudice of the City of New York and its inhabitants, in a manner so far unbecoming the high office which he holds, as to render him unfit to continue in the office of mayor."[6]

Because the grave charges were based on circumstantial evidence, the Joint Legislative Committee was divided and did not call for Walker's removal from office. Nor did Judge Seabury recommend Walker's removal. Yet, the charges were serious and could not be ignored. Was removal the only recourse? Should Walker be lightly slapped on the wrist, allowed to finish his term, and perhaps run for reelection so that the judgment of the voters could determine Mayor Walker's fitness for office? Such was the dilemma Governor Roosevelt faced.

In his defense Mayor Walker wrote a 27,000-word letter to "His Excellency Franklin D. Roosevelt." The mayor insisted that the Seabury investigation had been entirely politically motivated and created "to divert public attention from those responsible for the dreadful condition of affairs throughout the nation."[7] The mayor replied that he was a special target for hostility, misrepresentation, "malice," "slander," and "rancorous illwill."

He urged the governor to note that he was a popular mayor, that Seabury had been repudiated at the polls while he, Mayor Walker, had been chosen by a wide margin in the last election. "This distrust that he manifests for popular government he wants you to assume and, in spite of the votes of the people who supported me, to remove me from office.... It is sound American doctrine that the will of the people as expressed by their votes is not brushed aside to satisfy prejudice, a craving for publicity, or personal dislike, of political complainants. I respectfully submit that all the charges herein should be dismissed on the merits."[8]

But the hearings, with several interruptions, continued through twelve sweaty legislative sessions in the sultry heat of an August in Albany. Walker still had some popular support, but for Roosevelt the political landscape was tense. If he dismissed Walker, he risked Tammany's ire and perhaps loss of a pivotal state in the presidential sweepstakes. But upstate New York, and the rest of the country, wondered whether this pampered son of the Roosevelt family had the backbone to make hard decisions. They would not be disappointed.

During one break in the proceedings at a conference at Governor Roosevelt's desk, Walker, in an aside that revealed his growing frustration, said to reporters, "This fellow Seabury would convict the Twelve Apostles if he could."[9] And in a remark reminiscent of President Richard Nixon during the Watergate investigations of the 1970s, Walker, while on a break from the proceedings, strolled around the garden of the Hall of Governors with his close friend the prominent attorney, Dudley Field Malone, and remarked. "Dudley, you know that I am not a crook, and that this is just a political move. If I were a crook, why, during the last year or more, have I been compelled to borrow large sums of money from my friends to support my wife and some twenty-eight dependents and a lot of other people? Had I been a grafter, it must be perfectly plain to everyone that I could have accumulated millions."[10]

Yet, Walker intuitively knew that Roosevelt would dismiss him. His political sensibilities were such that he could recognize that on balance, while not without its political dangers, dismissal of Mayor Walker was the right political move for presidential candidate Roosevelt.

To his suite at the Hotel Ten Eyck in Albany, Walker invited George Ringler, a trusted reporter for the New York *Daily News* to see if the journalist had any insights or, indeed, any information as to the direction of the governor's thinking. Ringler reported that a well-placed source declared "that if Walker was smart he would resign."[11]

On August 27, Seabury and Walker boarded the same train en route for a weekend respite in New York. Walker was ill and his condition worsened when the next day he received the not unexpected news that his brother George, a TB patient at Saranac Lake, had died and that the body was being shipped to New York. On Thursday, September 1, an ill and saddened Mayor joined his sister, Nan, at the funeral services. Walker confided to some of those who had come to pay their respects to the deceased and to show continued sympathy for the beleaguered mayor that, "I think Roosevelt is going to remove me."[12]

A Mayor Resigns

After George Walker's interment at Calvary Cemetery, Jim invited his sister to take a short walk with him. "Sis," he said, "I'm going to resign." At a meeting of twelve or more Tammany leaders, including Max D. Steuer and Al Smith, the latter, when asked for his opinion, said straightforwardly, "Jim, you're through. You must resign for the good of the party."[13] Jimmy deserved better of Al. As governor, Smith was appalled by Walker's private behavior and warned him time and again that the debauched lifestyle Walker enjoyed would bring him down. Yet, Walker had displayed loyalty to Smith by making the latter a contender for the presidential nomination at the Democratic National Convention. So it was with a certain "I told you so" attitude that Smith administered the *coup de grace* and Walker resigned. With two giants of New York's Democratic Party — Alfred E. Smith and Franklin D. Roosevelt — hostile, little wonder, then, that in his resignation the legendary graciousness of Mayor Walker failed him.

> Walker Resigns, Denouncing the Governor; Says He Will Run for the Mayorality Again, Appealing to "Fair Judgment of the People"

This was the five-column headline in *The New York Times* of September 2, 1932, when Mayor Walker resigned his office. In explanation Mayor Walker held that by going to Albany once again to be questioned by the governor he would "demean" himself. He bitterly asserted that

"Instead of an impartial hearing, the proceedings before the Governor developed into a travesty, a mock trial, a proceeding in comparison to which even the practice of a drumhead court-martial seems liberal."[14]

Jimmy Walker was the first mayor in New York to resign as charges against him were being investigated. By his resignation the able Joseph V. McKee, the aldermanic president, became interim mayor. Walker kept alive a possible third run for mayor of New York City as an ultimate effort to vindicate himself by letting the electorate judge whether or not he was fit to fill the remainder of his term. Had he been ousted by the governor, he would have been ineligible to run for office in New York again.

Public comments on Walker's resignation were predictable but cautious. State Senator Samuel H. Hofstadter, chairman of the Joint Legislative Committee under whose leadership Judge Seabury carried out the investigation, made no comment at all. Publisher Paul Block, who had befriended the mayor with "beneficences," held that Walker "had no chance to prove his innocence." Former Mayor John Hylan, whom Walker defeated but later made a justice, was gracious, "I regret that Mayor Walker was forced to resign. In my opinion the mayor's resignation carries no admission of guilt." Governor Roosevelt was not surprised at the resignation but, statesmanlike, withheld comment until he could study Walker's statements. For his part, Samuel Seabury exulted that the resignation in the face of the record against Walker was the "equivalent of a confession of guilt."[15]

For ten days Walker uncharacteristically avoided public appearances. He divided his time between his suite at the Mayfair Hotel and the Larchmont estate of Alfred Cleveland Blumenthal, a wealthy realtor with a specialty in brokering movie theaters. Blumenthal liked nothing better than to surround himself with celebrities, starlets, and others in whose spotlight he could shine. During these awkward days for the former mayor, Blumenthal provided a temporary haven.

An hour after his announcement, Jimmy Walker wired Betty Compton, who was in Paris, and with mutual delight they made plans to meet in Europe. On August 10, Walker left for Europe aboard the Italian liner *Conte Grande* accompanied only by his dog, his valet, and George Collins, a former secretary. Walker declared that the trip abroad was for his health. This time one can believe him.

Walker's intention had been to seek renomination as mayor at a special convention, win the election, finish out his term as mayor of New York City, divorce Allie, and marry Betty. But the latter was not happy and asserted that another election would further ruin Jimmy's declining health, and by giving up politics the two could arrange an earlier marriage. After a good deal of wavering, Betty proved persuasive, and Jimmy and Monk spent some idyllic time together in Paris.

But, was it Betty who was decisive in permanently removing Walker from politics?

In New York, Tammany sachems were having second thoughts about running Jimmy Walker for mayor once again. Acting Mayor McKee, with support from a lower court, held that a special election was illegal and that he should serve the remainder of the mayor's term. Exemplary and intelligent though he was, McKee's political connections were all wrong inasmuch as he was the protégé of Bronx boss Ed Flynn, a Roosevelt supporter and therefore out of favor with the anti–Roosevelt sentiment in Tammany. New York's political boss, John Francis Curry, and Brooklyn's political boss, John H. (Uncle John) McCooey, were not about to get behind the candidacy of McKee irrespective of his unquestioned qualifications.

But Curry and McCooey could not now get enthusiastic about Walker. Why back a loser? That he was a loser was made eminently clear when Monsignor John P. Chidwick, at a Catholic funeral mass for a political leader, declared in the eulogy, "Would to God every man in public life would understand that he is an example, a model and a guide to young people who are apt to be drawn to him. Not only in official life, but in private life, should a man be clean and pure."[16] Since it was widely believed that Chidwick spoke for Cardinal Hayes and that the church hardly regarded Walker as one whose life was "clean and pure," the not-so-subtle message was that the return of Jimmy Walker was unacceptable to the church.

Walker returned to the United States on the *Bremen* still unsure whether he would seek renomination. But when news reached him that support in Tammany was eroding, church leaders were not supportive, and Roosevelt would not share the speakers' platform with him, Walker changed his mind. While aboard the *Bremen* he learned that Tammany stalwarts had chosen Surrogate Court Judge John P. O'Brien, and Walker played the role of "good sport" and wired O'Brien, "Perfect nomination. Very happy."[17] When at dockside he was asked whether he would support the Democratic ticket, and he replied that he was for the entire Democratic ticket: Roosevelt for president, Herbert H. Lehman for governor, and John P. O'Brien for mayor of the city of New York.

In the November election Roosevelt won handily. He carried all but six states and won by a popular vote of 22,809,638 to Herbert Hoover's 15,758,901.

A few days before the election Betty Compton and her mother returned to New York for a short stay during which they allegedly took care of remaining financial affairs. On November 10, Jimmy Walker joined

Betty and her mother in first-class accommodations aboard the *Conte Grande* for Italy and the French Riviera. Walker left New York with little fanfare; no politician was on the wharf to see him off and he had little money in his pocket. How then could he afford first-class staterooms for the transatlantic crossing? For the three years he lived in Europe, he lived well, where did the money come from? Had the elusive Robert T. Sherwood stashed away several hundred thousand dollars in assorted European bank accounts? The mystery remains.

"Letters I Forgot to Mail"

In Nice, Betty encouraged her Jimmy to write his memoirs, which would bear the tentative title, "Letters I Forgot to Mail." But just as Jimmy would not deal with the day-to-day, hard and unglamorous work of administering the city of New York, so he could not sit long enough and engage in the solitary task of writing a book. Nothing came of the project.

Via transatlantic telephone Jimmy told his wife, Allie, that she would have to file for divorce in Florida or he would file in France. On March 21, Allie tearfully complied. Allie and Jim never saw or spoke to each other again. She received no money from him except the $10,000 he left in his will. Her remaining years she spent reclusively managing a religious bookstore in St. Patrick's Roman Catholic Church in Miami Beach. She died in Florida, at the age of seventy, in 1956.

In Cannes, in April 1933, "wearing neither hat nor spats but with the red ribbon of the Legion of Honor in his lapel,"[18] Jimmy Walker married Betty Compton in a civil ceremony. Betty was almost twenty-nine; her husband was nearly fifty-two. In the eyes of the church the civil ceremony was not recognized, and Jimmy and Betty were technically living in sin. Inasmuch as they did not marry in a non–Catholic religious ceremony, they were not excommunicated.

In the November 1933 election, New York City voters thoroughly repudiated Tammany and overwhelmingly elected as mayor Fiorello La Guardia. With the latter's election Tammany was decisively defeated, and while it remained a factor in New York politics for some time to come, its teeth had been effectively pulled. By the 1960s it lost its bark as well as its bite.

As the fortunes of Tammany declined so in a parallel way did those of Jimmy Walker. In March 1934, Jimmy's home at St. Luke's Place was sold for nonpayment of taxes, and law suits were pending against him for nonpayment of bills. The federal government was making a case against him for income-tax evasion. That summer Dr. William H. Walker, the ex-mayor's brother, died in an automobile accident. Jimmy and Betty Walker settled in a home in Surrey, England, a suburban community not far from London to which he commuted frequently by bus rather than limousine. In March 1935, when Jimmy and Betty visited Eddie Cantor, who was staying in London's elegant Dorchester Hotel, the comedian was surprised how much Jimmy had aged. "He was broken, suddenly old."[19]

To many visitors Jimmy increasingly expressed a kind of longing for New York and hoped he would one day be able to return. When the U.S. government announced that it was dropping its tax suit against him, he and Betty began to plan a return to New York.

Eight thousand people led by Boss Curry welcomed the Walkers home on October 31, 1935. Some Tammany diehards insisted that if Walker chose to do so he could be mayor once again. But Walker was in failing health, and politics was no longer his governing passion. Betty and Jim moved into an apartment at 132 East Seventy-second Street, and, in March 1936, they adopted a baby girl and, a year later, a baby boy. In 1937, Walker's friends in New York's government arranged for him to qualify for a $12,000 pension. His health improved; he was invited to a private talk with President Roosevelt at the White House and once again became a popular speaker much sought after on the lecture and banquet circuit.[20] He even hailed La Guardia as "the greatest mayor New York ever had."[21] La Guardia reciprocated the goodwill by appointing Walker labor arbiter of the women's cloak-and-suit industry. The job, which paid $20,000 a year plus $5,000 in expenses, required that he maintain harmony among labor and management in that turmoil-prone industry.

However, Betty was not happy, and in a surprise move in March 1941, she filed for a Florida divorce. She charged extreme cruelty. A year later she married Theodore Knappen, a prosperous consulting engineer, by whom, in January 1944, she had a baby boy. Seven months later, at the age of forty, Betty died of cancer. For fifteen months Knappen and Walker tried to raise the three children together, but the absurd arrangement could not work. Eventually, Knappen took his son and Walker his adopted children. Nan Burke, Walker's sister, brought her two children, and the household of six got along remarkably well. He gave up his job as arbiter in the clothing industry and appropriately became president of Majestic Records. When asked whether he would be putting out a recording of "Will You Love Me in December as You Do in May?" the ever wise-cracking former politician aptly replied, "I've been hired to plug the company not sabotage it."[22]

In 1946, Walker's always-precarious health took a sudden and rapid turn for the worse. On November 12, after a speech before the Grand Street Boys Association, Walker returned home so tired that his sister sent for his personal physician. After several days of nausea and dizziness he fell into a coma, was given the last rites of the Roman Catholic Church, and was taken from his home to Doctor's Hospital. He never regained consciousness and died of a brain clot on November 18. He was sixty-five.

A year earlier, in a *New York Times* interview, journalist S.J. Woolf observed: "Age has not withered New York's Peter Pan, nor have setbacks soured him. The former Night Mayor has become the Toastmaster of the Town, and a complete public dinner now means everything from soup to Walker."[23]

The Tragedy of Jimmy Walker

Walker's place in the history of New York City is hardly a heroic one. Yet, he was not a bad man. He was lax and laid back in performing his duties as mayor, and in his work habits, or lack of them, he set a bad example for his subordinates. Jimmy Walker was a sinner who retained a soft spot in his heart for those who sinned in their public or private lives. In short, he set the tone in city hall that seemed to encourage less than due-diligence upon those working for the city of New York. He was, as New York's master builder, Robert Moses, observed, "incapable of sustained effort."[24]

So great was his popularity that when criticisms began to mount, Jimmy Walker was unable to comprehend why he was coming under fire. But it soon became clear that snappy dressing was no substitute for hard thinking, that a wink was not policy making, that a wise-crack was no alternative to critical thought, and that taking frequent vacations were no substitute for concentrated effort. As the Depression deepened, Jimmy did not know how to respond to jobless, homeless, and often hungry New Yorkers. He had compassion for the city's poor, but he tended to see them as individuals who needed a favor, a quick fix, or a temporary assist to get them on their feet. With no philosophy of government, he failed to provide a safety net for New York's beleaguered, nor did he even realize that such a safety net was needed. The traditional Tammany response, a vote in exchange for a hand out or a menial job, was no longer responsive to mass unemployment, and impoverishment.

Was Jimmy Walker a crook? While he did not seek to enrich himself in public office, his popularity was such that money was literally thrust upon him, and he neither looked at the source nor at the reasons for what he tirelessly called the "beneficences." Did the money he received influence his judgment, or bankrupt the city, or indeed jeopardize the well-being of its citizens?

Socialist Party leader Norman Thomas, perhaps his severest critic, wrote in 1932, the year of Walker's resignation, "the City of New York is not in bad financial condition ... and it has not been in bad financial condition during the Walker administration."[25] For the most part the corruption during the Walker years consisted of levies on the private sector by politicians who had the power to award a contract, provide a zoning variance, or give permits to start building. These are serious enough charges inasmuch as whatever money was passed to politicians under the table was later charged to the city in overstated bills for often-shoddy work. Walker probably knew but cared little that incompetent people were holding jobs that had been denied those who had taken and passed competitive civil service examinations. Those who served Tammany well could be rewarded with important jobs in the municipal bureaucracy. Thus, one James F. Geraghty, a Bronx district leader, as head of the Division of Licensed Vehicles, endangered the well-being of New Yorkers by accepting graft in exchange for giving taxicab licenses to ex-convicts. Charles L. Kohler was rewarded for his incompetence in monitoring corruption as health commissioner by being named budget director by Mayor Walker. Walker also tolerated Dr. William F. Doyle, a veterinarian known in the press as the "horse doctor," who posed as an architect and appeared before the Board of Standards and Appeals to plead for permits from the board. His only competence being his connections with Tammany and his ability to spread a little graft where it would do the most good and enable Doyle to accumulate $2 million in three years. He eventually did go to jail for a brief stay.[26]

One student of municipal government in America has asserted, "Walker exploited the mood of his times ignoring the tasks of office." He was among those mayors who "diminished the office [and] brought few aspirations to the office; and acquired no affirmative objectives from [his] acquaintance with the opportunities of office."[27]

For every bribe taker there is a bribe giver. For every influence peddler there is someone seeking to tilt the political machine in his or her favor. Walker was mayor at a time when business boomed and market forces became ever more sophisticated, and the amount of money available to seek preferential treatment was never greater. Compared with some Wall Street types who swindled small investors of their savings by promising seemingly feasible ways of getting rich, Jimmy Walker and his cronies were but nibbling at the edges of a system they did not invent but which they did not have the strength of character to resist.

Governor Roosevelt was not the prime mover in Walker's near ouster. Roosevelt dragged his feet until his hand was forced. He knew that Walker was but the most visible symbol of a system of corruption carefully camouflaged and nourished by the Tammany political machine. Jimmy Walker was "machine made," and he lived and governed by the code of Tammany Hall. But he knew no other way. Indeed, was there another way? It was not until government and personal budgets tightened, not until austerity was in the saddle and New Yorkers became aware of how they had been short-changed by Tammany in government services, including police protection, transportation efficiency, park land availability, to say nothing of a host of government services a city in depression required, that the finger pointing began. Fortunes were being made on every hand, and it is not surprising that those who felt left out also felt entitled to a share. When Paul Block established a "beneficence" for Mayor Walker, what he was doing was nothing more or less than he might have done for any other personal friend with fewer financial resources and less financial savvy. But his mistake was that the mayor of New York City should be above temptation. Walker liked the high-life and, under cover of his popularity, succumbed. Jimmy Walker's crime was that he heard and saw no evil.

Part IV

JAMES MICHAEL CURLEY: AMERICA'S FOURTH WORST MAYOR

And this is good old Boston
The Home of the bean and the cod,
Where Lowells talk to the Cabots
And the Cabots talk only to God.

Toast, Holy Cross Alumni Dinner, 1910

12

The Making of a Political Boss

The Emerald Isle's greatest export was its people. In 1847, a year before the Irish potato famine, Boston had a population of 260,000, including 5,000 Irish. By 1857, the population of Boston had grown to 310,000, including 50,000 Irish. The Boston Irish had grown from one-fiftieth to a sixth of the population and accounted for more than a third of the city's registered voters. By 1884, their numbers equaled that of the Yankee population and, in that year Boston elected Hugh O'Brien its first Irish mayor. In 1885, Patrick Maguire, boss of Boston's Ward 17, was the first Irish Catholic to deliver the city's Fourth of July oration. Senator George Frisbie Hoare wrote anxiously to Henry Cabot Lodge, "Unless we can break this compact foreign vote, we are gone."[1]

Catholic and Irish, they seemed to have little to commend them to their Yankee neighbors. They had come to escape Ireland's poverty and free themselves from the burden of British bigotry. But no red carpet treatment awaited them in America. Few Irish could be blamed if they felt that their escape had been largely illusory. Boston, the birthplace of liberty, seemed to be anything but welcoming to Irish immigrants, who were greeted, likely as not, with notices reading, "No Irish or Negroes Need Apply," as they sought work in their new country.

Irish immigrant women, indelicately called "biddies," "pot wallopers," or "kitchen canaries," most often became maids in fashionable Back Bay homes where they earned two dollars a week and lived in an attic that was often ice-cold in the winter and stifling hot in the summer. Irish immigrant men, "clodhoppers," "Micks," or "Paddies," as they were insensitively called by the Boston Brahmins, often brought their picks and shovels with them from the *Ould Sod* and went to work as laborers, longshoremen, or blacksmiths or as waiters, heavers of coal, diggers of canals, or workers on the intercontinental railways. The Yankee population welcomed their labor but abhorred their presence in their city on a hill.

Unlike New York, where the immigrant build-up was more diverse if not more gradual, the Boston immigrant, during the latter half of the nineteenth century, was nearly always exclusively Irish. Moreover, the Irish faced an entrenched Yankee aristocracy who could claim, with a good deal of truth, that they initiated the American Revolution, nourished a political and literary meritocracy second to none in America, and were the guardians of constitutional government. These Boston Brahmins, as they came to be called, felt superior to other Americans let alone to newcomers from Europe. But in the end, their very political traditions and orientation worked to the benefit of the Irish newcomer to Boston.

The sense of fair play among Boston Brahmins was such that "Boston's established Yankee aristocracy neither raised nor sought to exploit with vigor the issue of Irish Catholicism."[2] They refused, for example, to flock to the anti-Catholic, anti-immigrant policies of the Know-Nothing Movement, widespread in mid-nineteenth century America. Instead, the "good people" of Boston sought reconciliation and accommodation to the wave of Irish Catholic immigration. Moreover, belatedly perhaps, important elements in Boston's Yankee aristocracy began to see in the Irish immigrants an inspiration for the reinvigoration of Boston's political and economic life.

The Irish responded to the economic bind in which they found themselves by finding a place in civil service as firefighters, schoolteachers, or police officers. They also found a niche in local politics. The Yankee aristocrats of the city could not begrudge the newcomer for flattering them by example and by likewise playing the political game. When James Michael Curley asserted, "Politics is my business," the Boston Brahmins understood.

A Boy in Boston

Michael Curley, young Jim's father, came from Galway, Ireland, to Boston in 1865 at the age of fourteen. In the same year his mother, Sarah Clancy, arrived from Connemara at the age of twelve. Patrick "Pea-Jacket" Maguire, boss of Ward 17, helped Michael find work as a hod carrier for ten cents an hour, eleven hours a day. Sarah, who had arrived with her sister, found work as a maid with an up-scale family in Beacon Hill. When Michael was twenty-one, he and Sarah were married and found a place to live in a three-tiered shanty at 28 Northampton Street, a rat-infested, tuberculosis-ridden slum in Roxbury made up of wooden tenements that lacked adequate heat or toilets. During abnormally high tides, outhouses would overflow, foul the neighborhood, and bring disease. For this, they paid rent of $6 a month.

In this rough and squalid environment, to the Curleys were born three sons, first John and on November 20, 1874, James Michael. In 1879, a third son was born only to die of disease in 1881. As an Irish politician, James Michael would never forget the environment in which he spent his youth, and the prejudices to which he and his fellow immigrants had been subjected. As a formidable candidate for public office, he would fan the flames of communal resentment endemic in such an environment. In his book *Inside U.S.A.*, the journalist John Gunther would assert that it was not surprising that James Michael Curley would become the "undisputed champion of the local Irish.... His rise was an absolutely proper and inevitable phenomenon."[3]

Growing up in Roxbury, "the corned beef and cabbage Riviera" he later called it, was not easy, and James Michael Curley's happy years as a boy were few. In his autobiography, he commented, "I can recall few cheerful incidents of my early childhood, when I lived on the mudsill of society."[4] Often shoeless and close to hunger he would scavenge in the coal dumps for bits of coal to provide much-needed fuel during Boston's often harsh winters. During the summer James Michael and his buddies would swim in the nude in the polluted waters of the South Bay. He obtained his elementary school education first at Yeoman Primary School and then at the Dearborn Grammar School. In later years, he remembered that at these schools the janitors were almost exclusively Irish while his teachers rarely were. Classes were huge, consisting of between fifty and seventy pupils in one room. He was a good student and excelled in the speaking of famous speeches from Daniel Webster, Abraham Lincoln, or William Shakespeare at school assemblies. Considering his later reputation as a political bad boy, James Michael Curley was a good boy in school.

Curley's days at the Dearborn School were winding down inasmuch as he had to leave school to make some money when his father died in 1884. Typically, James Michael began his career as a newsboy. After school he would hitch a ride to the downtown office of the Boston *Globe,* pick up a bundle of newspapers, and return to his corner of Northampton and Washington streets from which he hawked his newspapers. On Saturdays he worked as a delivery boy for the Washington Market on East Lenox Street. The eleven year old was paid three cents for every basket of groceries he delivered.

When Curley was twelve, he went to work for Stephen Gale's drug store where this boy of all work sometimes put in as much as sixty hours a week sweeping the floor, delivering prescriptions, and working behind the soda fountain. He would start work at seven in the morning and continue until half-past eight before leaving for the Dearborn School a mile away. He would have lunch at home with John, his older brother, since his mother was generally away at her own job as a cleaning woman in an office building. He would return to the drugstore where he would work until one-thirty and then off to the Dearborn School once again, and back to the drugstore where he worked between half-past four and six o'clock. Then, he traveled back home for dinner and another dash to the drugstore to work until ten at night. For his fifty-seven hours of hard work, he received $2.50. At fifteen he completed the ninth grade at Dearborn, left Gale's Drug Store, and took a better paying job at the New England Piano Company, where he lived.

The most important job of James Michael's youth was as a delivery boy for the C.S. Johnson Grocery Company. Driving "an old gray horse which wouldn't hurry if you lit a fire under him," he delivered groceries not only in Roxbury, but also in Back Bay, Dorchester, and Hyde Park.[5] He worked as a delivery boy for eight years and earned $11 dollars a week. Since he often had to carry a barrel of flour up three or four flights of rickety tenement stairs, he worked out his well-trimmed, 5-foot, 11-inch body in a local gym to develop his biceps and his back muscles. During this period he took the examination for the fire department and passed with flying colors, but he was too young for the job. So, he remained at C.S. Johnson's a bit longer.

That he gave up two nights a week for two years, enrolled in the Boston Evening High School, and read Dickens, Thackeray, and Shakespeare, and the Boston *Transcript*, the newspaper of the "proper Bostonians," is evidence that he had better things in mind for himself than being a delivery boy. He taught Sunday school, served as usher at St. Philips Catholic Church on Harrison Avenue, and joined the Ancient Order of Hibernians, where he became chairman of a social committee to plan picnics, minstrel shows, church suppers, and dances. He served on the general committee that made arrangements for the St. Patrick's Day parade. He would not miss a St. Patrick's Day for the next fifty years.

This youthful Irish kid was strong, nimble on his feet, and, if need be, quick with his fists. "I stood a lean but wiry five-feet-eleven, and had learned something of the art of self-defense. I wore an 'Iron Mike' [a derby] and dressed as conservatively as a modest budget would allow. I smoked cigars, but did not imbibe of the elixir of sociability ... I had no time for girl friends.... I raised funds for welfare projects and went around the neighborhood visiting the sick and needy."[6] Although athletic in appearance, Curley was not an athlete and neither played nor understood football or baseball. Like Mayor Frank Hague of Jersey City, he was not companionable nor was he easy to get to know nor easy to like. He had no nicknames, affectionate or otherwise.

It is difficult to determine just when and where Curley determined upon a political career. His youth seemed to suggest that he would do no better nor no worse than other Irish young men who would lead life in obscurity. Yet, Curley appeared to have a natural talent for being a "pol." As he carried out his self-chosen assignments for the Ancient Order of Hibernians, he began to make inroads into the life of Boston's Irish community. During the eight years he spent as a grocery delivery boy for C.S. Johnson, he did not merely deliver groceries but became familiar with the lives of the families on his route. He was helpful, obliging, and when he could, did a favor. "For James Michael Curley, the springboard to political power in 1890s Boston was the operation of a horse-cart delivery route for a grocer. It took him all through the city, and at every stop he exercised his political charm to impress his personality upon the customer."[7] Before he could vote, James Michael Curley was a politician.

"Public Service Is My Business": The Making of a Boston "Pol"

Just how and exactly when James Michael Curley embarked upon his "uproarious years" in politics is the stuff of myth and legend. Politics was so natural to him that whether he was selling groceries or selling himself to the voters, he learned to stroke the customer and/or the voter with a word, smile, or gesture. And, more importantly perhaps, he gave value for value received. "Public service is my business, he stated.[8] As a grocer he conscientiously "delivered the goods"; as a politician he likewise did so whether he promised a job, a bucket of coal, or a Christmas dinner.

While memory may be an unreliable witness to history, how Curley, near the end of his career, remembered getting into politics offers an engaging image of a politico as he saw himself many years later:

> I used to drop into "One-Arm" Peter Whalen's tobacco store on Northampton Street (now a vacant lot) and listen to the conniving politicos plan their strategy. I was hanging around one night when Michael

> Cunnif, a banker-politician, asked me whether I could help Galvin in Ward
> 17.... At this time I was still working for C.S. Johnson Grocers, and spent
> as much time buttonholing customers in Galvin's behalf as I did in sell-
> ing, wrapping or delivering groceries. After work, I rang every doorbell in
> the neighborhood.[9]

Galvin, nevertheless, lost that fight.

Initially reluctant, Jim Curley was pushed into politics by the politically saturated environment in Whalen's tobacco store, pulled into politics by his own realization that his future was in politics not in groceries,
and forced into politics by C.S. Johnson, who became understandably
resentful that Curley was giving short shrift to the business of delivering
groceries. But Curley, already intoxicated by politics, could not choose
but run for political office the rest of his life, and that made all the
difference in his life, as well as that of Boston and Massachusetts.

James Michael Curley's first foray into politics was to go after the
entrenched but unpopular boss of the Ward 17, Patrick James "Pea-Jacket"
Maguire. A tailor by trade, he had come to Boston twenty years before
James Michael's parents and found that he had more of a career in politics than in tailoring. He administered favors and patronage with a measured hand, a job, a basket of food, or a bucket of coal for a vote. Because
men could vote and women could not, the former were favored and the
latter essentially ignored. When Curley's father died, "P.J." refused his
mother either sympathy or assistance since she had no political *quid pro
quo* to offer. Curley would not forget.

Dressed in a secondhand rather foppish suit of clothing, James
Michael Curley, this young politician and still fumbling speaker, waged a
vigorous, if amateurish, campaign for the Boston Common Council. John
Dever, the new boss of Ward 17, irked that young Curley had the "chutz-
pah" to be a foot soldier for Galvin, was determined to deny Curley any
of the usual facilities for holding a political meeting including storefronts,
ward rooms, or assembly halls. Curley was forced to rely on doorbell-ring-
ing and street-corner rallies. He carried a bucket of paste and plastered
his own posters throughout the ward.

When Curley began his political career, bullies in the employ of rival
political leaders heckled speakers, intimidated voters, paid derelicts to vote
repeatedly, and brought gangs of hoodlums to political rallies so as to cheer
for their candidate and drown out rival speakers and, if need be, stuff ballot boxes. But in his naiveté he did not recognize that Dever's lieutenants
controlled the actual count at the ballot box. By the time they finished
"counting" the votes, Curley had lost the election. Next year, he vowed,

he would be more sophisticated, meet strong-arm tactics in kind, and go on to destroy the ward boss's influence while building a political base of his own. Using brute force and cunning he would eventually triumph.

In 1899, in his third attempt at running for a council seat, Curley, now better known and his speaking ability substantially improved, was also not above using his fists and his friends in shouting matches and raw exhibitions of force. For example, Curley learned the importance of having his name first on the ballot to be assured of the votes of those who were not entirely literate. Curley and his devotees filed first, but throughout a long night had to stave off with fists and clubs attempts by rivals to steal the first line on the ballot. They were unsuccessful, and Curley went on to his first taste of political victory.

When young Curley joined the race for the Boston Common Council, it was the lower house of the city legislature and was made up of three members from each of the city's twenty-five wards who were paid but $300 annually. The powers of the council were limited to debating issues and sending recommendations to the powerful nine-member board of aldermen who examined the recommendations of the council and, if it approved, sent them on to the mayor for final action.

Curley used the momentum of victory to pay a visit to New York to study the workings of Tammany Hall, the powerful and Irish-dominated political club of that city. New York's Tammany Hall at the time of the Curley visit was under the thumb of Richard Croker, a legendary political boss. Croker lined his pockets freely, and for sixteen years he was the man to see and to pay off when a political favor was needed, a municipal ordinance bent, a bid on a construction project favorably acted upon, or to receive advance notice on city construction that may have a bearing on land values. Under Croker's leadership, "Tammany would wield a greater and more shocking degree of power over the lives of the people of New York than it ever had in the past or ever would in the future."[10]

James Michael Curley, a fast learner, recognized the need to cultivate three important political skills, that is, the skill to do favors for voters and thereby control their vote, the skill to make widely known his kindly beneficence, and the skill to prosper for his role in helping others prosper. These lessons Curley brought back to Boston where he organized his own club, likewise called Tammany, which formed the beginnings of his political base. The Roxbury Tammany Club, he assured the press, would be tailored to the needs of Boston.

Although a freshman on the Boston Common Council, he announced that he would become a candidate for chairman (ward boss), of the Ward 17 Democratic Committee. But for a political upstart this was a risky venture. He sought the help of Tom Curley, a namesake but no relation and a man who believed that he had been entitled to be boss of Ward 17 instead of John Dever. James Michael made a deal with Tom that if he helped James Michael win in the campaign for ward boss, then the latter would give up his seat on the Boston Common Council and help Tom win it. James Michael went on to become the youngest ward boss in the city.

In his early days as a politician Jim Curley learned how to do himself good by doing good. That is, he instinctively knew that to shore up his base among the poor, mostly Irish poor of Boston, he would have to show immediate results. No long-term, pie-in-the sky promises for him but specific actions that could be taken immediately. His first recommendation, seemingly trivial, was to grant Saturday afternoons off to city employees. Curley got the credit for having made a fair and humane proposal that the mayor could not veto. He proposed indoor toilets in public schools, a gymnasium for the Ward 17, a public hospital for the city's consumptives, an eight-hour day for Boston workers, and measures to end the backup of sewage into the apartments of families living in his ward. At Christmas he distributed baskets of food and buckets of coal, and hot holiday meals to the needy of his ward. "Curley took the notion of the ward boss as a benevolent figure and used it to craft a popular persona."[11]

Curley also played to the growing power of labor unions as when early in his career he opposed the policy of docking the pay of outdoor workers when adverse weather conditions prevented them from working while indoor workers could continue to receive their pay. Curley earned the backing of labor unions when he urged vacations for municipal workers and union wages for all city mechanics. He learned early in his political career that it was not enough to help individual poor; it was equally important that the media should know about it and report it favorably. His publicity skills were such that they would carry him far beyond the political boundaries of Ward 17 and the Boston Common Council.

Since he could not yet afford to be a full-time politico and had been fired by the C.S. Johnson Grocery Company, Curley had to find a means of having an income to support himself. As a result, in addition to working on the council, serving his constituents at his Tammany Club, and performing his functions as chairman of the Ward 17 Democratic Committee, he needed to look for work. For a time he worked as a salesman for a wholesale bakery company, briefly operated a saloon, and finally with his brother, John, opened an insurance agency which remained his nominal occupation while pursuing his more compelling political career. The brothers became agents of the New York Life Insurance Company and opened an office in downtown Boston. He spent four days at the insurance agency, one day at the Boston Common Council, and, even in his first year, he did very well financially.

At his Tammany Club he offered naturalization classes for immigrants and intervened on behalf of constituents who had gotten into trouble with the law. He spent hours with lawyers, judges, and police officers to secure lighter sentences if his constituent could not be freed altogether. He raised bail, intervened in probation matters, stayed evictions or repossessions, and, when he could, he saved some constituents from getting criminal records. Most importantly, in a city with chronic unemployment, he spent a good deal of time finding jobs for distressed men and women. He boasted, "In the course of two years, I secured jobs for about seven hundred men and women."[12]

In 1901, as promised, he gave up his seat on the common council to allow Tom Curley to try to win it. Tom won while James Michael Curley ran and was elected to the general court, or state legislature. As a member of the state legislature, Curley would have the opportunity of working on a broader political canvas, and he relished the prospect of doing so. There was much to do.

At the time Curley was elected to the general court, there were proposals before it to legalize a ten-hour day, fifty-eight-hour week for women and children in business and industry. There was, likewise, a proposal to ease the Sunday laws for the sale of soft drinks and liquor. The state and city were vying for who should build a subway addition in Boston, how it should be built, how much it should cost, and how to pay for it. Union labor was growing fast and marched on the state legislature to assure the passage of a law that would permit fifty thousand voters to submit a constitutional amendment directly to the people on the ballot. Labor won. It was in the state legislature that Curley met some of the prominent Republicans of the state. He impressed some, repulsed others, but was ignored by none.

But Curley had no over-arching political philosophy and brought no legislative agenda with him to the Massachusetts legislature. Quite the contrary, right from the beginning he recognized that his two years in the legislature would be but an interlude in his career, a stepping stone to perhaps more influential positions. Curley climbed the political ladder because of the effectiveness of his personal connections and not because he reflected the philosophy of either of the major political parties. As he reached for higher office, he was as much hurt as helped by the highly personal loyalty he attracted.

Although a member of the state legislature, he did not neglect his newly formed Roxbury Tammany Hall. It became a personal fiefdom in which members in effect pledged personal fealty to James Michael Curley. Roxbury Tammany Hall "nourished no competitors and encouraged no threats to the authority of the boss or to his uninterrupted tenure in office. He made the Roxbury Tammany Club Curley's personal machine.... There were no committees, no kitchen cabinet, no personal advisers on policy, [and] Curley made all the decisions."[13]

On a personal level, Curley was now doing quite well. His mother had a good home; he had money in the bank. He was recognized as a "pol" with important leadership qualities from the other ward bosses, and they elected him chairman of the Democratic Ward Committee. His political future looked bright. But one term in the Massachusetts House of Representatives was enough.

In 1903 he announced his candidacy for a place on Boston's prestigious nine-man board of aldermen. To be elected to the board, Curley would have to wage his first citywide campaign. But, in his haste to do good for himself by being good to others, he nearly tripped over his own zeal. Were it not for his natural political talents a lesser political Svengali might have found that the political magic which he had practiced with so sure a hand had now deserted him. But James Michael Curley would thrive on adversity and use political setbacks to sharpen his political skills.

"He That Filches from Me My Good Name ... Makes Me Poor Indeed"

The episode that nearly tripped him up had to do with finding jobs for Bartholomew Fahey and James Hughes, two strong and healthy men who worked as volunteers for the Roxbury Tammany Hall but, to make a living, wanted to be letter carriers in Boston. There was little doubt that these two men could deliver the mail, but could they pass the civil service examination required for mail carriers by the United States Postal Service?

To the Yankee establishment and other good-government types, the system of requiring civil service examinations for government offices at all levels was for the purpose of removing thousands of positions from the grasp of political machines to be used by them as political fodder to capture elections. The Brahmins of Boston were sure that by requiring a merit system based on competitive examinations and thereby providing a level playing field by which all job seekers could be objectively evaluated, the public would be better served by ensuring that only meritorious men and

women were appointed to government service. To the Boston Irish, however, the civil service examination system was just another obstacle put in
place by the Yankee establishment to hinder the legitimate progress of the
immigrant. Could a paper-and-pencil test measure the ability of candidates with good legs and stout hearts to deliver the mail swiftly despite
the gloom of night and the heat of day?

On October 15, 1902, James Michael Curley and Tom Curley assisted
Fahey and Hughes by helping them fill out and file their applications for
the civil service examination to be given in December for letter carriers.
But fearing that because their protégés were not fully literate and might
not pass the written civil service examination, Jim and Tom, on December 4, 1902, entered the Federal Building and took the examinations for
them. James Michael impersonated Bartholomew Fahey and Tom impersonated James Hughes.

The Curleys were recognized, and the case came before Federal Judge
Francis Cabot Lowell, of the Brahmin Lowells, a judge from whom the
Curleys could expect little sympathy. On noon of February 25, 1903, the
Curleys, Fahey, and Hughes "surrendered" to the federal marshal. Bail was
set at $2,500, a sum Curley thought vindictive and further evidence that
the Brahmins were out to "get" the Irish. This was the first time a member of the Massachusetts State Legislature had ever been criminally
arrested. The Curleys were represented by a Yankee lawyer, Heman W.
Chapin, who demanded a $3,500 fee. To raise the money the Roxbury
Tammany Club staged a minstrel show and with the proceeds paid the
lawyer. Chapin argued, incredibly, that the law did not bar a proxy from
taking a federal exam. Moreover, the lawyer asserted that no fraud was
intended nor was a fraud perpetuated upon the federal government. The
intent of the Curleys had been only overzealousness in getting jobs for
men who could clearly do the work and desperately needed jobs.

Judge Lowell was neither amused nor persuaded. The two Curleys
were found guilty of a crime against "the peace and dignity of the United
States of America" and were sentenced to sixty days in the Suffolk County
Prison, better known as the Charles Street Jail. When Curley heard the
foreman of the jury pronounce him guilty, "a slight shudder seemed to pass
over him."[14] Yet, the Brahmin judge had been lenient since the maximum
penalty he could have imposed was two years in jail and a $10,000 fine.
Numerous appeals followed, and it was not until November 7, 1904, nearly
two years after the impersonation had taken place, that Curley was taken
away in manacles and incarcerated in a jail cell.

The cheers from the crowd at the Tammany Club must have still been
ringing in his ears from the party held the night before when James Michael

Curley entered his cell. And he must have felt reassured when sixty days later he emerged again to the cheers of his political supporters. "Curley pledged that he would venture beyond the constitutional, the legal, the bureaucratic, and when he walked out of the Tammany Club onto George Street, scores of shouting supporters stood in the snow waiting to let him know they approved."[15]

The Charles Street jail was a house of correction for minor offenses and had little by way of amenities by which prisoners could keep themselves occupied. It did, however, have a decent library, and books could be ordered from the Boston Public Library. James Curley quickly cultivated prison warden Fred H. Seavy, a loyal Democrat, and spent his sixty days of confinement in some comfort. The Curleys occupied the most spacious cell available and took daily exercise and salt-water baths. They were allowed more than the usual number of visitors, who often brought baskets of food to supplement the prison diet.

James Michael Curley was now twenty-nine-years old and at an age when he had no career other than a political one on which to build. During his appeals (1903) and later (1904) from his prison cell, Curley campaigned vigorously for the Boston Board of Aldermen. With his back literally to the political wall, Curley could do no other than to use his oratorical skills to persuade others that what he tried to do he undertook not in his own self-interest but on behalf of two poor, unemployed, but otherwise deserving men. "Curley could convince others that an unlawful means to achieve an end was right, if it could be established that the end itself was just and desirable.... What appeared to be personal disgrace and misfortune was turning into a political blessing."[16] Although now tainted as "jail birds," men with prison records, Tom Curley won a seat in the state senate, and James Michael Curley won his seat on the board of aldermen.

However, the Republican state senate, claiming that the newly elected senator was, by virtue of having served a prison term, unworthy of a place in the senate, refused to seat Tom Curley. Fearing a parallel attitude on the part of the board of aldermen, when, on January 6, 1905, James Michael stepped out of jail, he jumped into a waiting carriage and hastily made his way to city hall, where Daniel Whelton, president of the board of aldermen, likewise proposed to offer a resolution to bar him from the board. Curley raced to Whelton's second-floor office and asked if he proposed to go through the resolution to bar him. When Whelton responded affirmatively, "Curley pointed to the window and remarked, 'If you do, you will go through that window.'"[17] The resolution was never offered. He would serve as alderman for five years.

Over the years Curley's flamboyant political style was such that scandal seemed to follow him wherever he went. Some scandal was of his own doing, as he cut political corners with a swagger and a seeming indifference to public opinion. But Curley was not at all indifferent to public opinion. He was well aware that the sixty days he spent in jail left a wound, which his opponents would never let heal altogether but would remind the voters of Massachusetts of it over and over again. Among his responses, James Michael Curley would loftily declaim these lines from Shakespeare's Othello:

> Who steals my purse steals trash; 'tis something, nothing;
> 'Twas mine, 'tis his, and has been slave to thousands;
> But he that filches from me my good name
> Robs me of that which not enriches him,
> And makes me poor indeed.[18]

Shakespeare would be, however, an insufficient defense against the Republican opposition, hostile factions among the Irish, rival Democrats, and Boston Brahmins who thought that Curley's political tactics were making a mockery of democracy and bringing disgrace to the Athens of America.

13

The Mayor of the Poor

At age thirty-one, shortly after he was released from jail and took up his aldermanic duties, James Michael Curley met, and after a two-year courtship, married Mary Emelda (Mae) Herlihy of Burke Street, Roxbury. The couple married at 4:30 in the afternoon on June 27, 1906, at the St. Francis de Sales Church by Reverend Cornelius J. Herlihy, the bride's first cousin. From the church the wedding party, a small group of fewer than twenty, went to the Herlihy home for the reception.

Curley was not yet the celebrity he later became, and his wedding was crowded out among the lurid headlines describing the murder, in New York, of Stanford White by Henry K. Thaw the day before. It was only in a five-inch column on page eleven in the *Globe* where the wedding was mentioned and casually noted that the groom was president of the Roxbury Tammany Club and leader of Ward 17. The once and future politician of Massachusetts would never again escape the tender ministrations of the media.

After a dinner at the Essex House the couple made their way to North Street Station en route to their honeymoon trip that, according to Curley's autobiography, would take them to Montreal, down the St. Lawrence River to Lachine Rapids, then on to Lake Louise in Banff, and Chateau Frontenac in Quebec. They saw a rodeo at Medicine Hat in Saskatchewan, cruised up the Columbia River to Vancouver, and then came back to Buffalo, New York, from whence they made excursions to Niagara Falls, the Thousand Islands, and Saratoga Springs, where they attended the annual convention of the Ancient Order of Hibernians. But it was not all tourism. As Curley boasted or confessed in his autobiography, "I visited every town office or city hall possible, picking up pointers from officials."[1]

That he visited town halls and city halls was probably true, but could a relative newcomer to politics afford a thirty-day honeymoon? Historian

Charles Trout thinks not. Trout has asserted that Curley's honeymoon lasted no more than thirteen days and that he and his bride never traveled beyond Niagara Falls.[2] Curley's tendency to embellish, to exaggerate, and to portray himself in contexts that bordered on the grandiose may undermine his credibility, yet the seven-league boots which he chose to wear were part of his effort to achieve legitimacy among his followers and in the broader political environment of Boston.

Following their honeymoon travel, the couple made their home in a five-room wooden cottage at 114 Mount Pleasant Avenue in Roxbury. "We didn't have a pile of money. But we had faith in each other."[3]

James Michael Curley: The Man

Jim Curley, an impressive man about six feet tall, weighing over 200 pounds, and ruggedly handsome, carried himself with the air of a statesman. His hair at the time of his marriage was jet black and matched his eyes. But over the years his hair grayed handsomely, and his virile bearing made him attractive to women and to men. "He can bow over a lady's hand with the assurance of a Chesterfield, or with equal ease swing a fist into an opponent's chin in a street brawl."[4] Curley was a formal man. He had no nicknames and few persons ever called him "Jim." He was always "James Michael Curley," or just "Curley."

He was devoted to his family and his church and had no women in his life other than his wife and daughters. He drank and smoked moderately and played golf occasionally but vigorously. Despite his religious zeal, he was disliked by William Cardinal O'Connell, who despised the graft and corruption for which he alleged Curley was responsible, but he also disliked Curley's urban populism, his appeal to the poor, and his attempts to shake up traditional Boston politics. The Curleys lived modestly, but midway during his first term as Boston's mayor he built an ostentatious, seventeen-room house at 350 Jamaica Way. The house would haunt Curley's political career as questions would be raised as to who paid for it, how it was financed, and what did the house say about Curley's concept of government and political leadership.

Curley was self-educated and highly cultivated. He attended the symphony and discoursed knowledgeably on sculpture and Oriental jade, but he did not seem to have developed a passion for paintings. He read voraciously, had a retentive memory, and was impressive in his seeming mastery of classical literature, which he quoted at length and which he generously interspersed in his speeches. Because he rarely spoke from a completed text, his speeches seemed spontaneous even when they were not.

Curley's was a voice that could reach the shanty as well as lace-curtain Irish, the ordinary men and women of Boston, the Brahmins of Boston's Back Bay, and the students and teachers on the Harvard campus. Scrubwomen and teamsters, street-car conductors and stevedores, housewives and letter carriers, police officers and firefighters, and schoolteachers and civil servants were caught in the magnetism of his voice and personality. He always reassured his listeners that he relished his role as "mayor of the poor." For the most part, they believed him. His voice "booms and reverberates from the diaphragm, rises and swells in crescendo and sinks to a whisper as he strums upon the nerves and emotions of any audience."[5]

Just as he was self-taught in book learning so he was self-taught in public administration. He developed an exceptional administrative ability but, as we shall see, did not always direct such talent to the nobler purposes of politics. While politics was his business, he was no businessman. When in office, the money rolled in; when out of office, the money dried up. He was a sucker for get-rich-quick schemes but got burned each time he invested in risky deals.

Curley was a family man and left the political wheeling and dealing for the political arena. While at home he played the role of "father knows best." Mayor Jimmy Walker of New York had two adopted children later in life, and Mayor Bill Thompson of Chicago had none at all. James Michael Curley and his wife, "Mae," had nine children: James Jr., Mary, Dorothea, twins John and Joseph, Leo, Paul, George, and Francis. While they were growing up James Michael Curley gave to them as much time as he could. But, theirs was a hard lot as they were treated with special consideration by their teachers and coaches and often with disdain bordering or cruelty by other children when their father got into political scandals, ran for political office, or otherwise made his views known.

Tragedy struck James Michael's family life with an eerie regularity. His twin sons, John and Joseph, died only a few days old in 1922. Fourteen-year-old Dorothea died of lumbar pneumonia in 1925. On June 10, 1930, his wife, Mary, at age fifty-five, died after a two-year battle with painful arthritis and cancer. In January 1931, James M. Curley Jr. died at the age of twenty-three from a pulmonary embolism following a gallbladder operation. In 1945, Paul G. Curley, his eldest surviving son, died of a heart attack at age forty-two. In early 1950, Mary at forty-one and Leo at thirty-four would die of a cerebral hemorrhage on the same day. But these personal tragedies were in Curley's future. He lived in the political present and set his sights on becoming Boston's mayor.

En Route to City Hall

By the time Curley ran for mayor of Boston in 1913, he was a prominent politician, an energetic campaigner, and had a proven track record that suggested that he had much to offer Boston's voters. He had served a stormy five years on Boston's board of aldermen, where he provoked his staid colleagues by accusing them of being "subhuman reactionaries." Prodded into action, they approved liberalizing visiting hours in city hospitals, offering a business course in high schools, providing pensions for firefighters, developing a playground in Curley's Ward 17, liberalizing truancy laws so that young truants were not hustled off to prison for skipping school, and putting union labels on all city horseshoes.

Curley's fellow aldermen often found it hard to keep up with the nimble techniques he devised to get the measures he cared about adopted. It was common, for example, not to pay street workers on rainy days when they could not work. Curley wanted them paid by the week as were foremen and clerks who, in bad weather, continued to work indoors and earn their paychecks. When Curley introduced an order barring payments on rainy days to workers working indoors as well, his fellow aldermen were incensed and eventually approved an order paying all a weekly wage irrespective of the weather.

Curley urged statewide old-age assistance plans, fought to retain the five-cent fare on street railways, and recommended abolishing ferry charges for the boat trip to East Boston. He advocated the inspection of factories for the health and safety conditions in which employees worked. He pressed his aldermanic colleagues to abolish convict labor and to increase wages and provide shorter hours for government workers. He inveighed against department heads who ousted older workers to make room for younger ones. And, sarcastic and solemn at the same time, he urged his fellow aldermen to display toward blue-collar Bostonians "the same broad liberal treatment we accord horses."[6]

He sponsored numerous food fests for his supporters and his "Annual Curley Christmas Tree" event for the children of Ward 17 was invariably a huge success. He distributed toys and mittens and thousands of sugary Christmas candy canes. His formula for winning the hearts and minds of his constituents appeared to be jobs for men and gobs of candy for the children. It was a formula hard to beat. He was a tough and relentless campaigner and was not above making personal attacks appealing to class and religious antagonisms, or even blackmailing opponents for real or alleged sexual misconduct.

When Tom Curley, his namesake and former cell companion, lost his seat in the state senate, he expected James Michael to be generous by paving the way for him to assume either the presidency of the Tammany Club or the chairmanship of the ward committee. James Michael tenaciously held on to both jobs and a bitter, long-term hostility between these two erstwhile political allies ensued. In 1907, Tom Curley announced that he would run against James Michael for both positions. He did so and lost. For the rest of their political careers, Tom and James Michael were vigorous political enemies.

In 1909, the Good Government Association sought to diminish the power of the ward bosses by promoting a new city charter that replaced the seventy-five–person common council and the nine-member board of aldermen with a single city council of nine members. In the first election of the new city council all members were elected at-large and without party labels. The "Goo-Goos," as Curley called the members of the Good Government Association, were sure that Curley's vote-getting ability was limited to Ward 17. But, they were wrong. Moreover, Curley took no chances. To confuse the voters and to obfuscate the issues he produced his own slick brochure "sponsored" by a nonexistent group that, with tongue in cheek, he called "The Better Government Association." In the confused babble of political charges and counter charges, name-calling and vituperation on both sides, Curley, to the surprise of the "Goo-Goos," won a clear victory for a seat on the new Boston council.

However, Curley was restless and sought to test his vote-getting ability by running for the United States House of Representatives. Curley thought that his quest to become Boston's mayor would be furthered by taking a detour and running for a seat in the U.S. Congress. In March 1910, he announced that he would seek to replace the incumbent Joseph F. O'Connell, who held the congressional seat from the Tenth District.

According to the journalist Joseph F. Dinneen, a Curley critic and then admirer, Curley's decision to run for Congress was made by chance while he was being shaved in Mike Fitzgerald's barbershop. In the next chair, also being shaved was former Congressman William S. McNary of South Boston who had been defeated by Joseph O'Connell. It was his thought that Curley's vote-getting ability would be enough to unseat O'Connell, and, in a vicarious sort of way, McNary would have achieved revenge for his defeat. Moreover, McNary assured Curley that he would support him in his congressional campaign. According to Dinneen, Curley decided to make the run for Congress then and there.

Sitting in the chair on the other side of Curley was Standish Willcox, who was destined to play an important role in Curley's political career. A courtly, well-spoken Protestant, Willcox had a flair for drafting speeches for one who could deliver them flawlessly. Thus, the two men established a life-long relationship with Willcox as Curley's man-of-all seasons for twenty-two years.

McNary, however, dissembled — he went back on his word to support Curley and not run for Congress himself. His intent was to make the Democratic primary a three-way fight among Curley, O'Connell, and himself. McNary hoped that Curley and O'Connell would split the Roxbury/Dorchester vote between themselves while he, McNary, breezed in with a heavy vote from South Boston. A raucous campaign followed with Curley flaying both opponents with humor, sarcasm, and an attack on their records and allegedly duplicitous acts.

Curley went on to win the primary handily and proceeded to defeat his Republican opponent, J. Mitchell Galvin, with a vote of 20,345 to 15,783. But McNary would not take his defeat gently. Instead, he urged members of the Massachusetts congressional delegation to deny Curley his seat because he was a convicted felon. Inasmuch as the House of Representatives, for the first time in sixteen years, now had a Democratic majority, the 250-pound James Beauchamp "Champ" Clark was the new Speaker of the House. Curley went to Clark and sought from him a favor, namely, to reject the request of the Massachusetts congressional delegation to deny Curley a seat in Congress. Because Clark complied, and tabled the request, a lasting friendship and a political alliance between the two men developed. Clark went even further and assigned the new congressman a seat on the important Foreign Affairs and Immigration Committee.

Curley, reviled as a corrupt political boss, made a record in Congress that would identify him as an urban liberal and a harbinger of the great divide between urban and rural values, prohibition's "wets" and "drys," foreign-born and native-born Americans, and the secular and the fundamentalist.

The Curley/Clark alliance was further tested when the former supported the latter at the 1912 Democratic Convention when the fight over the presidential nomination became a fight between "Champ "Clark and Woodrow Wilson. Through Curley's efforts as "Champ" Clark's New England campaign manager, Clark won nearly every Massachusetts delegate to the convention and also was successful in other New England states, including Rhode Island and New Hampshire.

When the Democratic Convention convened in Baltimore in summer 1912, "Champ" Clark had 436 delegates to Woodrow Wilson's 248. But a presidential nominee of the Democratic Party was required to win two-thirds of the convention's delegates, and, while Clark would go on to win a majority of the delegates, he could never muster the two-thirds vote of the delegates he needed to be nominated. Curley worked the convention floor diligently for Clark but on the forty-sixth ballot, the Democratic Party nominated Woodrow Wilson as their standard-bearer.

How much of Clark's defeat was a disappointment to Curley? In his book *The Rascal King*, Jack Beatty conjectures that had "Champ" Clark been elected, surely Curley would have merited a sub-cabinet or even a cabinet post. But, because Clark lost, Curley "would remain a provincial figure, never to mount the national stage."[7]

But did Curley really want the national stage? Did he feel comfortable upon it? In an unusual arrangement, despite his election to Congress, James Michael Curley continued to serve in 1911 on Boston's city council as well. Thus, he appeared to recognize that his political future was in Boston and Massachusetts rather than in Washington. Curley ran and won a second term in Congress, but no sooner was victory achieved than his ambitions shifted once again toward Boston, where John Francis "Honey Fitz" Fitzgerald as mayor was strengthening his political base with ample access to patronage and the leverage to reward supporters with lucrative city contracts. Curley could see that under "Honey Fitz," "Boston's sizeable financial outlay and its desirable political appointments provided ample resources on which to build a political machine."[8] From Curley's perspective, there was more boodle to be had in Boston than in Washington, D.C., and he intended to oust "Honey Fitz" from city hall and preside over the largesse "The Hub" made possible.

Besides, Curley was bored in Congress.

"Toodles' Ass" and Curley's First Campaign for Mayor

In his political campaigns, James Michael Curley often posed with his wife and children in the background by way of advertising to the voters his commitment to family values and to his own unblemished record of devotion to the woman he married. So it was not surprising that when word was leaked to him that "Honey Fitz" Fitzgerald, the mayor of Boston and the occupant of a post he coveted, was having an affair with a nightclub cigarette girl, Elizabeth "Toodles" Ryan, Curley would make the most of it.

Although his second term as mayor had been an unusually successful one, Fitzgerald, the first Boston mayor without beard or mustache and the first to serve a four-year term, had been confiding to anyone who would linger awhile in his office that he would probably not seek a third term as mayor but would, instead, run a year later against Henry Cabot Lodge as United States Senator from Massachusetts. Inasmuch as reelection as mayor was essentially a sure thing and success in 1916 against Lodge more risky, Fitzgerald remained ambivalent. For thirty-nine-year-old James Michael Curley, the mere hint that Fitzgerald might leave the fight for mayor to others as he pursued loftier aims was enough for Curley to trigger his announcement that he would seek to become Fitzgerald's successor as mayor of Boston.

However, Curley's independence and flamboyance frightened the ward bosses, who saw their patronage and influence drying up if Curley became mayor. With their considerable clout both in the Boston media and among the state's and city's politicians, the ward bosses got Fitzgerald to reverse his decision, and on November 28, 1913, Fitzgerald announced that he would, on second thought, run for the mayor of Boston once again. This would prove to be a major mistake. Fitzgerald did not accurately take the measure of his potential opponent.

Curley, instead of withdrawing from the race as most of the ward bosses assumed he would, appeared more determined than ever to make the race for mayor. "For one hundred or more times in the last two years," Curley told his audience at the Tammany Club, "the mayor has told me that he would not be a candidate for reelection. I entered the campaign three weeks before Mayor Fitzgerald announced his candidacy. I am not opposing him. He is opposing me. I had supposed Fitzgerald would keep his word, although I knew he had broken his word with others; but I supposed that he would keep his promise with a tried friend."[9] With a theatrical flourish, he declared that only death could keep him from making the race.

To get Curley to drop out of the race, "Honey Fitz" sought the help of William Cardinal O'Connell. The cardinal, in a private meeting with Curley, asked him to drop out of the race for mayor and leave the post open for a third term to "Honey Fitz." The cardinal asserted that Curley was young enough to wait out the four years and then be assured of election. But Curley would not listen to the cardinal. Instead, Curley found an opportunity to abort Fitzgerald's plans to run for a third term as Boston's mayor.

Fitzgerald's nemesis came in the form of Daniel H. Coakley, a rather dapper and disreputable attorney, who years before had had a run in with "Honey Fitz" and had sworn eternal hostility to him. The ravishingly beautiful cigarette girl, Elizabeth "Toodles" Ryan, engaged the legal services of Coakley in a $50,000 breach of promise suit against Henry Mansfield, the forty-year-old owner of the Ferncroft Inn who allegedly promised to marry her. She revealed that her job at the Ferncroft Inn was not so much to sell cigarettes as it was to use her beauty to entice men to the upstairs gambling room to take their chances at the illegal roulette table. At the trial the evidence failed to convince the jury that Mansfield had really promised to marry her, and the jury could not reach a verdict.

What was significant to Coakley, however, was not Mansfield's intentions, but the fact that "Toodles," prodded by his questioning, enumerated her many admirers and included John Francis Fitzgerald, Boston's mayor, among them. She described how they danced in a tight embrace and how he would press passionate kisses upon her. Coakley quickly realized that he now had a weapon with which he could stop Fitzgerald's campaign in its tracks, and his own unsavory character was such that he knew how to use the devastating information. He gave the information to Curley, who instinctively knew what to do with it. Curley recognized that, in an election, he would clearly lose to Fitzgerald, but perhaps careful use of a potentially damaging material would get the latter finally to drop out of the mayoralty race.

On December 1, Curley had a black-bordered letter delivered to Mrs. Fitzgerald at her home on Wells Avenue, cautioning her that unless her husband dropped out of the race he would release the scandalous details of her husband's infatuation with the twenty-three-year-old "Toodles." While there had been some vague talk that Fitzgerald, on occasion, was a pushover for pretty women, nothing very damaging had, heretofore, been disclosed. But with "Toodles" the evidence appeared unambiguous. For Fitzgerald the situation was grossly unfair. How much his infatuation with "Toodles" went beyond a hug, a squeeze, a kiss, or a dance cannot be known, but for Mrs. Fitzgerald, however limited his involvement with "Toodles," it was too much, and she insisted that he avoid public humiliation and comply with Curley's demand that he pull out of the race. Besides, Mrs. Fitzgerald had welcomed her husband's premature announcement that he would not seek reelection as Boston's mayor with a substantial measure of relief. Perhaps a year or so away from the political arena would be good for both of them.

Had Fitzgerald been in good health he might have been in a better position to resist his wife's importunities. But he had been seriously injured and nearly killed when he inspected a fire that broke out in the Arcadia lodging house, one of the many firetraps housing the city's poorest. While he was inspecting the burned-out Arcadia and other hovels, the fifty-year-old mayor collapsed and nearly fell down a flight of stairs and was taken to a hospital. Bulletins from the hospital revealed that the mayor was not recovering rapidly and was not sleeping well. But was his failure to recuperate as the physicians had expected because of his mental or physical wounds? Fitzgerald felt the charges were unfair and that Curley, a young upstart, had been both reckless and unscrupulous in his use of the titillating material. His first inclination was to fight back.

Curley relentlessly pursued his advantage. He announced that with the help of James Walsh, a Fordham University history professor, he would deliver three lectures: "Graft in Ancient Times versus Graft in Modern Times," "Great Lovers in History: From Cleopatra to Toodles," and "Libertines in History from Henry the Eighth to the Present Day." In the first lecture, he compared alleged financial wrongdoing under Fitzgerald with parallel financial chicanery in ancient Rome. "Honey Fitz" had had enough and, on December 18, Mayor Fitzgerald reluctantly announced that he was withdrawing from the mayoral race on the advice of his physician who recommended a long rest. The remaining lectures were never given, John F. Fitzgerald's days in the political limelight would end, and he would never again win an election. To avoid disgracing the family, "Honey Fitz" announced that he would not run for mayor, an election he could have easily won. As the verse that made the rounds of the Hub asserted: "A whiskey glass and Toodles' Ass/Made a Horse's Ass out of Honey Fitz."

After the political dust settled, Curley's opponents chose Thomas Kenny, a rather stolid, fifty-year-old president of the city council as their candidate. Supported by the Good Government Association, Kenny ran a dignified, if dull, campaign and was no match for Curley, who took no political prisoners. Curley surrounded himself with a brass band, a loud chorus, and popular guest speakers. In Curley's corner, too, was John L. Sullivan, the "Boston Strong Boy" and former heavyweight champion of the world. While seldom sober, John L. on the platform still lured an audience who came to see a sports celebrity even if the price they paid was to listen to a political harangue from Curley.

Using scare tactics that his listeners were unlikely to believe, Kenny insisted that Curley would remove every city employee in order to make room for his Tammany Club supporters. He went on to describe James Michael Curley as a "dictator," as "unscrupulous," and as one of the most dangerous men to be at the helm of a great city. Kenny challenged Curley to name all the contractors who had contributed to his campaign and to reveal the identity of those who had endorsed a $20,000 note which Curley had drawn from a local trust company.

Curley did not entirely ignore Kenny's allegations but neither did he rise to the bait by answering them. Instead, Curley formulated a platform of his own, one which would appeal to the instincts of good government supporters while retaining his hold on his vast constituency among the urban poor. Thus, he pledged an economical, honest, efficient, and clean government, the object of which would be to reduce the tax burden of Bostonians. But Curley continued to emphasize those projects that Boston's voters could translate into well-paying jobs. Thus, he pledged that he would develop port facilities, encourage industry to come to Boston, extend transportation, enlarge sewer and water mains, and require a forty-foot minimum width on the construction of new streets. Curley promised to eliminate the juvenile correctional facilities in West Roxbury and on Rainsford Island. Since the bulk of those in these institutions were the sons of urban poor, their parents liked what they heard. But Curley had no real need to spell out a carefully crafted platform. Most of Boston's voters knew instinctively that with Curley in city hall, the masses would have greater access to power in Boston. To the ordinary voter, "good government" was code for the wholesale elimination of jobs, and, try as he might, Kenny just could not get beyond this perception. "The power to provide jobs was the key to Curley's power."[10]

Curley wanted to be all things to all people, and so three days before the election he cynically renamed his Tammany Club as the "Pro Bono Publico Club," meaning that his "new" organization was established for the "public good." After the election, the Pro Bono Publico Club disappeared from public view. How many voters were swayed by this change of name is hard to assess, but that so transparent a tactic attracted many voters is hard to believe. However, it does tell us something of the lengths to which James Michael Curley would go to get elected and how little he thought of the memory or loyalty of the ordinary voter.

Curley's candidacy failed to appeal to the "better element" among Boston's voters who were turned off by his dirty campaign tactics, which included contrived sexual scandal and hiring gangs of hoodlums to break up Kenny's meetings. The wives of Kenny's campaign workers received a message saying that if they thought their husbands were out campaigning they had better investigate further. Curley alleged that the husbands were visiting women of dubious virtue at a notorious boarding house on Columbus Avenue. When some of the wives attempted to investigate by showing pictures of their husbands to the building caretaker, the latter would assure the wives, as Curley had paid him to say, that indeed their husbands been frequent visitors to the boarding house. Nor was Curley above sending a gang of toughs to sabotage Kenny's rallies. At one such, the toughs shouted such obscenities that women hastened from their seats in droves. Paid toughs, working for Curley, would jeer Kenny when he attempted to speak.

During this first campaign for mayor, seven out of nine of the city's newspapers opposed him. The aristocratic Boston *Transcript* was sure that a Curley victory "would be the most humiliating experience in the history of the city."[11] The Boston *Post* asserted that Boston's voters were faced with a clear choice between "Kenny or Curley, honest and scrupulously clean government or the ways and means of Tammany."[12] But once Curley hit his stride there was no stopping him. As Kenny faded, Curley seemed to catch his second wind, and on the freezing cold evening before election day, Curley's twelve-car entourage covered every ward in the city of Boston in a matter of five and a half hours during which he spoke to 20,000 people.

To former mayor "Honey Fitz" and still-powerful ward boss Martin Lomasney, Curley's two chief rivals among the Democrats, the choice was not at all clear. They hated to see Curley win the post of mayor of Boston, nor could they abide a Republican victory. Fitzgerald initially supported Kenny, but as he saw that his candidate could not possibly win the election he remained essentially neutral. Lomasney waited until the morning of the election to endorse Curley.

On January 13, 1914, the coldest election day in Boston's history, Curley voters came out in numbers large enough to ensure his victory by a vote of 43,362 for Curley and 37,542 for Kenny. On February 2, 1914, before three thousand roaring partisans, mayor-elect James Michael Curley delivered his inaugural address at Tremont Temple. In Curley's inaugural speech he promised honest government. In dulcet tones he solemnly declared, "I am a firm believer in the value of publicity, and as sunlight destroys microbes that lurk in dark and damp places, so, in my opinion, by making the city's business become the property of all, rather than officeholders alone, it will result in the elimination of graft and corruption and the development of efficiency and economy which at this time is imperative."[13] Because he suspected that "Honey Fitz" had secretly aided Kenny, Curley was relentless in his attack at his predecessor as the audience roared their delighted approval — the hostility which Curley directed against Fitzgerald in his oration reminded one of the angry hissing of a riled tomcat."[14] Not content with defeating his rival, Curley sought to humble him, and he did so.

It was Curley's intention to retain his seat in the United States House of Representatives until March 3, 1915, when his term in Congress ended, while serving as mayor of Boston. His excuse for doing so was that if he kept his seat in the House of Representatives he could continue to fight against immigration restriction. In retrospect, however, the $7,500 salary he would continue to receive likewise looked attractive to him. He was, therefore, disappointed that the House Republican minority leader, James

Mann, began proceedings to oust him from his seat as representative from the Twelfth Congressional District and would not countenance "double dipping" in this fashion. On February 24, 1914, three weeks after he had been sworn in as mayor, a motion was made in the House of Representatives to strike his name from the congressional membership rolls. In a predated communication to the House of Representatives, Curley sent a letter of resignation so that the record would show that he voluntarily resigned in view of his election as Boston's mayor rather than having been forced out of Congress.

The Mayor and the "Goo-Goos"

Because Curley's margin of victory was respectable but not overwhelming, the new mayor approached the problems of his city by making a big show of his zeal for reform, efficiency, economy, and fair and balanced appointments. He asserted that he would "fire all loafers, goldbricks and payroll patriots."[15]

With the cheers of his Tammany supporters still ringing in his ears, Curley went to city hall, signed the oath book, and seemingly began to run in all directions at once. If there was a method or consistent thread in what he was doing, only Curley knew what it was. But perhaps that thread was to throw up enough sand to get into the eyes of his friends and enemies so that now one and now the other praised and reprimanded him, scolded and congratulated him, loved and detested him, one at a time and then again, all at the same time. "His administration became one of highly efficient and effective confusion with the Good Government Association and the Finance Commission carefully watching and examining every move that he made, constantly frustrated by the sleight of hand that they could not follow or explain to the people. Money appeared as if by magic and disappeared the same way."[16]

His working day began at about 10:00 A.M. and often did not end until after 10:00 P.M. One night, as he was leaving city hall after a long day in which he had seen hundreds of job and favor seekers and personally determined how best to treat their petitions, the scrub women were already on their knees scrubbing the floors of city hall to clean it up for the next day. Shaken by this sight, and remembering his mother on her hands and knees, the next day he raised their wages and ordered long-handled scrubbing brushes so that no woman would ever after have to get down on her hands and knees in city hall. In his relations with the press, he had no cronies and granted no individual press interviews. Instead, he held a press con-

Major James Michael Curley (right) and son James Jr. riding in the Evacuation Day parade on Beacon Street on March 17, 1917. Courtesy of the Boston Public Library, Print Department.

ference for all journalists during which he reported what he had achieved and responded individually to their queries.

By personally passing judgment on the request of each supplicant who came before him, under Curley the city hall became a place crowded with men and women seeking a job, promotion, or helping hand. Curley learned and remembered the names of thousands of petitioners; he left no one in doubt as to where he or she stood, and no one could doubt that Curley had been responsible for the action taken or withheld. Indeed, Curley expected to be repaid with their loyalty and their votes. Curleyism thus became the process of weaning power away from most of the ward bosses and placing power directly in the hands of the mayor. Curley's contribution to Boston politics was the creation of the first citywide political machine, which would replace the localized machines of the ward bosses. But it was a Curley machine, not a Democratic machine, in that it revolved around Curley and rose and fell in influence and importance as his political prospects waxed or waned. Unlike New York City's Tammany Hall, which was a machine for the Democratic Party and only temporarily under the ministrations of the Democratic political leader of the time, Curley's Tammany could not be transferred to any other candidate.

"My idea is to put the city on a business basis," Curley intoned to the surprise of many and to none more so that the members of the Good Government Association. When he made a grandstand play by inviting Louis D. Brandeis, then a prominent reformist and an advisor to the Interstate Commerce Commission, to join the new administration as city auditor, the "Goo-Goos" were impressed. But Brandeis demurred, expressing his appreciation of the offer but asserting that there was too much unfinished business in the nation's capital requiring his attention. When Curley invited John A. Sullivan to be the city's corporation counsel, urban reformers everywhere were astonished that Curley seemed to have metamorphosed from a political caterpillar to a civic reformer butterfly. Sullivan had been the former chairman of the state-appointed Finance Committee charged with the responsibility of policing the spending habits and practices of Boston's mayors, and he had been a thorn in Fitzgerald's side during his tenure as mayor. That Curley had embraced Sullivan appeared to portend a change for the better in Curley. But in fact, Sullivan had been playing a double game. Even while secretly helping Kenny write his campaign platform, Sullivan had also given important support to Curley. Whether Curley had been more impressed with Sullivan's political versatility or with his reform credentials, the fact was that Sullivan's appointment was a pleasant shock to the reform element in Boston.

Curley achieved a number of policies. He set up a credit union for municipal employees, closed the worst homes for juvenile delinquents, called for a municipally owned pasteurization plant, and strengthened building codes and fire regulations and used these codes to close several of the city's sweatshops. Six hundred city employees, mostly Fitzgerald loyalists, found that they were either fired or reassigned. He dropped the Fitzgerald contractors and appointed new ones, who were warned that they must deliver quality in the goods and services they provided or they would be ousted without further ceremony.

Although he had dismissed a number of departmental heads and made a great show of insisting that he would have only those who had demonstrated their loyalty to Curley working for the city, he actually dragged his feet in making the most of the political spoils now at his disposal. The "Goo-Goos" were initially impressed, and the Boston press, unable to believe what was happening, heaped praise upon him. Curley had visited the Marine Park aquarium, yet "no fish have died, resigned or been suspended."[17]

In a manner reminiscent of the mayoral administration of "Big Bill" Thompson of Chicago, Mayor Curley launched a barrage of public works projects. City streets were paved by the mile, new parks and playgrounds replaced rat-infested slums, the electric streetcar system was expanded and tunnels were dug under streets, and hospitals were modernized, cleaned, and painted. But who would be the beneficiaries of this largesse? Curley cut out the ward bosses, who had traditionally been the middlemen in allocating contracts to "deserving" political supporters and handing out jobs to Bostonians of demonstrable voting loyalty. But now the ward bosses were exasperated when Curley administered these lucrative contracts and dispensed patronage without consulting them. They rode to city hall only to be turned back. Curley would not receive them; "within a year the ward bosses were, with the exception of Martin (Mahatma) Lomasney, operating like sick chickens with terminal political diseases."[18]

Among his high priorities as mayor, Curley was determined to promote Boston as a good place for commerce and industry. To "boom Boston" he proposed a fund to which private individuals of substantial means would subscribe. But as people of wealth dragged their feet and only reluctantly, if at all, contributed despite Curley's arm-twisting, Curley was not above using similar tactics among the agencies in Washington. Although the vote had been barely counted but with his election as Boston's mayor assured, Curley took advantage of the window of opportunity he still enjoyed as a member of the House of Representatives to return to Washington to lobby on behalf of the city of Boston. Before boarding the afternoon train to Washington, D.C., he announced to a crowd seeing him off at the station, "I am going to confer with Secretary Daniels to get that supply ship for the Charlestown Navy Yard. That will insure employment for a great army of workers there for at least thirteen months."[19] He successfully lobbied Franklin D. Roosevelt, then the Assistant Secretary of the

Navy, to award a contract to build a ship in the Boston Naval Shipyard. He was also successful in lobbying Treasury Secretary McAdoo to locate a Federal Reserve Bank in Boston. Clearly, Curley was a "can do" kind of guy.

The good-government reformers initially liked what they saw: namely, a businesslike mayor who had embarked on a program of civic improvement while weeding out incompetent and ineffective municipal workers and inviting reformers of proven track record, like Brandeis and Sullivan, into his administration. But it would not be long before disillusionment would set in. Tax rates shot up on banks, newspapers, and businesses. Contrary to his promise, Curley's was not an open administration. Instead, in his daily press briefings he put a spin on what he was about, and there were few ways to check his activities. Indeed, the Finance Commission, which had been established in 1907 as an independent budget and tax watchdog, was woefully understaffed and could not possibly undertake a review of the civic projects Curley initiated. "The commission operated with a thoroughness bordering on slow motion, and when it sent its accountants to check into one program, Curley made use of their slowness by immediately starting a dozen new programs."[20] The accountants did find that Curley was awarding contracts to loyalists and not to lowest bidders and proved that the quality of materials was less than the contracts required. But the commission was helpless to do much about these discrepancies inasmuch as a complete report would be a decade away.

Governor David Walsh, the first Irish Catholic to hold statewide office in Massachusetts, was determined to keep James Michael Curley in his place in view of the latter's one-time support of his opponent. The Boston "Goo-Goos" and Governor Walsh worked together to push a reform charter through the state legislature which would undermine the authority of the mayor of Boston. Curley would not let this go by without a fight. He opposed a modification that would have strengthened the hand of the ward bosses, the same group he had brought to heel. The most dangerous aspect of the new charter was the proposal that the mayor could be recalled through the means of a special election. Curley argued long and eloquently but fruitlessly against the adoption of the reform charter. Walsh and Curley remained bitter enemies, but Curley reaped satisfying revenge by working with Lomasney to bring about Walsh's narrow defeat for election as governor for a second term.

Moreover, when the "Goo-Goos" and Walsh, in his lame-duck status as governor, tried to get the legislature to recall Mayor Curley, the latter amazingly enlisted support from "Honey Fitz" by agreeing to support him in his campaign to unseat Senator Henry Cabot Lodge, and from

"Mahatma" Lomasney, by appointing his brother Joseph Lomasney to the schoolhouse commission. But the recall proposition was roundly defeated at the polls. For recall to occur a majority of those registered to vote, not of those voting, needed to support the measure, which in 1915 was 57,000. Only 48,000 voted to remove Curley, and only 35,000 supported him. Of the city's twenty-six wards, Curley carried but eight. Thus, Curley narrowly escaped being recalled as mayor, but the closeness of the vote marked it as one of Curley's more serious rebuffs at the hands of the voters. Curley generously thanked both of his former adversaries.

Haunted House

On March 17, 1915, St. Patrick's Day, midway through his first term as mayor, construction started on Curley's Georgian colonial brick mansion. Located on two acres on Jamaica Way, its 10,000 square feet would eventually contain 21 rooms, including a 20-by-32-foot oval dining room paneled in mahogany and at its center a crystal chandelier, 28 carved mahogany doors, Italian marble fireplaces, a huge 2-story bronze chandelier in the foyer, an elegant 3-story spiral staircase, 5 bathrooms, and a heated garage. While no longer a Brahmin stronghold, Jamaica Way was an area of huge estates and rolling lawns bordering a lovely pond outlined by a beautiful park road. The area had been landscaped by Frederick Law Olmstead some twenty years earlier and, while bucolic in character, was, like New York's Central Park, entirely within the city limits of Boston.

As Curley tells it, he initially did not know what kind of house he wanted when he learned that the estate of Henry H. Rogers, chief executive of Standard Oil Company, was putting his former summer home at Fairhaven, Connecticut, up for auction. Built at a cost of some $200,000, the house was of no immediate use to Rogers' heirs, and a highway had been planned which, if built, would destroy the house. Curley and his associate, Standish Willcox, decided to take a look. Curley wrote:

> I shall never forget buying the beautiful tile fireplace. When the contractor removed it I asked him how much he wanted for it. He told me to make an offer. Before leaving Boston I had counted out a thousand dollars, mostly in one-dollar bills, and wrapped a five-dollar bill around them. I told the foreman I would give him this huge roll, and he agreed immediately. Incidentally I might mention that the purchase included the Dining Room, the staircase, the twenty-eight carved mahogany doors and a few other odds and ends. At auction I also got the tongs and other fireplace equipment, which I thought were brass, but which turned out to be gold-plated.[21]

In due course the artifacts he bought and shipped to Boston were included in what came to be called the "House with the Shamrock Shutters," which were etched into each of its thirty white blinds.

When the family finally moved in, here is how Curley lovingly described his house:

> The oval shaped, hand-carved mahogany paneled dining room, with its marble Grecian columns, is forty-feet long and has a fourteen-foot ceiling. Its chandelier, with delicately carved Irish Waterford glass hung on silver chains, is flanked on the ceiling by carved moldings. The outstanding feature of the house is the winding staircase which rises two stories without any visible support.[22]

The house must have given James Michael Curley a great deal of personal satisfaction. He now had an elegant residence of which he and his family could be proud. But was it a house fit for a mayor of Boston?

The ostentation of the Jamaica Way house would make its occupant a target of political opposition. Conjecture continued throughout his career as to how, on a mayor's modest salary, he could pay for it. Curley's flamboyant home was a symbol of how this first generation son of dirt-poor Irish immigrants could rise in a single generation and was, perhaps, an expression of his acceptance by the "better element" of Boston. The shamrock cut-outs were, however, a thumb in they eye of James Michael Curley's up-scale neighbors. Behind the shamrock shutters, his neighbors thought, this Irish upstart was thumbing his nose at them.

For his part, Curley remembered that in his youth, as he looked for employment, he read signs, "No Irish Need Apply," and as an adult recognized that there were still some neighborhoods in which no Irish could buy a home. Through his elegant home he was delivering a message to one and all that not only had James Michael Curley arrived, but with him all of Boston's Irish as well. Had he moved into his new house quietly, had the house been less ostentatious, and had he not thumbed his nose at his rich neighbors, there might have been less interest in how he had financed the house on a modest salary of a mayor. But that was not the Curley way. He was asking for trouble. He knew it would come. He relished the trouble rather than let it diminish his enjoyment of the house with the shamrock shutters. To the Boston Finance Commission, however, the esthetics of the house were of far less interest than its financing. How could a man earning $10,000 a year as mayor, the Finance Commission wanted to know, afford to buy a house on which the land alone was worth $10,000?

Mayor James Michael Curley was, if not an honest administrator, a thoroughly capable one. Yes, he lined his own pockets, and in building a grand house he literally feathered his own nest with kick-backs from contractors. But as did few others, he understood the finance as well as the politics of city administration and so could smother inquiries and cut corners and enrich himself while at the same time transforming the topography of the city, putting people to work, and building a political machine that would keep him in the limelight if not always in office for nearly two generations. Curley used his knowledge of the details and technical aspects of the business of running a large city like Boston to make it impossible for the Finance Commission, the state-created agency to serve as a watchdog over the finances of Boston, to follow a clear trail of corruption.

Herbert Marshall Zolot, in his detailed and excellent doctoral study, *The Issue of Good Government and James Michael Curley: Curley and the Boston Scene from 1897–1918*, succeeded remarkably well in identifying civic corruption in Boston under James Michael Curley. Some of these elements may be briefly summarized:

By allowing favored contractors to substitute cheaper materials for specified-better grade materials, profit margins could conveniently be increased.[23]

Under Curley, the city administration privately awarded a great deal of work to favored contractors that should have been put out for open bidding.[24]

Through the device of split contracting, a department divided a large job into small contracts, which the city let directly to individual contractors without asking for bids.

Habitually, Curley's administration used its authority to steer contracts in the direction it desired. For the purchase of laundry machines, Joseph McGinnis, the architect in charge of determining improvements, deliberately set specifications that favored the Poland Laundry Machinery Company. The American Laundry Machine Company protested to no avail.

It was routine that the city did not receive the quality it paid for. Forty dozen of the fifty dozen brooms purchased by Boston's street cleaning service from the New England Broom and Supply Company failed to meet contract specifications. The brooms were accepted anyway.[25]

The lion's share of the bonding of contractors who wanted to do business with the city went to Peter Fitzgerald and his son Edwin R. Fitzgerald. With Curley's blessing, the Fitzgeralds held a near monopoly of Boston's bonding business with a share of 95.6 percent. What had the Fitzgeralds done to deserve Curley's confidence? Peter J. Fitzgerald was

Francis L. Daly's father-in-law, and Edwin P. Fitzgerald was Daly's brother-in-law. The Daly Plumbing Supply Company was instrumental in making Curley's shamrock house a reality.

Francis L. Daly of the Daly Plumbing Supply Company and Marks Angell (also known as Max Angelovitz) of the Roxbury Iron and Metal Company had been Curley loyalists in Curley's Ward 17 Tammany Club. Daly had represented the ward in the state legislature, and Angell had been largely effective in turning out the Jewish vote for Curley. When Curley ran for alderman, Angell assured the Jewish people of Roxbury, "Whenever trouble comes to the Jewish people in Roxbury, Alderman Curley is always ready and willing, and does his utmost to help us."[26]

Angell was a special favorite of James Michael Curley, and Curley allowed his buddy free access to the offices of city hall. Angell was not at all bashful about taking advantage of it. He would swagger through one office and then another urging its administrators to sell its junk to Marks Angell's Roxbury Iron and Metal Company. Curley himself intervened on Angell's behalf and urged the Transit Commission to allow the Roxbury Iron and Metal Company to handle its junk without competitive bidding. In addition to the junk Roxbury Iron and Metal collected from the city, the company sold to the city, without competitive bidding, lead pipe, pig lead, tin, and solder.

Investigation by the Finance Committee revealed that Curley had, for a time at least, held a half-interest in Angell's junk business. If Angell was becoming a rich man through the buying and selling of junk, could James Michael Curley be far behind? Indeed, Curley, while mayor, was also becoming wealthy.

Curley's arrangements with Francis L. Daly followed a parallel pattern. Daly's Plumbing and Supply Company carried on considerable business directly with the city of Boston, and Francis Daly's brother sold electrical supplies to all city departments. Investigation by the Finance Commission revealed that Mayor Curley participated in the Daly firm as a silent partner in direct violation of the city charter, which prohibited an official of the city government from participating in the profits of a firm conducting business dealings with the city.

Curley had become a copartner in the Daly firm while he was preparing to run for mayor. Daly had revealed in testimony before the Finance Commission in 1917 that on September 2, 1913, for $8,000 he had bought out his partner, Daniel P. Sullivan, of the firm of Sullivan and Daly. He insisted that he obtained the money from a conveniently dead but destitute relative. At about the same time, Curley had drawn $4,100 from the Federal Trust Company and $3,900 from a $4,000 loan from the Mutual

National Bank. Curley, however, denied that he had taken such large sums to invest in the plumbing business; instead, he said, he used the money to purchase stock from Nathan Eisman who, like Daly's uncle, was conveniently dead. The mayor asserted that he made a good profit of $12,500 from the stock deal. In a mayoral campaign speech on January 17, 1914, Curley admitted, "I am a partner in the Daly Plumbing Supply Company, from which concern I net a sufficient income to render me independent of political office."[27]

As journalist Joseph Dinneen has asserted, "Even before the Irish conquered Boston, Yankee Brahmins had not been entirely unskilled in channeling part of the city's revenue into their own pockets and bank accounts. Curley did not devise the spoils system. He inherited it.... He added his own ingenious improvements to the system and found many novel ways to defeat the Finance Commission."[28]

"'Governor, did you pay for that house?' John Henry Cutler, the ghostwriter for *I'd Do It Again,* asked Curley in 1956. He had the largest brown eyes I've ever seen on a person, Cutler said, and he gave me a wink as if to say of course he didn't pay."[29]

Censor in Chief

Just as Boston Brahmins were responsible for creating the Finance Committee to monitor the financial affairs of Boston, so this group had established the Watch and Ward Society to monitor Boston's morals. Curly outwitted the former and outdid the latter.

An important aspect of Curleyism was the mayor's unhesitating foray to protect the people of Boston from viewing films or reading books or seeing live entertainment that he considered immoral. While he did not invent "banned in Boston," he did contribute to its development to make Boston a laughing stock of the nation, while assuring that what was banned in Boston would be seen or read nearly everywhere else in the United States.

In taking an extreme position, was Curley expressing his own view of how best to improve the morality of Bostonians, was he pandering for votes the conservative elements among Irish Catholics, or was he tweaking the nose of Boston Brahmins under whose narrow vision "banned in Boston" became an infamous slogan?

Boston's Watch and Ward Society had been, since 1878, watching over the morals of Bostonians. With the Protestant elite in positions of leadership, the society presumed to tell Bostonians what they could read or see on stage or on the screen. As time went by, the influence of the organization waned, but Curley, an Irish-Catholic mayor, preferred to adopt the society's techniques of censorship when he would have been better advised to allow them to fade away. Curley was not a religious zealot, yet he anchored his censorship in what he declared to be the basic moral principles as expressed by Cardinal O'Connell, and as he, Curley, understood them. This must have surprised His Eminence inasmuch as James Michael Curley was, to say the least, no favorite of his Bishop.

Boston's new mayor, the very same who used "Toodles" Ryan to drive "Honey Fitz" from his campaign for a third term as Boston's mayor, the mayor who, as a candidate, was not above raising sexual scandal to a fine art, sought to ban late-night dancing in Boston because of the perceived threat that it "ruined young girls." Under his moral guidelines "bare feet, suggestive jokes, impersonations of effeminate persons, depictions of drug fiends, disrobing scenes, Salome dances, and plays teaching lessons in immorality were banned in Boston."[30] Under such broad moral guidelines, Curley banned Isadora Duncan, who showed her bare legs, as well as the ballet dancer Pavlova, who did likewise. Mary Curley also assumed the role of censor and had her husband pull down the curtain on Mary Garden's rendition of *Salome.* "I want this show stopped. It's nothing but burley."[31] What Mary found immoral James Michael Curley banned.

But by allowing the movie *The Birth of a Nation,* a D.W. Griffith apparent tribute to the Ku Klux Klan, to be shown, Curley dealt a body blow to the movement for civil rights among blacks and made sure that censorship had found a comfortable home in Curley's Boston. While "Big Bill" Thompson banned the movie in Chicago, Curley refused to follow that example.

It is hard to explain Curley's inconsistency and insensitivity. He had an opportunity to ban the film and so reward Boston's fifteen thousand African-Americans who supported him in large numbers for mayor of Boston. Surely, he would have banned the film had it shown Irish-Americans with all their warts. As a member of Congress, he had been a leader in the fight against immigration restriction and had been proud enough of his record of support from immigrant minorities to make it an element in his mayoralty campaign. In a hearing called by Curley, the fledgling National Association for the Advancement of Colored People (NAACP), led by Moorfield Storey, its first and white national president, argued that the film would "discredit the Negro race all over the country."[32]

Jack Beatty, whose *Rascal King* provides an excellent description of Curley's role as arbiter of artistic expression in Boston, explains that Storey was vulnerable in his argument because, while he argued vigorously on behalf of African-Americans, he was an equally vigorous opponent of immigration. Thus, in Curley's judgment, Storey was a flawed advocate for African-Americans. "A man with these known views should not have pled the case against the film before Curley."[33] At the conclusion of the hearing, Curley asserted, quite falsely, that he did not have the power to ban the scenes, and so the racist screed *The Birth of a Nation,* with a little cosmetic editing, played in Boston. African-American protests against the showing of the film resulted in one of the most violent racial incidents in Boston, when, at the show's premier, black protesters clashed with city police officers. The blacks of Boston solicited the support of Massachusetts Governor David I. Walsh, but little did it help them. *The Birth of a Nation* played in Boston for six and a half months—three hundred and sixty performances in all.

One can say many harsh things about James Michael Curley, but was he a racist bigot? Did he subscribe to Jim Crow traditions, which then guided white-black relationships? While he probably shared the racial prejudices of the day, more likely his judgment to allow the showing of *The Birth of a Nation* was based on a feeling that he probably could afford, temporarily at least, to offend Boston's small black community and so better curry favor with Irish and other ethnic minorities who were not without racist prejudices of their own.

Over the years, Curley sought to make amends to Boston's black community. For example, he lobbied on behalf of an African-American army lieutenant to gain his burial in Arlington National Cemetery, the first black military war hero to achieve such distinction. Later, in 1917, Mayor Curley submitted an antilynching bill to Senator Henry Cabot Lodge. Also in 1917, the year before he would run for reelection, the mayor issued a proclamation to honor the one-hundredth anniversary of Frederick Douglas, the black abolitionist, by naming a square in the black section of Roxbury after him. In the last year of his first term, Mayor Curley named an African-American to be an assistant registrar and another to be an assistant corporation counsel. "Thus, when it came to token recognition of blacks, Curley readily took opportunities to portray himself as a friend of African-Americans."[34]

With Curley maybe nothing profound was involved, instead, maybe only monetary gain was at stake. Louis B. Mayer, then a bit player in the film industry, owned a theater in Haverhill, Massachusetts. Mayer later boasted that he made $500,000 from the New England rights to *The Birth of a Nation.* This half a million dollars may have been crucial to Mayer's rise in the film industry. Did Curley have his hand in the till as well? Was he signaling to the movie industry that he was not really so serious about film censorship after all and that Boston might be a very receptive venue for the making as well as the and selling of films?

Curley had been in office almost six months when World War I began. At first, the conflict caused few ripples in the environs of Boston, but, with its traditionally large Irish population, support of a wartime alliance in which England played a leadership role made the zeal for war initially unpopular in Boston. The Easter week uprising in Ireland touched Boston's Irish more deeply than did the war itself. The Irish in Boston much preferred to greet leaders of the Irish rebellion than leaders of the allies. And Mayor Curley, recognizing that there were no votes for him to be had in London or Paris, was not quick to assume a leadership role when prominent foreign leaders came calling to win moral and material support in their cause. Curley was, however, much less reluctant than "Big Bill" Thompson of Chicago to embrace the allied cause. As late as June 1917, two months after the United States Congress, at the urging of President Woodrow Wilson, declared war on the Central Powers, Curley was still fulminating against what he called a "war for commerce." But, when he realized that despite their support of the longings of Ireland's Irish for independence from England, 80 percent of South Boston's Irish had voted for Wilson, Curley saw the political uses of supporting the war effort. "He embraced the war in its most Wilsonian aspect, as democracy's crusade against despotism."[35]

Where "Big Bill" Thompson had to be dragged to a reception of Marshal Joseph Jacques Joffre who, with a distinguished entourage, began a tour of the country to win moral and material support for the war, Mayor James Michael Curley was among the leaders of those who would wine and dine this French hero of the Battle of the Marne. A half-million Bostonians cheered Marshal Joffre as he and the mayor, sitting in an open touring car, wound through the streets of Boston. Later, as her proud parents beamed, nine-year-old Mary Curley presented the marshal with a check for $175,000 for the war orphans of France. While Curley gave his full support to the war effort, he refused to be drawn into the overzealous chauvinism that trashed all things German. He would allow no attacks on German-Americans, and he defended the rights of Socialists and pacifists to dissent.

14

Winning Isn't Everything —
It's the Only Thing

If Curley counted on Marks Angell and Francis Daly for the sources of illicit income, he counted on Joseph Pelletier and Daniel Coakley to bail him out of trouble. Pelletier, who had been his long-time political ally, and Coakley, who had shared with Curley the romantic fling "Honey Fitz" was having with "Toodles Ryan," served as his personal lawyers before the Finance Committee. Between Pelletier and Coakley, the Finance Committee was whip-sawed so as to be unable to bring Curley to justice. It was not loyalty to Mayor Curley that kept Pelletier and Coakley working on behalf of their client but that Curley's was the respectable front for a sexual scam of considerable proportions.

Coakley, Pelletier, and Nathan Tufts, district attorney of Middlesex County, were part of a triumvirate in a sexual entrapment racket. It worked something like this: A prostitute hired by the trio would lure a rich, elderly, vulnerable gentleman to a hotel room and when the pair were in *flagrante delicto,* an irate "husband" or "father" would burst in, or the police would demand entry and charge the man with fornication or contributing to the delinquency of a minor. The "mark" would be told that an alienation of affection suit could be avoided only by hiring as lawyer one Daniel H. Coakley, who would endeavor to persuade one of the district attorneys not to prosecute. Pelletier and Tufts developed a substantial income by accepting generous bribes, usually negotiated by Coakley, not to prosecute. From one seventy-five-year-old bachelor who had fondled a sixteen-year-old girl, Coakley got $300,000, while the love letters of another victim were good for $150,000. In view of their successful scams, the trio got ever bolder. Why did Curley look the other way?

213

The "Fatty" Arbuckle Caper

On the evening of March 6, 1917, Paramount Pictures gave a dinner at the Copley-Plaza Hotel in honor of Roscoe "Fatty" Arbuckle, who had recently signed on with Paramount. Among those who came to Boston to honor the comic of the silent screen were 125 Paramount exhibitors from the New England area, including Adolph Zukor, Hiram Abrams, and Walter Greene, the three owners of Paramount, and Jesse Lasky, its vice president, as well as Marcus Loew, who controlled the largest circuit of theaters in the United States. Joseph Levenson, a prominent Boston attorney, served as toastmaster and introduced the rich and famous such as Roscoe Arbuckle. Despite severe pain from an infected leg, the verdict of the society columns in Boston's newspapers was that "Fatty" was "as great a success as an after-dinner speaker as he is in comedy."[1]

After the dinner was over and Arbuckle, desperately needing rest and his infection requiring care, retired for the night. But for a select few the night was not yet over. Hiram Abrams, one of the Paramount presidents, threw a late-night frolic for some special guests at the suburban Mishawum Manor, a "house of ill-fame," presided over by "Brownie" Kennedy, a madam of many talents and many aliases. Among the select gathering in the suburban village of Woburn, Massachusetts, were Zukor, Abrams, Greene, Lasky, toastmaster Levenson, and theatrical managers Harry Asher and Edward Golden. Dessert, following a chicken and champagne dinner, came on a huge salver, which had been carried into the room to the tune of a popular piano melody. When its cover was removed, out popped a seductive young woman "wearing only a few small pieces of parsley and a sprinkling of salad dressing" while fourteen other seductively smiling, naked young women mingled with the guests.[2] When the party ended near dawn, Abrams paid "Brownie" Kennedy, the professional hostess, $1,050 for 52 bottles of champagne and other party favors, and the movie men went their own way. But they would eventually pay much more for their party.

Two months later, while in Portland, Maine, Abrams received an urgent telephone call from Mayor Curley advising him that a serious matter had come up with regard to the party at Mishawum Manor and that he should return to Boston at once. In a meeting at Boston's Hotel Touraine, Curley, accompanied by Coakley, told Abrams that some of the young women at Mishawum Manor had been under the age of consent, that the husbands of others were bringing alienation of affection suits against the Paramount executives, and that the district attorney of Middlesex County, Nathan Tufts, was investigating the charges. "Brownie"

Kennedy had already been brought to trial. "Brownie," wearing a pair of flimsy pajamas, was arrested as she tried to flee through a window. She got away with a fine of $100 and a suspended sentence of six months. The moguls of the movie industry would not get off so easily. The mayor introduced Coakley as someone who could help.

After Abrams agreed to Coakley's demand for a $10,000 retainer, Coakley speedily arranged a conference with Tufts, and soon after Curley, Coakley, Abrams, and his lawyer met with the district attorney in his Cambridge offices. After calling Abrams and his associates "licentious Jews," Tufts said he would drop the investigation if the complaining husbands would drop their suits. Daniel Coakley estimated that $100,000 would silence the husbands, and be enough to cover his own fee and the fees of the husbands' lawyers. Abrams, after conferring with his colleagues, sent checks to all the lawyers and their clients. Curley was not among those receiving a check, "but what other motive than money could he have for lending his office to this sexual shakedown?"[3]

Godfrey Lowell Cabot (1861–1962) was the veteran treasurer of the Watch and Ward Society and as such looked after the moral behavior of Bostonians. Since 1914, Cabot had been following the badger games of Pelletier, Coakley, and Tufts, and with the naughty details of the Mishawum caper titillating Bostonians, Cabot was more determined than ever to destroy the sexual shakedown artists. In that immoral triumvirate of Coakley, Pelletier, and Tufts, he found enemies worth fighting. He would make it his life's business to stop the blackmailers.

If, as the saying goes, "the Lowells talk only to Cabots, and the Cabots talk only to God," a man by the name of Godfrey Lowell Cabot was assuredly a man above reproach. Prim, prudish, and prissy, Cabot was among those who feared sex even as he was hypnotized by it and mired in guilt feelings over his own eroticism. But what if all Bostonians shared his erotic guilt, and, horror of horrors, what if they acted out their eroticism, and with men and women who were not their spouses? Cabot viewed it as his life's mission to impose sexual discipline upon those Bostonians who were not fortified with the Lowell/Cabot genes enabling them to resist temptation as he could. Thus through the Watch and Ward society he would scuttle rampant sexual expression where he could find it — mostly in what Bostonians read but also in what they saw on stage and screen.

Cabot, nearly sixty years old, certain that he could not win his fight against Pelletier and associates during his lifetime, wrote to the two executors of his will instructing them to carry on the fight after his death. But Cabot was to live long enough, he died at the age of one hundred one, to see Pelletier, Tufts, and Coakley disbarred. Coakley later served time in prison. Although neither disbarment nor imprisonment ended the political influence of Pelletier, Tufts, and Coakley, Cabot remained proud through his long life that disbarment of these men was his greatest achievement.

Curley's fingerprints were nowhere to be found in the sexual entrapment racket, nor was he a direct player in the sex-scandal ring. But he must have known of its existence and, by failing to blow the whistle, held Coakley and the district attorneys hostage to his own reckless and often amoral pursuit of wealth and power. But did Curley, a man whose family was his fortress and shield against the outside world, get a sexual charge out of being on the fringe of sexual scandal? Did he simply take the money, uncaring of its source? Or, was it a matter of arrogance and a sense of power that he could get away with it? Was his dabbling on the fringe of sexual scandal not only a campaign tactic and a source of money but also an expression of Curley's own erotic nature? Indeed, was his lust for political power a substitute for his suppressed erotic needs?

Political Wilderness: Curley Out of Power

"I am a candidate for reelection," Curley announced to the Tammany Club in a ninety-minute speech on New Year's Eve, 1916, "and I have not the slightest fear of the outcome." In reality, he had a great deal to fear.

If James Michael Curley was aware that he faced an uphill battle for reelection, he did not show it. Instead, he faced the voters with assurance that in the last analysis Bostonians would have no other for which they could logically cast their vote. Not for the last time would he be wrong in his assessment of his prospects.

Curley's confident outlook that he would easily be reelected should have been jolted when the powerful ward boss Martin Lomasney embarked upon a campaign to deny him reelection. Even when twelve Democratic Irish ward bosses agreed to support the candidacy of a rather colorless undersecretary of treasury Andrew J. Peters, a graduate of St. Paul's and Harvard, a conservative Yankee Democrat, and a Curley neighbor on Jamaica Way, Curley still felt he would be reelected.

Lomasney, however, took no chances. He prevailed upon the popular Congressman James A. Gallivan of South Boston to make a hopeless run for the Boston mayoralty, and he also persuaded Congressman Peter Tague of Charlestown to do so. Since the congressmen could run for mayor of Boston while retaining their seats in the United States House of

Representatives, they had little to lose by challenging Curley and much to gain by currying favor with Lomasney. This blatant attempt by Lomasney to divide the Irish vote was evident to Curley, who burst into Lomasney's office at the latter's Hendricks Club to demand an explanation. "'I put them in to lick you,' the Mahatma [Lomasney] said frankly, signaling his bully boys to surround the visitor."[4]

Curley was undeterred. He confidently and vigorously campaigned throughout the city with indoor and outdoor rallies and denunciatory newspaper ads. Although as a campaigner Peters was dull beyond belief, he won the election as Lomasney's strategy of splitting the Irish vote was successful. The vote tally was as follows:

Peters	37,900
Curley	28,000
Gallivan	19,400
Tague	1,700

As it turned out, perhaps Curley was lucky in his defeat. Mayor Andrew J. Peters was a man who liked the honor of being mayor but not the hard work that went into the job. Peters preferred golfing and yachting to the confinement of city hall. Moreover, he had the misfortune to be mayor of Boston during the serious post–World War recession of 1919 to 1921 and during the headline-grabbing Boston police strike, which Governor Calvin Coolidge broke by asserting: "There is no right to strike against the public safety by anybody, anywhere, any time."[5] As writer Joseph Dinneen noted with regard to the recession and the police strike, Peters "looked around blinking, bewildered and uncomprehending, not knowing what had happened. He never did figure it out."[6] Robert Sobel, a biographer of Calvin Coolidge, concurred. He wrote of Peters, "He was a clumsy politician who often seemed baffled by what was going on around him ... [and] he hadn't much of an idea how to be an effective mayor. As a result, this well-meaning dilettante presided over an administration every bit as corrupt as those of Fitzgerald and Curley — but those mayors, unlike Peters, had been effective."[7]

Nothing Save the Votes: Curley's Return to Political Power

In 1918, in a rare error in political judgment, Curley hastily mounted a campaign to wrest the Democratic nomination away from Congressman James A. Gallivan, who Curley believed was chiefly responsible for his defeat in his quest for a second term as mayor. The challenge was ill advised. Gallivan was popular with his constituency, and Curley, now living in the splendid house he built for his family on Jamaica Way, was no longer a resident of Gallivan's congressional district. But the defeat was a cleansing purgative for Curley. He had failed to think through the pitfalls of a campaign for Congress and was ill prepared for the fight. Once defeated, he could concentrate on a return to his first love, the office of mayor of Boston. From his office at the Hibernia National Bank where he now worked as its president, Curley looked jealously at the office he preferred in Boston's city hall, and, in 1921, against considerable odds, he waged a successful campaign to win the office of mayor once again.

Before Governor Calvin Coolidge went to Washington, D.C., to serve as vice president, he signed a charter revision barring any Boston mayor from running for a second consecutive term. But even without this amendment, Peters had no chance of reelection. The "good-government" people would not support a corrupt mayor while the Democratic ward bosses would not support Peters because he failed to share the spoils of office with them. Such ingratitude could not go unpunished, and so Lomasney and his cronies turned to the sixty-six-year-old John R. Murphy, Peters's fire commissioner, as their candidate.

Hostility to another term for James Michael Curley from nearly all the Boston newspapers, and the zeal of the "goo-goos" to thwart Curley's return as Boston's mayor, seemed to whet Curley's determination to make the race. With a *sang froid* that was something to behold, Curley calmly announced, that in face of the political corruption evident under Peters, he would run for mayor once again and as the reform candidate! The backers of Murphy were sure that Curley's candidacy was but "the dying flutter of a small crow."[8]

Murphy made much of his maturity and experience, while Curley emphasized his youth, age forty-eight, and vitality. Curley portrayed himself as a devout Catholic while he mocked Murphy as one who ate meat instead of fish on Friday. And, as he was wont to do, Curley and his underlings spread the canard that Murphy was about to divorce his wife of many years so that he could marry a well-built-sixteen-year-old beauty.

Curley's "dirty tricks" continued unabated, and he was unabashed about using them. Thus, he hired Harvard students who went into Catholic neighborhoods and announced they were Baptists who were seeking votes for Murphy. He paid $2,000 to A. Z. Conrad, a minister in the Ku Klux Klan, to attack Curley viciously from the pulpit so that Curley could ostentatiously denounce him as a Catholic basher. Since the 1921 election was the first in which Massachusetts women could vote, Curley paid them special attention and urged his wife to join in the campaign. She did so effectively. In one stage-managed performance, repeated time and again, with his wife on one side of him and the American flag on the other, Curley would reach out with both arms and embrace his wife and the American flag. Screaming approval invariably followed, especially when Curley supporters planted in the audience led the cheers. Thus did Curley publicly demonstrate that he loved his wife and his country.

Curley recognized that in this campaign he needed to reach out beyond the Irish vote and beyond the women's vote, and so he courted African-Americans, Poles, Jews, Italians, and Portuguese. When, during the campaign, the opera singer Enrico Caruso died, Curley attended a memorial meeting of twenty-five thousand Italians on the Boston Common and cried so that all would notice that he shed real tears over the passing of the Italian tenor. Murphy made a more tepid response by merely expressing his sympathy.

When the votes were counted on a cold and stormy night, the tallies at 8:30 P.M. showed Murphy holding a lead of 7,500 votes. Although the newspaper headlines declared Murphy the winner, Curley learned from the election commissioners that fourteen districts which were likely to be supportive of his candidacy had delayed reporting. Curley refused to concede. When the votes of those precincts were duly counted a bewildered Murphy and a confused Boston found Curley the victor with a plurality of 2,698 votes. Ward bosses, who had bet between them $128,000 on a Murphy win, groaned despondently. As Curley told it in his autobiography, "Houdini the Great wired me: 'As I know what it means to present an apparently impossible stunt, accept congratulations from a fellow stunter.'"[9]

The Further Adventures of James Michael Curley

During his second administration as mayor, James Michael Curley continued the free-wheeling spending and the loose application of conflict of interest ordinances that had been characteristic of his first mayoralty. He embarked on an unprecedented public works program and expanded the city hospital by building new maternity, pediatrics, and pathology buildings. He widened a number of streets, especially those around city hall. Public bathhouses and recreational areas were built to make them available to the needy of Boston. He set up a retirement fund for city laborers and doubled their wages.

Curley routinely and methodically received a cut from every city contract, and as Boston became beautiful, Curley became rich. At the rate at which he built it was not long before the city ran out of public money with which to continue his ambitious program of public works. Boston's business people were in a fury when they realized that Curley planned to raise business taxes to continue his public projects. The Finance Committee was swamped with projects that required auditing and for which they were totally understaffed. What they came up with often were so inane as to make a laughing stock of its members. For example, the Finance Committee charged Curley with fraudulently spending $28,841 on local parades. Curley was able to demonstrate that, as mayor, "Honey Fitz" had spent even more. Thus, the Finance Committee was kept off balance, and its members were often the subject of disparagement and ridicule.

Because Curley resented the Republican initiative, which he correctly understood to be aimed especially at him, that denied Boston's mayors a second consecutive term, and aware that he could not possibly get the law amended or repealed, in 1924, midway in his mayoral administration, he sought the governorship of Massachusetts. But, in 1924, the political tide was in favor of Republicans.

Curley's Republican opponent for governor was Alvan T. Fuller, a wealthy car dealer who, despite initially identifying himself as a Theodore Roosevelt "Bull Moose" reformer, became a staunch conservative. And, in the conservative climate of the 1920s, this was enough to win for Fuller the governorship of Massachusetts. Moreover, Curley, in his slash and burn campaign tactics, scarcely crowned himself with either glory, decency, or integrity. In the past Curley had supported an amendment to the United States Constitution that would limit child labor in factories. The child labor amendment was making its rounds among the states and required staunch supporters if it were to be adopted. Curley, however, proved to be a disappointment to its adherents. When autocratic and ultraconservative William Cardinal O'Connell came out in vehement opposition, Curley likewise declared his opposition in a vain attempt to win votes despite his convictions to the contrary and despite his reputation as being a mayor of the poor.

Curley thought he found another issue in the reinvigoration of the Ku Klux Klan. Although never very strong in Massachusetts, Curley inveighed against the KKK night after October night and, as he did so, fiery crosses were conveniently burning in the background. This gave Curley the opportunity to intone, in that eloquent voice of his, "There it burns, the cross of hatred upon which Our Lord Jesus Christ was crucified — the cross of human avarice, and not the cross of love and Christian charity."[10] But Massachusetts had never seen so many fiery crosses to which Curley so frequently pointed. Those crosses had been set by party hacks in the pay of James Michael Curley and timed to burn conveniently for Curley's oratorical flourishes during which he tried but failed to hang the label of klansman around Fuller's neck. Fuller's Catholic wife spoke in her husband's defense, and his generous contributions to Catholic causes were cited in his favor.

During the campaign, Curley proved as handy with his fists as he was with his tongue. Thus, when he encountered Frederick Enright publisher of the Boston *Telegram,* the only local newspaper supporting Curley in his 1921 campaign but now a fierce opponent and a Fuller advisor, he punched the 6' 4" Enright and knocked him down. Curley held Enright responsible for bringing up the time Curley spent in jail and reinforcing the memory with a picture showing Curley in prison stripes. Curley also brought a libel suit against Enright when the publisher asserted that the mayor had paid some $35,000 as a bribe to some brokers to avoid a court case that would have led to Curley's further imprisonment. Curley won the court case, and Enright lost his newspaper. In the gubernatorial election that followed, Curley was defeated.

Despite his loss to Fuller, Curley still had a year longer to serve as mayor of Boston, and he was determined to make the most of it. What better way of crowning his second term as mayor than by spending and spending on a program of building roads, paving streets, landscaping parks, establishing new playgrounds for the poor, and making hospital improvements. But now the state legislature had set limits on the amount Boston could borrow, and so, despite higher tax rates, Curley could not raise the money he needed to finance the capital building he thought necessary for the welfare of Bostonians.

When the bankers refused to lend the city any additional money, Curley resorted to some unorthodox methods to pry the money loose. Thus, to one banker he declared, "Listen, there's a water main with floodgates right under your building. If you don't know where it is, your architect can tell you. You'd better get that money up by three o'clock this afternoon or those gates will be opened pouring thousands of gallons of water right into your vaults."[11] The banker provided the money.

Another time Curley needed money to meet Boston's payrolls, and again the same banker refused. Curley admonished the bank president, "You'd better get that money up. The watergate is still there, but before I come to that I have a better idea. I'll have six hundred city employees lined up outside your bank tomorrow with checks for their salaries. That will make a line about a mile long; and I'll advise all of the city contractors who have accounts in your bank to be in that line too, with their employees who have money on deposit to transfer their accounts to other banks. You don't want to see a run on your bank, do you?"[12] Curley got the money.

When, a bit later, Curley needed payroll money once again, Curley said to the niggardly banker, "I have a nice picture of you, and I have a good picture of that beautiful estate you have in the country. If I don't get the money to meet the payroll, I am going to print those pictures. Under your picture I'll have a caption, 'This is the man responsible for payless paydays for city employees'; and under the picture of your beautiful house the caption, 'This is where he lives.' When a man gets hungry, he's likely to do something desperate. I'd keep away from that house if I were you." The city's workers were paid on time.

Curley used his last months as mayor to plan for the next mayoral election. If he could not run again, who should run in his place? Early in 1925, Lomasney, "Honey Fitz," and Curley met at the former's initiative with a view of deciding upon a single candidate so as to assure a Democratic victory. Lomasney proposed his protégé Joe O'Neil as an ideal compromise and as one who could bring the competing Irish factions into harmony. Curley rejected O'Neil and in his place put up Theodore A. Glynn, his fire commissioner. Although Glynn received some campaign funds, Curley was intent on a double game.

Instead of Glynn, he clandestinely backed the candidacy of a Republican, Malcolm E. Nichols, a Boston accountant who had the support of Republican ward boss Charles Innes, a good friend and sometime mentor of Curley. The latter assured the former that with Nichols as mayor only good things could happen to Curley. For one thing, Nichols would be easy to control while mayor, and for another he would be easy to defeat when and if Curley chose to run for mayor once again. Both predictions came to pass. With seven Irish Democrats competing for mayor, the result was an unusual victory for the Republican Nichols. During Nichols's term, half his appointees and half the contractors were Curley's men. Nichols made no major move without consulting Innes, who in turn often turned to Curley for further guidance. As Nichols' term neared its end, Republicans seemed to repudiate him. Said one critic, "Mal [Malcolm Nichols] is the fifty-third card in the pack — a joker."[13]

Curley, it seemed, had it all. Although no longer mayor, he was once again president of the Hibernia Bank, and the power behind the Nichols mayoral administration. Money appeared plentiful as Curley drew his salary as a corporate executive while the contractors continued to provide Curley with his "share" of the booty from building projects for which the city of Boston had been over-charged. But, Curley was not a happy man.

He preferred the political hustings to the comfort of a leather swivel chair behind a huge mahogany desk as befits a bank president.

Out of the Wilderness and Into Politics

James Michael Curley could not breathe except in a political environment. Out of political life, he was prey for notorious promoters of get-rich-quick schemes, nearly all of which failed. When, in 1929, he ran for mayor for a third term, Curley was desperately in need of money. However, what should have been an easy victory turned out to be a victory for which he would have to fight. His opponent was none other than William Cardinal O'Connell, who put forward the candidacy of an arch-conservative Frederick W. Mansfield, the fifty-two-year-old president of the Massachusetts Bar Association and former attorney for the American Federation of Labor. While the cardinal did not overtly support Mansfield, that the latter was also the cardinal's personal lawyer and chief lobbyist with the Massachusetts state legislature was not lost on the voters. Mansfield would not have run without the cardinal's approval. Although a dull speaker, that it was widely known that he was the cardinal's choice made him a formidable candidate.

To confuse the voters even more, Mansfield encouraged Tom Curley, James Michael Curley's cellmate of twenty-five-years past, to run. Mansfield expected, quite reasonably, that two Curleys in the race would confuse the voters and take some of the vote away from James Michael thereby enhancing his own chances for victory. Although still hostile, Tom Curley decided that there was little for him to gain by remaining in the race and withdrew. Mansfield, all but certain that he would lose in a two-candidate race for mayor, beat about for another candidate and came up with Dan Coakley, the former Curley ally but now a lawyer disbarred for blackmail and a Curley enemy. But Coakley could serve Mansfield well. The latter was proper but dull; Coakley was dapper and had a venomous mouth. But that mouth was no match, as it turned out, for Curley, who promptly described Coakley as "Dapper Dan, the leprous creature" and dubbed the Mansfield/Coakley alliance as "Freddy Mansfield and his manikin."

In Boston politics, however, it was hard to keep score even with a scorecard. Boston's potential voters were shocked when "Mahatma" Lomasney, formerly a stalwart Curley foe challenged the cardinal and announced his support of Curley "with no ifs, ands, or buts." Since the Republicans did not enter a candidate in the 1929 Boston mayoralty contest, the struggle was mainly between Mansfield and Curley. As the campaign neared its close, 25,000 people assembled to cheer James Michael and to hear "Honey Fitz" sing his "Sweet Adeline" and do his celebrated Irish Jig. When Mansfield sought to strike back by revealing Curley's shady financial dealings, the voters did not listen. Instead, Curley received 116,500 votes to Mansfield's 97,000 and Coakley's 2,900. Thus, in 1929, Curley was swept into office for his third term as mayor. But there would be little for him to cheer about.

On January 6, 1930, at Symphony Hall, Curley, for the third time, took the oath of office as mayor of the city of Boston. Because Boston, like the nation, was in the grip of the Great Depression, Curley, in a ninety-minute ceremony (fourteen times longer than that of New York's Mayor, Jimmy Walker) promised a "work and wages" program which he thought would help Bostonians cope with the ever-deepening Depression. With help from a state-approved bill to permit Boston to borrow beyond its legal debt limit, Curley launched into what he did best, that is, spend on a lavish program of public works, which helped create jobs for the armies of Boston's unemployed even as he skimmed substantial sums from each of the contracts.

Personal tragedy struck when in June 1930, his wife Mary, died of a lingering cancer. Six months later, twenty-two-year-old James Michael Curley Jr., a student at Harvard Law School, died of an embolism during a gall bladder operation. Curley was also politically frustrated because Joseph B. Ely, a Democrat but a Curley enemy, had been elected governor of the state. A Republican governor, Curley thought, would be easy to beat, not so a Democrat who would be seeking a second term. Perhaps personal tragedies and perceived political frustration explain the appointment of his chubby, wealthy, but corrupt neighbor, Edmund L. Dolan, as city treasurer. The extent of his corruption reached into nearly every corner of Boston's city government:

Dolan was the secret boss of the Mohawk Packing Company, which had a contract to supply Boston's city institutions with meat. It did so at prices a third higher than those in retail butcher shops.

He was the mastermind of the Legal Securities Corporation, a private company that bought and sold municipal bonds including those of the City of Boston. As treasurer Dolan sold the bonds to his company, and as head of Legal Securities he sold bonds from other cities to Boston; "and his fury of activities—buying and selling to himself in reality—brought him a fee on each transaction."[14]

Edmond Dolan, as city treasurer, reaped a huge reward when a private contractor on city work accidentally flooded the basement of a General Equipment building. General Equipment's insurance offered to settle with the city for a $20,000 payment, but the amount listed on the settlement was for $85,000. The *Finance Commission* found that the insurance company had collected $20,000. What had happened to the rest of the money? Did Curley and Dolan split the ill-gotten windfall?

With his family life disrupted and scandal mounting, Curley arranged for a well-publicized trip to Europe. He took his twenty-three-year-old daughter Mary and Edmond Dolan with him. The former he took for comfort, the latter to keep him out of the reach of investigators who were boring in on Dolan's corrupt bargains. He also took Mary's friend Lauretta Bremmer, who would become his daughter-in-law. Standish Willcox, Curley's long-time amanuensis and confidant, made sure that everybody worth informing knew of Curley's grand tour of Europe.

In Europe, Curley stopped briefly in County Galway to seek out his impoverished relatives, and then had a state dinner with the president of the Irish Free State. After visits with officials in England and France, he went to Italy, where he had a private half-hour audience with Pope Pius XI who awarded Curley a silver medal, a bronze medal to Edmond Dolan, and rosaries to the ladies. Curley and the Italian premier, Benito Mussolini, were scheduled to meet at the Gigi Palace for but ten minutes, but the audience lasted more than a half hour as the dictator and the mayor, two ego-maniacal men, seemed to share a high regard for each other's pomposity. As were so many others, Curley appeared especially dazzled by Mussolini. "I never met anyone in such a position," Curley declared after he left the meeting, "who was more profoundly interested in the welfare of his people; the progress and prosperity of his country. As a practical economist he amazed me."[15] While others became disenchanted with Benito Mussolini, the Italian dictator remained a favorite of James Michael Curley. Curley and his entourage returned to New York aboard the *Leviathan* and promptly boarded a train for Boston.

Curley had been born with a penchant for politics and a seemingly political silver spoon in his mouth. But he recognized that his image as a political power appeared to be tarnishing. As he boarded the train in New York en route to Boston, he learned that New York Governor Franklin D. Roosevelt occupied a suite on the same train on his way to assess his political fortunes in Massachusetts preparatory to making a bid to be the presidential nominee of the Democratic Party. Never one to miss an opportunity, Curley sent his card to the Roosevelt suite and was invited to pay a call.

Curley and Roosevelt

When at the conclusion of a meeting of Democrats held at Magnolia, Massachusetts, on the North Shore in the summer house of President Woodrow Wilson's *eminence grise,* Colonel Edward M. House, Curley shocked most of the other Democrats when he announced, "Franklin Delano Roosevelt is the hope of the nation."[16] For his abandonment of Al Smith and his unqualified support of Franklin Roosevelt in the 1932 campaign for the Democratic presidential nomination, Curley was branded a traitor by Smith supporters and denounced as the Irish Benedict Arnold.

So great was the continued enthusiasm for promoting a fellow Irishmen into the White House rather than a Yankee patrician, that at a meeting of the Ancient Order of Hibernians a resolution was passed without debate that the mayor was a traitor. "For the first time in his three terms as mayor, the corridors were empty. He was shunned, snubbed, ignored."[17] During the St. Patrick's Day parade in South Boston, snowballs were thrown at Curley for daring to dump Al Smith. "James Michael Curley," according to the Worcester *Telegram,* "is the most battered political casualty of the Massachusetts primary."[18]

State Democratic Chairman Donahue, acting on behalf of Governor Ely and Senator Walsh, created an all–Smith slate of delegates to the national convention in the state's presidential primary. Thereupon Roosevelt invited Curley to organize a competing pro–Roosevelt slate. Although Curley tried valiantly, he knew that his fight was futile and the pro–Roosevelt delegation went down to overwhelming defeat. Curley appeared to be at the nadir of his political career. A vast audience of twenty-five thousand saw the pro–Smith delegates off to Chicago in June 1932, and Curley did not even have a pass to get into the Chicago stadium as a spectator. But Curley would have the last laugh.

Mayor Curley went out to Chicago at his own expense and talked the Puerto Rican delegation to allow him to be its chairman. To the surprise of Governor Ely and Senator Walsh, there was Curley sitting right behind them on the convention floor when the call came from the platform: "Puerto Rico— Chairman Alcalde Jaime Miguel Curleo," and Curley shouted back, "Puerto Rico casts its six votes for Franklin Delano Roosevelt."[19] With Roosevelt winning the nomination, Curley once more returned to the center stage of Massachusetts and national politics. Now the cheers, as he left the train in Boston, were for him and for Roosevelt while Walsh, Lomasney, Ely, and "Honey Fitz" were all on the sidelines. On his return to Boston, he began his first speech with the salutation, "Senors and senoras."[20]

Roosevelt, however, realized that he needed the regular Bay State Democratic organization if he was to win the state from Hoover. Roosevelt prevailed upon Governor Ely, who had made the nominating speech for Al Smith, to lead the campaign for Roosevelt in Massachusetts. Ely agreed, but only if he had the assurances that he, not Curley, would direct the campaign. Unwelcome to lead a Roosevelt campaign in Massachusetts, Curley agreed to take on a strenuous campaign of public speaking and public appearances on Roosevelt's behalf in the mid and far west. Curley denounced Hoover for encouraging General Douglas MacArthur to fire on the Bonus Army when veterans, mostly of World War I, attempted to demonstrate in Washington, D.C., for payment of bonuses they had been promised. Curley accused Hoover of prolonging the Depression by neglecting to take appropriate and timely remedial action. When Roosevelt came to Boston on November 1, 1932, Curley returned from exile in the American heartland. As election day approached, it was James Michael Curley who introduced FDR to a capacity rally of fifteen thousand at the Boston Arena.

On election day, November 8, 1932, Roosevelt swept Hoover out of office by a seven million-vote margin. In Massachusetts, he got 800,000 votes to Hoover's 737,000. Surely, Curley thought he would then break loose from provincial Massachusetts politics and be rewarded for his efforts with a distinguished cabinet position. At Warm Springs, Georgia, where Roosevelt swam in the warm waters in a vain attempt to strengthen his legs weakened from polio, Roosevelt allegedly offered Curley the position of secretary of the navy, but no announcement was to be made until four months later when, in March 1933, Roosevelt would be inaugurated. On January 2, 1933, when Curley returned from Warm Springs, he received word of the death of Standish Willcox of a diabetic condition. Curley had been preparing to take the ever-loyal Willcox to Washington with him, but now all he could do was to prepare a lavish Episcopal funeral.

The promise to make Curley navy secretary became unstuck when James Roosevelt, representing his father, arrived in Boston to attend the funeral of Calvin Coolidge. After the funeral services, James Roosevelt advised Curley that his father had been forced to withdraw the navy offer. Actually, the promise of such a distinguished cabinet post as Secretary of the Navy was not one based on reality inasmuch as Curley's efforts in behalf of FDR were not as effective as Curley liked to believe.

James Roosevelt, however, assured Curley that he could have the ambassadorship to France or Italy. When, after Roosevelt's inauguration, the two finally met, Curley advised the president that he would prefer to be ambassador to Rome rather than to Paris. Roosevelt was noncommittal

President Franklin D. Roosevelt (right) talking with Governor Curley during a campaign tour in Brockton, Massachusetts, 1936. Courtesy of the Library of Congress. Prints & Photographs Division, LC-USZ62-119019.

and advised Curley to think over his choice. In the meantime, when news spread of Curley's possible appointment to be the American ambassador to Italy, strong opposition came from Cardinal O'Connell who believed Curley was unsuited to a post that was in such proximity to the Vatican. Roosevelt advised Curley that opposition also came from Mussolini, the pope, and the king. Curley stormed out of Roosevelt's office, deeply disappointed.

He next heard from FDR by letter that the best he could do was to offer Curley the ambassadorship to Poland. But as news of this proposal leaked to the press, one newspaper asserted, "The President must be anti-Polish." Another declared, that "Curley would pave the Polish corridor." The ambassadorship to Poland, relatively insignificant as it was, was opposed by Curley's enemies. Roosevelt, somewhat taken by surprise by the unpopularity of his decision, asserted, "What is there in Poland Curley would want to steal."[21] Curley believed that the proffered appointment was an insult that should be filled with a Republican enemy. It was, he believed, a four-year exile. He was not wrong. "If Poland is such a god-dam interesting place," he undiplomatically told the president to his face, "why don't you resign the presidency and take it yourself."[22]

While James Michael Curley had been an early supporter of FDR, the latter was distrustful of the former and was put off by Curley's reputation as a corrupt politician. In February 1933, Erland Fish, president of the Massachusetts Senate held public sessions at Boston's Gardner Auditorium with the intent of calling public attention to the alleged corruption of the mayor and his treasurer, Edmund Dolan. In a climate that reflected the investigation in New York by Samuel Seabury against Mayor Jimmy Walker, the Fish probe encouraged Republicans and anti–Curley Democrats to berate Curley for his alleged corrupt practices. Not wishing to bring discredit on his new administration, Roosevelt gleefully left Curley dangling in the wind.

Curley and Roosevelt were, in reality, a political odd couple. Curley was more comfortable with Irish machine politicians than he was with patrician reformers like Franklin Roosevelt. FDR, on the other hand knew, that Curley could not be trusted where financial honesty was important. It is unlikely that Roosevelt would seriously have fought for Curley's appointment as Secretary of the Navy or for important ambassadorships in France or Italy.

While Curley developed a deep dislike for Roosevelt, he was smart enough to continue courting the president, who made up for the shabby treatment accorded Curley by giving Boston a disproportionate share of federal help for that city's harbors, rivers, parks, hospitals, and roads. Roosevelt's advisors worried also that a large proportion of what was allocated was lining Curley's pockets. They were not wrong. Boston's economy-minded political establishment, Republicans and conservative Democrats alike, looked askance at what they saw were the free-wheeling spending proclivities of the New Deal, especially when much of the money flowing from Washington to Boston went through the hands of Mayor Curley. As a popular doggerel that made the rounds in Boston suggested:

> The King is in the White House
>   Handing out the money.
> The Queen is on the front page,
>   Looking very funny.
> The Knave is up in Boston,
>   Picking up the plums.
> While the country alphabetically
>   Is feeding all the bums.[23]

Curley's third term as mayor would end January 1, 1934. Because state law forbade him from succeeding himself, he aligned himself once again with Charlie Innes to attempt to reelect the pliable Malcolm Nichols until Curley could lawfully run once again for mayor. But, this time, Fred Mansfield, still a favorite of the cardinal, thwarted the Curley-Innes plot to elect Nichols and became mayor of Boston.

Although he would soon be sixty, politics flowed in the bloodstream of James Michael Curley, and so he cast about for new political challenges. Curley's intuitive but timely support of Roosevelt for president paved the way to his first and only term as governor of Massachusetts. His two years as governor were to be as tumultuous as they were historic.

King James I: Governor of Massachusetts

On January 3, 1935, James Michael Curley took the oath of office as the fifty-third governor of Massachusetts. When he rose to deliver his inaugural address the thunder of applause from his supporters could not be abated until he took the gavel from Leverett Saltonstall, Speaker of the House, and pounded the lectern so that he could get on with his remarks. His speech was interrupted twenty-six times by cheers. However, when he called for reducing the size of the legislature to half of its existing membership, holding biennial rather than annual sessions, and dissolving the popularly elected Governor's Council, which had the power to confirm his appointments, it signaled to his opponents that what Curley sought was akin to royal decree rather than democratic debate.

His overarching ambition and love of the panoply of military pomp led some to describe him as "King James I of Massachusetts." To others, his authoritarian preferences reminded them of his contemporary, Huey P. Long, and so they called him "The Kingfish of Massachusetts." Still others, remembered his continuing admiration for the Italian dictator Benito Mussolini, and so they dubbed him the "Irish Mussolini." Massachusetts under Governor Curley's leadership became "a virtual dictatorship" as "Jim Curley [held] Massachusetts in the palm of his hand."[24]

Such were the trappings of the Massachusetts governorship that Curley could command the chauffeur driven twelve-cylinder Lincoln and roam the state highways while ignoring the speed limits. His gaudily attired state troopers were dressed in uniforms reminiscent of the soldiers of old Mexico. More than once the Lincoln with the *S-I* tags was involved in an accident one of which involved the death of a motorcycle escort. To give an address at the tercentenary commencement at Harvard in 1935, the governor arrived with an escort of red-coated cavalry known as the "Dandy Lancers." He entered Harvard Yard with the pounding of drums and the blare of trumpets as if it were a Roman amphitheater rather than a college campus. But showman extraordinaire that he was, it was generally acknowledged that Curley gave the best speech of the day. "Never in the proud Bay State's history was the man in the street given such a show from the Governor's office. He watched his Excellency's actions as avidly as he followed the progress of the Boston Braves and the Boston Red Sox during the baseball season."[25]

From behind a desk once occupied by Calvin Coolidge, Curley tried to deliver on his "work and wages" promises as he tried to mirror the essentials of the New Deal. Bellicose and histrionic, Curley promised much but delivered relatively little. To keep Massachusetts under his control, Curley appointed those whose chief qualification for the job was loyalty to Curley. For civil service commissioner he turned to Tom Green, the political boss in Charlestown and a real estate tycoon who, with his family, Curley once described as "the James Brothers," popular outlaws of the "Wild West." With Green in charge, the civil service examination became a mockery as soon as it was known that one could readily pass if one had the Curley blessing. Curley replaced the highly regarded Payson Smith, the commissioner of education, with a small-town superintendent with Irish roots. For commissioner of agriculture he appointed an Irish grocery salesman who had joined the Grange. As state librarian, he appointed Margaret O'Riordan, an officer in the Hibernian auxiliary and a member of the Democratic state committee who had devotedly and selflessly campaigned on Curley's behalf. But this appointment was too much for the press to accept when it was learned that she owned no books and that her reading consisted of *True Romances* and *Spy Stories*.

Governor Curley successfully nagged President Roosevelt for grants to fund public works so that he could put the unemployed to work. When hospitals and other institutions were built, Curley could hardly wait to reward his followers with jobs. When some hospitals complained that they had more attendants than patients, he ordered that some of the attendants be put to work growing vegetables. Mobs of the unemployed hounded him at his Jamaica Way home each morning as he eased himself through the crowd to his waiting Lincoln. They followed the governor into the state house and lined the marble stairs pleading for jobs. Curley gave and created jobs for more than 100,000 persons.

Although the state legislature was Republican-controlled, Curley was able to squeeze through legislation reducing the hours in state institutions from seventy to forty-eight hours a week. He managed to get the legislature to liberalize the workman's compensation law; he legalized horse racing, and he succeeded in turning over the job of determining the location of a new race track to his neighbor, Edmund Dolan. Because of Cardinal O'Connell's hostility, Curley's attempt to adopt a state lottery fizzled.

Although he did not get everything he wanted, during the legislative session of 1935, the longest up to that time in the state's history, James Michael Curley clearly became the master of the legislative body. "He swung the whip without mercy when lashing was necessary, and he handed out the lumps of sugar when expediency indicated that course."[26]

The "get Curley" crowd consisted of President Roosevelt, Boston Mayor Frederick W. Mansfield, William Cardinal O'Connell, U.S. Senator from Massachusetts David Walsh, and former Massachusetts Governor Joseph B. Ely. Democrats all, formidable politicians, they detested Curley for his flamboyance, corrupt practices, and huge ego. While the finance commission continued its efforts to "get the goods" on Curley, the governor was now in a good position to weaken the commission, and he did so with a political virtuosity that bordered on genius reminiscent of how Mayor Hague paved the way for a judgeship for his son. Before long, the reconstituted finance commission announced that the files on Curley and Dolan that had been turned over by the "get Curley" crowd had been "lost."

But Governor Curley's popularity continued to grow especially when he demonstrated both energy and administrative skill as when in 1936 he took charge of rescue efforts brought about by widespread flood waters in western Massachusetts. He dispatched the National Guard; declared a state of emergency; set up temporary shelters; arranged for the delivery of much-needed food, clothing, and medicines; and arranged for emergency bank loans. He made his presence known as he went from one emergency site to another and even muddied his beloved Lincoln in an attempt to provide relief and hope to flood victims. "For almost one hundred hours straight, he was on the scene of the misery to cheer up the unfortunate and handle specific problems on the spot. Newspaper reporters followed him on his sleepless prowl of the flooded areas, detailing for readers how his presence and sympathy kept spirits high."[27]

The Long Goodbye of James Michael Curley

Despite widespread acknowledgment that the governor had abused the power and trappings of office, in 1936 Massachusetts voters were quite prepared to reelect him for another term as governor. But Curley shocked his supporters and surprised his enemies by announcing that he would spurn the opportunity to run for governor, even though reelection was a sure thing, to try for a far more dubious victory in a race for the U.S. Senate. This was the biggest political miscalculation of his career and the beginning of a long political twilight. While he would be elected to several important posts, Curley never regained his influence and seemed to linger too long in the political shadows, thereby eroding the fondness many still had for this charismatic politician.

Specifically, in a boss-dominated state Democratic convention, Curley finessed Marcus Coolidge out of renomination for United States Senator. There upon Curley announced that he would try a run against thirty-four-year-old Republican Henry Cabot Lodge Jr., grandson of Wilson's nemesis who had opposed the League of Nations and Wilson's attempt to make the United States a member.

In his campaign, Curley had counted on the support of Father Charles E. Coughlin, the demagogic priest from Michigan. When the latter decided to form a new political party, the Union Party, and to run William Lemke of North Dakota for president and Thomas C. "Hamburger Tom" O'Brien, a Curley enemy, as vice president, Curley was taken by surprise. Curley's chance of victory was substantially dimmed when "Hamburger Tom" ran also for the Marcus Coolidge seat in the United States Senate.

Curley's mistake was not so much in attempting a run for the United State Senate when he was at the height of his popularity as governor of Massachusetts but in depending for his strategy on the "hate vote" that Coughlin represented. For all his administrative skills and political sagacity, Curley demonstrated a notable lack of integrity in relying for victory on the demagogic qualities of a Father Coughlin. Perhaps he saw in Father Coughlin, as he did in Benito Mussolini, a political model he would dearly love to emulate but whose danger in a democracy he could not recognize. In the election, Curley lost to Lodge by 136,000 votes. Deservedly, he was out of politics. However, phoenix-like he rose from the political grave to lose and win elections until his death. His victories were pyrrhic in that he never again really knew what to do with each win. He remained in politics because he could do no other.

His one solace was that on his last day as governor, with typical Curleyesque showmanship, he married a widow, Gertrude Denis. Unlike the quiet departure of other governors, who traditionally walked down the steps of the state capitol and onto the Boston Common, symbolic of giving up the indicators of power to mingle with the crowd, Curley was met by a cheering crowd of admirers who congratulated him on his marriage and presented him with a new Lincoln for the honeymoon.

In 1937, sixty-two-year-old Curley was defeated for mayor of Boston by his thirty-seven-year-old former protégé Maurice J. Tobin. In 1938, he was defeated by Leverett Saltonstall, a Boston Brahmin, for governor of Massachusetts. With three successive political losses, for U.S. Senator, Boston mayor, and Massachusetts governor, Curley seemed destined for political obscurity. Political reporter John Gunther commented, "Many Bostonians have become sick of that grotesque old man."[28] And so it seemed. In 1941, the law preventing a mayor from running for reelection was repealed, and the stage again was set for a new Curley-Tobin race. Although it was a squeaker, Curley lost once again.

In 1942, amidst the jeers of younger people with political ambitions, Curley ran for the House of Representatives once again, this time, against Thomas Hopkinson Eliot of the eleventh district. This grandson of Charles W. Eliot, the distinguished president of Harvard and a favorite of FDR, was a Protestant Yankee whom an Irish Catholic from Boston loved to destroy. Using his political savvy like a shillelagh, Curley won an easy victory.

However, dogging Curley's political career was the threat of legal action against him for allegedly using public money for private gain. While running for mayor against the youthful and popular Maurice Tobin, Mayor Mansfield, with support from the White House, brought legal action against James Michael Curley and his former city treasurer, Edmund Dolan. Mansfield brought two separate actions to increase his chances of gaining convictions against at least one of the accused if he could not win against both. Dolan was charged with stealing $178,000 from the treasury of Boston. The claim against Curley was that he had stolen $50,000 from the settlement of the General Equipment Corporation's insurance claim for water damage against the city. In a trial held before Judge Frederick Fosdick, an anti–Curley Republican, and with no jury, Curley's lawyers managed to get the first of thirty-four continuations for him. However, the publicity of the court action hung like a dark cloud over his campaign against Tobin. When Curley ran for governor against Leverett Saltonstall, Judge Fosdick took the opportunity to decide that Curley had "improperly" received $30,000 in the insurance settlement case. At once Curley appealed the decision to the state supreme court because the chief prosecution witness had given three entirely different versions of the alleged payoffs. But the appeal was too late as the Fosdick decision appeared to brand Curley as a crook to the disaffection of many voters.

Had the legal cloud under which he had been campaigning been lifted,

Curley might have defeated Tobin in the 1941 mayoralty campaign. But legal matters only got worse for Curley when the Massachusetts Supreme Court ruled three years after Judge Fosdick's decision that Curley would have to pay Boston a judgment of $42,629 in the General Equipment Company's insurance settlement case. A lower court set Curley's payment at $500 a week for eighty-six weeks and ordered him imprisoned if he failed to keep up the payments. In a separate suit, Edmund Dolan was sentenced to two and a half years in the Charles Street jail for bribing members of his jury.

Out of office, Curley was always short of funds. He lived well, saved little, and was a sucker for get-rich-quick schemes that never succeeded. It was hard to see how Curley could maintain the payment schedule imposed by the courts, and he seemed headed for jail. But Curley was not without friends. According to one perhaps apocryphal story, upon awakening on the day he thought would surely be the one during which he would go to prison, Curley looked out his bedroom window and found an orderly group of people who had spontaneously come forward upon reading about or hearing of Curley's financial problems to contribute what money they could. For a month, groups of people allegedly came forward, some more than once, to save their favorite politician.[29] The Boston Teamsters' Union held a testimonial dinner on his behalf and raised a substantial sum for Curley. As one man told a reporter who interviewed those in line, "I figured he could use some dough so I thought I'd drop by and kind of help him out."[30] With the "Luck of the Irish," Curley narrowly escaped serving jail time.

Curley in congress was ineffectual as his legal problems eclipsed his congressional responsibilities. The charges that finally landed him in jail had nothing to do with skimming the treasuries of Boston or of Massachusetts. The charges against him were seemingly minor, but the outcome was politically disastrous. Would his luck hold out?

Two years before Pearl Harbor, Curley was approached in Washington, D.C., in the lobby of the Mayflower Hotel by a stranger, one James G. Fuller. Fuller said he was an advisor to a firm called the Engineers Group, Inc., which helped manufacturers run the gamut of government regulations in their efforts to win contracts from the government for producing war materiel of various kinds. When Fuller described the credentials of a number of distinguished men who were involved with the enterprise, Curley was impressed, and his finances already low, he readily accepted the invitation to be president of this group. As collateral he put up essentially worthless brewery stock he owned with a par value of $35,000 for which Curley accepted a check from Fuller for $3,500. Curley should have known that something was amiss when the check bounced.

Financially unsophisticated, Curley accepted whatever excuse Fuller gave and permitted Fuller to use Curley's name as president, to print Engineers Group stationery with his name listed as president, and to rent office space in Washington, D.C. Curley served as president for but six months, and, late in the fall of 1941, he resigned from the presidency of the Engineers Group. During his presidency, he received no compensation and made no phone calls to Washington bureaucrats on behalf of the Engineers Group's clients. He did, however, tell three inquiring contractors to talk to Fuller and to phone a bank with regard to a loan to the Engineers Group.

In April 1942, a defense watchdog committee headed by Harry S Truman was looking into the behavior and activities of those seeking government contracts, and among those investigated was the Engineers Group. Uncovering the $3,500 bad check Fuller had given Curley, the latter was called before the Truman committee. The committee found that Fuller was an ex-convict and that the company had taken money from private firms but had not arranged for a single contract. At the end of the day during which Curley was examined, Truman assured Curley that he had nothing to fear from the committee.

However, Curley learned that President Franklin D. Roosevelt had heard of Curley's association with the Engineers Group and looked upon it as an opportunity to put Curley in jail. To that end, FDR ordered a further study by the FBI before seeking Curley's indictment by a grand jury. Curley got House Majority Leader John McCormack to intercede on his behalf and sought to put himself in a favorable light with FDR by supporting the latter's effort to win a third term as president. None of this worked for Curley. Instead, in September 1943, Congressman Curley, Fuller, and others associated with the Engineers Group were indicted on charges of violating the mail-fraud law. All were accused of "falsely representing themselves as consulting engineers, accepting advance retainers, promising contracts from the War and Navy Departments, the Federal Housing Administration, and the Soviet Government — and securing none."[31]

Curley won a delay of his trial long enough to return to Boston and run in 1944 for another term in the United States House of Representatives. In the rematch against Tom Eliot, Curley easily won by an even greater margin than he had two years earlier.

Although now ailing, FDR was preparing to go to Yalta for a historic conference with Winston Churchill and Joseph Stalin. Prior to his departure the president hosted a reception for new members of Congress. Curley, although no longer a new congressman, crashed the reception and demanded of the president, who was in no mood for a confrontation with

Curley, that the president order the case thrown out of court. "I am not a dictator," the president replied. "If I were I would have the case thrown out." To which Curley, under pressures of his own, rather ungraciously replied, "You are nearer to being a dictator than any other man who has ever filled the office of President."[32]

A few months later, Curley's lawyer was refused another extension of the criminal suit, and with pressure mounting and a jail term facing him, Curley became ill and went to the Bethesda Naval Hospital. Federal Judge James Proctor, upon receiving a medical deposition testifying to Curley's illness, which described Curley as having a temporary paralysis of an arm and leg, postponed the trial. Yet, in May 1945, Curley had recuperated sufficiently to be able to travel to Boston and file the papers that would make him a candidate for mayor that year.

In 1944, Maurice Tobin won election as governor of Massachusetts despite accusations that he had allowed the city's infrastructure, its housing, roads, transportation facilities, schools, police, and fire fighting services, to run down. In his place as mayor, the Boston City Council chose John Kerrigan, its president, as mayor. With Kerrigan as his chief opponent, Curley returned to the mayoral hustings boasting that he was "Curley the Builder" and that in his fourth term he would restore the services of which Bostonians had allegedly been deprived. Unless he was elected, he declared, Boston would become a "ghost town." The voters agreed. Curley's enemies were nonplussed that a seventy-year-old man, soon to be tried on a felony charge, would be reelected mayor of Boston by a respectable margin of 54,000 votes. Three weeks after his victory as mayor, Curley's trial began in federal district court in Washington, D.C.

Curley's lawyer demanded of the court to know why his client was being prosecuted for mail fraud when he had never written a letter on behalf of the Engineers Group, never collected a penny, nor charged to the company any expenses. The prosecution agreed, but still Curley's name was on the stationery, and the office had been rented in his name. In the midst of the trial, the judge called a recess to allow Curley to go home to Boston for his inauguration as mayor. After the inauguration, Curley was back in Washington, D.C., and the trial resumed. The jury, after more than twelve hours of debate, found Curley guilty of "conspiring and using the mail to defraud."

Judge Proctor sentenced Curley to prison for six to eighteen months, and then permitted him to go free on bail pending an appeal. Curley returned to Boston, where, perhaps unsurprisingly, he received a hero's welcome. A reporter for *The New Yorker* was so dismayed about this show of affection for a convicted felon that he wrote glumly, "Bostonians can see merits in James M. Curley not visible to anyone else."[33] But John Hanna, the chief analyst of the administrative office of the United States Courts wrote to *The New York Times*, "Few lawyers will doubt that Curley was prosecuted for political reasons and unfairly convicted."[34] The United States Circuit Court of Appeals and the Supreme Court turned down Curley's appeal in 1946.

The strain of the case weakened Curley's already declining health. He claimed he suffered from hypertension, gall bladder, arteriosclerosis, and diabetes, and he was rushed to a hospital where the last rites of the Roman Catholic Church were administered. Although certainly ill, Curley was still up to his old tricks. He was brought into the courtroom in a wheelchair and, to evoke more sympathy from the judge, wore a shirt with a collar size too large so that he would look thin, sick, and gaunt. Judge Proctor was not moved; instead, he ordered the mayor to be taken to Danbury Prison to begin his prison term. Curley was not permitted to make a statement, and Proctor ignored him when Curley cried out, "You are sentencing me to die! This is the death penalty!"

On the very night that Judge Proctor ordered James Michael Curley to Danbury Prison, Robert Bradford, the Republican governor, sent a message to the Republican legislature that Curley be guaranteed his full $20,000 salary and that John Hynes, the city clerk, be made temporary mayor until Curley's return. Hynes was guaranteed a return to his job as city clerk for life. The Massachusetts legislature quickly complied. For his part, Curley contributed his salary to charity for the time he was a "guest" at public expense in Danbury Prison.

Before Curley went to Danbury he had asked John McCormack, Democratic Majority Leader in the House of Representatives, to circulate a petition for a pardon to be delivered to President Harry Truman. All members of the Massachusetts congressional delegation except John F. Kennedy signed the petition. After Curley had served five months in prison, President Truman, in November 1947, granted Curley executive clemency in time to be home for Thanksgiving. By pardoning rather than merely paroling Curley, Truman made it possible for him to resume his political activities at once. He returned to Boston a hero. At South Station the band played "Hail the Conquering Hero Comes," and in front of his home on Jamaica Way, another band played "Hail to the Chief." Curley announced, "I come back ten years younger," and, as if to prove it, he proceeded to perform the duties of mayor with a renewed zest.

Mayor Curley had nearly $38 million to spend on public works, money that members of the council withheld from Temporary Mayor Hynes so that Curley could claim the political credit for spending the windfall. In a vain attempt to garner additional votes for still another rerun for mayor, he assumed the mantle of protector of the city's morals and condemned modern art and burlesque shows. Surprisingly, James Michael Curley, now a sick old man, seemed to have a good chance of defeating the former temporary mayor, John Hynes, who decided to become a candidate for the mayoralty. Hynes ran a campaign based on youth and honesty, enlisted the support of Harvard students who went door-to-door on Hynes's behalf. His former protégé and later enemy, Maurice J. Tobin, now Secretary of Labor in President Harry S Truman's cabinet, came to Boston in support of Hynes. When the results were counted, Hynes was elected by a scant 11,000 votes.

Although defeated, there was more magic in Curley's political life than in his personal life. During the ordeal of his trial over the Engineer's Group in 1945, Curley's thirty-two-year-old son Paul died. In 1950, his daughter Mary and son Leo died of cerebral hemorrhages an hour apart in Mary's apartment.

To help himself recoup from these setbacks, James Michael Curley went to Europe with his two remaining sons, George and Francis. Most of those who had followed his career assumed that the political music he made would now end. Not quite yet.

In 1951, he ran once more against Johnny Hynes. Had this been but a two-man race, Curley might have won. Instead, Curley was infuriated when Joe Timilty, who had been his military aide as governor, his police commissioner when he was mayor, and owed his wealth as a contractor to Curley, entered the race as well. Also, like a ghost at a Halloween party, "Hamburger Tom" O'Brien, Father Coughlin's vice-presidential candidate in the 1936 race, entered this political free-for-all. Timilty siphoned away votes that would surely have gone to Curley, but Curley also made a mistake by once again trying for the "hate" vote by assuring his listeners that he was a better supporter of the demagogic senator Joseph R. McCarthy than was "Hamburger Tom." Out of this political potpourri, Hynes emerged victorious.

On November 20, 1954, James Michael Curley celebrated his eightieth birthday. As a birthday present to himself, he entered the mayoral race of 1955 once again against Johnny Hynes. In this, his "last hurrah," Curley lamented that his seemingly timeless campaign techniques had become ineffective. Voters no longer listened to his "air-conditioned" voice laced with classical quotations. Oratorical virtuosity, the extemporaneous parry-and-thrust of political debate, political showmanship, even dirty tricks, he lamented, seemed wasted and did not win votes.

On November 12, 1958, Curley died. When his will was probated, it showed a net estate of $3,768, insufficient to cover the bequests he had made. Among those who paid tribute to Curley was Edwin O'Connor, whose novel *The Last Hurrah* appeared in 1956. Its hero, Skeffington, was based on Curley's career. When Curley read the novel he was at first infuriated but later intrigued as he began to view O'Connor's Frank Skeffington with some affection. In the novel, Skeffington, on his death bed, hears some visitors say that if he had it to do all over again he would no doubt do it very differently. To this, the dying man musters his last strength to say, "The hell I would!" In response to *The Last Hurrah,* Curley wrote his own autobiography to which he gave the title, *I'd Do It Again.* The movie, starring Spencer Tracey as Skeffington, was held over for a fourth week at Boston's Loew's Orpheum Theater when Curley died.

To the extent that politics is theater, Curley played his role well. But his big mistake was in staying on the political stage too long and hogging the curtain calls. Thus, he remained mainly a political actor and never reached the level of political sage that his real talent for politics suggest's he might have been. Curley exploited the sufferings and discrimination of Irish immigrants as well as those of other immigrant groups, but in the last analysis he "solved nothing; he moved toward no larger understanding; he opened no new lines of communication.... For more than thirty years, [he] ... kept the greater part of the Boston populace half-drunk with fantasies, invective, and showmanship."[35]

Epilogue:
Paradox of
Political Corruption

"The trouble with this house [of politics] is that it is occupied entirely by human bein's. If it was a vacant house, it cud aisily be kept clean." Thus spoke Mr. Dooley, the cartoon character of Finley Peter Dunne, as he saw things at the turn of the century. What he observed then pertains today as well.

The trouble with political corruption is that corruption is often in the eye of the beholder. As Theodore Roosevelt explained, "A leader is necessary, but opponents always call him boss. An organization is necessary, but men in opposition always call it a machine."[1]

The trouble with political corruption is that it often serves a useful function in that it keeps the wheels of government from squeaking.

The trouble with political corruption is that while it can never be completely eliminated, it must be carefully controlled and fought against so that, in a perverse sort of way, it can do the job expected of it.

Why People Vote for Crooks:
The Persistence of Political Corruption

In the days before television, voters and their children often came to political rallies from afar to be entertained, fed, and served free beer or booze. They came to see a parade, hear a band, and enjoy a picnic. During political speech-making they could ask provocative questions, taunt or cheer the candidates, laugh at their impossible promises, revel in the

241

heat of debate and argument, and so get an important feeling of participating in the democratic process. The quartet of mayors identified as
America's worst were political showmen who used their showmanship, at
least some of the time, on behalf of the city's hoi polloi while, at the same
time, serving themselves.

The four "worst" mayors in this volume had charismatic qualities
that parallel those described by the noted sociologist Max Weber. That is,
they were not necessarily charming men, although some were; they were
not merely lovable rogues or effective speakers; in Weber's terms, they
were willing to push the envelope of tradition and to break the cake of custom, sometimes in illegal ways, to keep themselves and/or their political
party in power, and in so doing often they paved the way for alternative
methods of doing the city's business.

These mayors, moreover, personified the eras in which they lived.
"Big Bill" Thompson in his girth and bravura was the living image of Carl
Sandburg's "City of the Big Shoulders."

When Al Capone and his eighteen bodyguards went to the races or a
football game, many Americans went out of their way to shake his hand.
Some even stood and cheered. "What were they cheering about?"[2] If the
voters of Chicago could cheer for Al Capone, it should not be a matter of
surprise that they would cheer "Big Bill," their mayor, despite, or perhaps
because of, his alleged ties to the mobster.

Frank Hague, who did not hesitate to announce to one and all, "I am
the law!" embodied the mayor as the sole authoritarian of his community.
In an age of dictators, Hitler, Mussolini, and Stalin, Frank Hague's long
reach extended well beyond Jersey City. Had American democracy been
threatened by a worsening depression or defeat in World War II, it does
not stretch the imagination that Hague might have emerged as a "made-
in-America" despot.

Jimmy Walker, dapper in dress, was a Tin Pan Alley songwriter, the
essence of the Age of Jazz and the Flapper Era. General affluence and the
dominance of a business-oriented populace who, during the 1920s, agreed
with John J. Raskob that everyone could be rich, led New Yorkers to overlook the fact that their mayor, at best, was indifferent to his duties, incompetent to perform them, and careless with the city's money.

James Michael Curley epitomized Boston just as it was turning away
from the elitism, sometimes called Brahminism, of an earlier time to Curleyism, a kind of shorthand for the political and economic ascendancy of
mainly Irish but of other Americans of recent immigrant origins as well.
Of the four worst mayors, James Michael Curley was probably the biggest
thief but the most able big-city mayor.

But Martin Lomasny, a Boston rival of Curley, succinctly explained to Lincoln Steffens why municipal political corruption exists. What voters want from a politician was not justice but help. "There's got to be in every ward somebody that any bloke can come to—no matter what he's done—and get help. *Help you understand; none of your law and justice, but help.*"[3]

If mayors are more likely to be corruptible than presidents, it is because of the street-level politics with which they deal. They need to be more accessible to the people, and in confronting the daily issues there are likely to be pressures for short-term solutions—improved public transportation, swifter snow removal, cleaner streets, and more parks, playgrounds, public swimming pools, and public schools. Cutting corners, bending rules, looking away, or winking an eye often makes the difference when determining who provides the goods and services a city requires at what price, in what quantity, and at what level of quality.

During prohibition people voted for crooks because of a certain empathy with them. Many Americans, immigrants as well as native born, voted for crooks because they wanted their beer at a local tavern before going home. So they winked and/or gave the password as they entered an illegal saloon (speakeasy). This made them a conspirator in crime, and so they looked the other way at the crime syndicate that transported illegal spirits over the border from Canada or across the Rio Grande from Mexico. They cheered when stills were broken by prohibition law enforcers but then went to the speakeasy for a drink just the same, where they could boast of the vicarious thrill of being an eyewitness to criminal behavior. And they winked further when the "capo" of the mafia "whacked" a police officer or a prohibition agent or a gangland rival.

When "Big Bill" Thompson declared that he could never find perfect people to fill a job and so had to be satisfied with those who were "serviceably sound," he was onto something. Cities, big and small, are run by ordinary men and women who are neither saints nor sinners, people who are simply "serviceably sound" rather than brilliant and who work in an environment filled with temptation for financial gain as the public interest rubs up against the self-interest of a market economy. But the merely "serviceably sound" men and women are not beyond temptation and so are corruptible. Because good people get caught up in questionable practices, one can sympathize with Hamlet when he said, "I am myself indifferent honest, but yet I could accuse me of such things that it were better my mother had not borne me."

In a federal system where political power is shared between the federal government and state and local governments, it is often difficult to determine who does or should do what. When a narrow special interest group needs help, it is often difficult to know which level of formal government can provide it or which will more readily do so. In the vacuum thus often created, a political Svengali, often the leader of a "political machine," steps in and, in exchange for a vote or some similarly important favor, can pave the way toward the solution of an admittedly modest problem but one which is of considerable consequence to the special interest pleader.

People vote for crooks because sometimes good laws are often contradictory. Or, one cannot precisely determine what the law means in practice. What exactly needs to be recycled? Sometimes, a good law is nearly unenforceable. Should the police arrest an elderly woman who illegally feeds pigeons in a public park? Should the police issue a ticket to a person who deposits a bag full of refuse in a city-provided trash can?

A law is sometimes a bad one because unintended consequences flow from it or because it has outlived its usefulness. How many people fall between the cracks of our immigration laws, which are often ambiguous as between someone who is a legitimate immigrant, that is, enters the country under the quota assigned to the country of origin, and the one who is a refugee? Moreover, if the latter, there is a difference in how the immigrant is treated if he or she is a political refugee seeking political asylum from a repressive government abroad or an economic refugee one seeking to better himself or herself by getting a better job.

Similar stories can be told of the seriously ill who fall between the cracks in Medicare or Medicaid and are denied the benefits that modern medicine can provide. People desperately in need of their social security check to pay the rent may find it delayed or not sent as a result of some bureaucratic snafu. Rather than try to untangle the web, why not corrupt an often all-too-willing bureaucrat or get someone else to do so? How tempting it is and has always been in this land of opportunity to "pay off" someone to look the other way. As Lincoln Steffens declared in *The Shame of the Cities,* "The spirit of graft and lawlessness is the American spirit."[4]

People vote for crooks because government is often far away, out of sight, and out of mind. That is, government is in Washington, D.C.; in Albany, New York; Trenton, New Jersey; Chicago, Illinois; and Boston, Massachusetts. To most people government is remote. They recognize government only at the margins, often in the form of a traffic officer, who keeps the traffic flowing and gives tickets to speeders, to illegal parkers, or to those who drive without seatbelts.

Government in the abstract can be clean, but where government touches the people there is always room for judgment. Was the car too near a fire hydrant and so illegally parked? Was the parking meter really working? Does a new home fully conform to fire-safety regulations? Was the seat belt secure? On another level, was the accused really at the site of a crime? Did the accused pull a gun? Thus, where government touches people intimately, there are judgment calls to be made, and these give rise to efforts to tempt law enforcement to look the other way by offering a ticket to a ballgame, cash for lunch, or preferential treatment in a restaurant.

In these circumstances, corruption forms a nexus between a citizen and his or her government. Who hasn't reveled and probably boasted about having had a ticket "fixed?" Or, what homeowner has not smiled inwardly while giving a building inspector a twenty-dollar bill for overlooking a minor violation of the building code in a newly built house? What street food vendor has not slipped the cop on the beat a few dollars or a hot dog with all the trimmings (sauerkraut and mustard) for overlooking the fact that he had poured dirty water into the streets? In truth, a city probably could not function unless some of these allowances are made. The political apparatus of government staffed by legally elected or appointed apparatchiks does not satisfy the incredibly diverse needs of Americans. Because some needs go unmet, a gray area develops which offers a fertile ground in which the seeds of political corruption can grow.

In a letter from Boston dated May 31, 1909, Lincoln Steffens, already prominent for his study of urban America in *The Shame of the Cities,* noted with some frustration, "One of the reasons cities and states and nations and civilizations are in their present situation is that the natural leaders of men in each community ... are not for but against the community.... Their special interests are not identical with the common interest. They run a railroad, provide gas or electricity, or any other public service not to serve the public, but to get dividends, and their reward is proportionate to the degree of their disservice."[5]

People vote for politicians they know to be corrupt because the political machine humanizes and personalizes all manner of assistance to those in need.[6] In the days before the New Deal, it was the political machine of Jersey City, Chicago, New York, or Boston that provided a much-needed bucketful of coal, basket of food, shelter, a temporary job, or even a rent payment. As "transactional" leaders, to use James McGregor Burns's term in his book *Leadership,* these mayors expected only a vote for a favor, loyalty for a job, party discipline for a easing the way to citizenship. In many ways, the corrupt mayors were also "transformational" leaders, again borrowing from Burns, in that as cities grew through migration from farm to city and from foreign shores to America, as employment opportunities vanished and new ones were created, they saw needs that were going unattended well before the reformers did so and quickly moved into the vacuum to ameliorate hardships even if only on a short-term basis. But corrupt mayors, such as those in this book, used their positions to build political support in a self-perpetuating cycle of civic corruption.

"Mornin' Glories": The Limitations of Reform

In 1902, that estimable rogue of Tammany Hall, George Washington Plunkett, pontificated that reformers "were mornin' glories—looked lovely in the mornin' and withered up in a short time, while regular machines went on flourishing forever, like fine old oaks."[7] Cynical though it may sound, Plunkett was right again. Reform movements, important as they are, appear not to have staying power, and for every reform enacted and put into place, there will be those who will take the initiative and find a way around the reform.

It is probably safe to say that no project — building a subway, developing a new highway network, constructing a bridge, or dredging a port — has had a virgin birth. Somehow, somewhere, someone has been paid off. But the question that also must be asked is whether the additional cost of construction is worth the *quid pro quo* by giving additional encouragement to builders and contractors to undertake risky financial, architectural, or construction projects they might prefer to avoid.[8]

Reform movements are "mornin' glories" precisely because there is no uniform agreement on what corruption is, how bad it is, or how much reform is needed. Throwing the rascals out is often more difficult than it appears and highlights the limitations of reforming American politics, especially at the municipal level, by making its political officials more accountable and its procedures more transparent to voters and taxpayers. If reformers are too conscientious and impose restrictions on what public officials may or may not do, they make of these public servants a group apart, and so people with unusual capacity, innovative ideas, and unconventional insights into political problems shun government and leave the public sector impoverished of talent. To the extent that employees in the public sector must behave substantially different from those in the private sector, to that extent public service becomes an activity with few privileges and many burdens. Those who work in the vineyard of government bear many obligations with which their opposites in the private sector need not concern themselves.

Political bosses, in the tradition of the worst mayors described in this book, are now few in number, and those that exist are both less colorful and less powerful. But, to the extent that each new bureau for highways, public health, welfare, parks, public works, water supply, hospitals, schools, street cleaning, fire, police, public transportation, or taxi regulation has a chief or career commissioner, many bosses must be dealt with to get anything done in the modern city, and mayors can no longer be certain that they will have the loyalty of the bureaucratic bosses who allegedly report to them. Reform does not abolish political power, but it does alter what one has to do to get it. "The legacy of reform," according to Theodore J. Lowi, "is the bureaucratic state."[9]

Good-government reformers, "Goo-Goos" as they are derisively called, are widely believed to be undemocratic in outlook and have their roots among the civic elites and not among people of humble origins. Reformers, in the eyes of many urban Americans, stand for efficiency, meritocracy, dominance of business methods, and preference of the native born not for the American of immigrant origins. Forces for "good government" generally seek to limit immigration, to delay admission to United States citizenship, and to limit the franchise by making voting a privilege for the relatively few rather than a right for the many.

Most reform proposals, such as civil service examinations for those seeking positions as firefighters, police officers, social workers, letter carriers, and cleaning and custodial help, seem to put in place an obstacle to achieving a modest enough job. There is an application to be made out, usually in the English language, a technique for taking an examination to be learned, and an arbitrary level of schooling to have been achieved. So-called corrupt mayors, on the other hand, look precisely to these positions as a means by which they can build a voting constituency, a system of patronage that will build loyalty to person or party. Thus, they take short-cuts; they see what the masses need and appear to provide it with few obstacles. Political machines tend to moderate class conflicts and transform politics into personal relationships, "humanizing and personalizing all manner of assistance to those in need."[10] Thus, the political machine is there "when a feller needs a friend."

None of this is to suggest that reform efforts are unimportant. Political corruption, like crabgrass, cannot be eliminated altogether and, as we have seen, may even have unintended desirable consequences. But political corruption can and must be constantly monitored and controlled as best it can. In the American political system of checks and balances, reform efforts toward "good government" check runaway political corruption which erodes the body politic, drives men and women of integrity from government service, undermines the quality of life in a community, destroys confidence in political institutions, and discourages participation in democratic processes. Monies derived from grants and taxation may be misallocated; city contracts for construction may be awarded to incompetent firms; and municipal safety may be adversely impacted if licenses to inadequately trained drivers are awarded on the basis of bribes rather than demonstrated skill.

Corruption exists because politics exists, but the former needs to be kept at bay so that the latter does not remain a dirty word. Reformers keep the feet of politicians to the fire of public opinion. Reform movements test the mettle of those who would serve in government and create a climate of public service that makes it at once an occupation of honor, dignity, and pride. In each of the administrations of America's four worst mayors, a line was crossed so that the community itself was besmirched, as ordinary men and women began to sense that the wave of corruption appeared to overwhelm their cities and needed to be curbed. Chicagoans often felt embarrassed that they lived in a city with "Big Bill" as mayor, and New Yorkers, after a while, laughed at, not with, Jimmy Walker. And so, they "blew the whistle" on Messers Thompson, Hague, Walker, and Curley.

The Whistle-Blowers

When corruption gets out of hand it takes a "whistle-blower" to identify sources of corruption, coalesce the organizations choosing reform, call the corruptors to account in some kind of judicial proceeding or public hearing, and demonstrate that corruption is less efficient and more costly than correctness. Whistle-blowers channel a community's frustration, impotence, and outrage into strategies that can succeed in "throwing the rascals out."

In New York City, Judge Samuel Seabury blew the whistle on Jimmy Walker. New York's governor, Franklin D. Roosevelt, would have preferred to leave Jimmy Walker alone so as to assure himself of the support of Tammany to further his presidential ambitions. However, Roosevelt's laid-back attitude toward corruption in New York City could not be sustained. The Citizens Union, the City Club, and other organizations were clamoring for political reform, and Roosevelt had to get out in front of the reform crowd and become the whistle-blower of last resort and encourage Judge Seabury to accumulate evidence of corrupt practices in nearly every branch of the government of New York City. Because of the Seabury investigations, Walker would be swept aside, and Fiorello La Guardia would be elected New York's reform mayor.

Chicagoans did not quickly drive their mayor, William Hale Thompson, from Illinois politics. Instead, his was a long goodbye. America's worst mayor, "Big Bill the Builder," was clearly exposed for political corruption in the 1923 trial of Fred Lundin, the poor Swede, who early on saw the possibilities of being the power behind Thompson's mayoralty. Chicagoans named them the "Gallagher and Shean of Chicago politics," after the popular vaudeville comedians of the day.[11] But, in 1923, despite a falling out between the two men, Thompson, now out of office after two consecutive terms as Chicago's mayor, returned from a vacation in Hawaii to help Clarence Darrow defend his erstwhile political mentor from charges of having accepted kickbacks from the Chicago Public School Board and for overcharging Chicago's schools for supplies and building materials and thereby waxing rich from ill-gotten gains. With a straight face, without a trace of outrage, Thompson testified on behalf of his former political ally so that the charges against Lundin were dismissed. Chicagoans, however, recognized that justice had been miscarried and that Lundin was merely a surrogate for equally damning charges against the mayor himself.

Chicagoans were not yet ready to blow the whistle on their mayor. Although "Big Bill" would be elected mayor once again, his campaign techniques became increasingly vituperative, his campaign speeches increasingly coarse, vulgar, and profane, and his promises ever more rash and scarcely to be believed. The reason it took so long for Chicagoans to "blow the whistle" on Mayor Thompson was that in his belly he understood that, to the mass of Americans, politics is a game, a spectacle, a means of recreation, and that the prizes of electoral victory go to the best performers. So Chicagoans forgave William Hale Thompson, "America's master political showman."[12]

By 1931, showmanship failed Thompson when he lost election to Democrat Anton Cermak. But, as he fell from grace, he left a legacy of open warfare on the streets among criminal gangs, the near bankruptcy of Chicago's financial structure, tax revolt, a revolving door among police commissioners, and charges of graft in his administration estimated at $30 million a year.[13]

Thompson became increasingly demagogic in an attempt to remain an actor in Chicago's political drama. In 1931, he attacked the Jewish businessman and philanthropist Julius Rosenwald, not because he was rich but because he was Jewish, and, in 1936, he continued his demagoguery by entertaining the Chicago Nazi Clubs by speaking at their picnic, in which he vilified "Reds and Jewish Bankers."[14]

It took a strong and well-disciplined Democratic Party to unseat Thompson. But, by the time they did so, Chicagoans were tired of their mayor, embarrassed by his excesses, nauseated at his open association with the hoodlums of organized crime, and well aware that this was not the mayor to steer them through the rough eddies of the Great Depression in which Chicago, like the rest of the country, endured. Nor was he the man to represent them in the forthcoming World's Fair, "A Century of Progress."

When, in April 1945, President Franklin Roosevelt died, Curley remarked, "Well, the son-of-a-bitch is dead." Little wonder that Curley felt this way in that the whistle-blower in Curley's case was none other than the president of the United States, who refused to intervene when Curley was charged as president of the Engineers' Group of using the postal service to defraud the government. Although the whistle-blower had been the president of the United States, Curley could not be pushed off the political stage where he felt most comfortable.

"Curley, in his prime, was an intelligent and forceful executive who conducted the city's business with vigor and competence."[15] Irrespective of his reputation as a corrupt politician, what James Michael Curley did for Boston's Irish was to give them control of that city's political machinery and the economic as well as political mobility such control made possible. He offered opportunities for lower-class Irish to advance that respectable channels denied them. But, by the time he got through with Boston, after his four, nonconsecutive terms as its mayor, Boston would never again be William Bradford's "City upon a Hill." But, then again, was it ever; and did anyone care?

James Michael Curley would go on to serve in Congress as well as mayor of Boston but increasingly, as Boston's Irish became more sophisticated and better educated, Curley became irrelevant and an embarrassment. With Curley as mayor, Boston received less and less of New Deal funds, which other cities sought to ease the burden of relief and recovery from the Depression. Without an important industrial base, Boston also had few war-related industries to absorb the unemployed. Thus, James Michael Curley was caught in a vise of his own making. His charismatic qualities began to lose their charm, and Boston's poor began to recognize that while Curley's oratory may have been fine and made them feel better, they were still poor. It was not that FDR was hostile to bossism in urban politics, but the wily president doubted Curley's loyalty and questioned his ability to deliver the votes of Boston or of Massachusetts to Roosevelt. Mayor Hague, America's second-worst mayor, was left alone by Roosevelt, who cynically allowed him to get away with political practices of unquestioned dishonesty because he could be relied upon to deliver Jersey City's and, indeed, all of New Jersey's vote.

Jack Beatty, Curley's biographer, summarizes his hero's life: "He spent his final years dying in the glow of his own fame as a funny, lovable, for-givably, roguish last-of-a-kind, having lived a politician, he died a celebrity."[16]

A common characteristic among America's four worst mayors is that they stayed politically active too long. None was readily weaned from the political stage they enjoyed so much. If Thompson was burlesque, Hague was vaudeville, Walker was comedy, and Curley tragedy. All were hypno-tized by the political offices they held, by the adulation of the voters, by the seemingly unending reach of their powers, by their own egos that led them to believe that they could live beyond the rules of political stagecraft. By being both producer and director they thought they could manipulate the voting audience by their whims, and all were astonished that, in the end, they could not do so.

As a result, all had to be pulled off the political stage, and all went rather ungracefully and ungraciously. None could believe that having mes-merized the voters once, they could mesmerize them seemingly forever. If, given the nature of politics, corruption offers some benign compensation, it was a mistake for the four worst mayors to assume that their activities were altogether beyond the reach of reformers. But, the voters were them-selves the main reformers, the real "whistle-blowers," as they grew in sophis-tication, education, and political maturity. It is in the nature of democracy to demand much of the voter, and despite the fact that at times it seems that American voters will never grow up, the fact remains that they do.

The emphasis in the fight against corruption in the past has depended upon the sagacity of reform-minded individuals and groups to provide some correction to the shoddy practices of corrupt politicians. But their achievements are rarely permanent. Today, the battle against political cor-ruption takes a more subtle approach by emphasizing ethics in politics and encouraging those who would act on the political stage to bring with them inner strength, security, and incorruptible integrity so that what they do and what they urge others to do are derived from their better natures and not from the day-to-day compromises that are the warp and woof of pol-itics. "Old-time" mayors like James Michael Curley, Jimmy Walker, "Big Bill" Thompson, and Frank Hague exploited the immigrant, the newcomer, the jobless, and the homeless to perpetuate themselves in power. "Old-time" mayors used tawdry means for tawdry ends— namely, to keep feed-ing from the public trough. "New-time" mayors, though no less political than their corrupt predecessors, use their offices to open new lines of con-tact with the urban masses and to offer solutions rather than promises and speak from their better natures to the better natures of the voters who elected them.

Notes

Preface

1. Melvin G. Holli, *The American Mayor: The Best and the Worst Big-City Leaders*, University Park: The Pennsylvania State University Press, 1999.
2. James Q. Wilson, "Corruption Is Not Always Scandalous," in J. A. Gardiner and D. J. Olson, *Theft of the City: Readings in Corruption*, Bloomington: Indiana University Press, 1968, p. 32.

Prologue

1. Quoted in Lloyd Wendt and Herman Kogan, *Big Bill of Chicago*, Indianapolis: The Bobbs-Merrill Company, Inc., p. 357.
2. "'Big Bill' Thompson Is Dead in Chicago," *The New York Times*, March 20, 1944.
3. Quoted in Wendt and Kogan, *op. cit.*, p. 358.
4. "When the Big Boy Goes," *Time* 67 (January 16, 1956): 19.
5. *The New York Times*, November 19, 1946.
6. Gene Fowler, *Beau James: The Life and Times of Jimmy Walker*, Clifton, N.J.: Augustus M. Kelley Publishers, 1973, p. 379.
7. Quoted in Herbert Mitgang, *Once Upon a Time in New York*, New York: The Free Press, 2000, p. 229.

8. Jack Beatty, *The Rascal King: The Life and Times of James Michael Curley*, Reading, Mass: Addison-Wesley Publishing Company, 1992, p. 3.
9. Francis Russell, "The Last of the Bosses," *American Heritage* 10 (June 1959): 91.

Chapter 1

1. William Allen White, *Masks in a Pageant*, New York: The Macmillan Company, 1930, pp. 484–485.
2. *Ibid.*, p. 486.
3. Lloyd Wendt and Herman Kogan, *Big Bill of Chicago*, Indianapolis: The Bobbs-Merrill Company, 1953, pp. 20–21.
4. *Ibid.*, p. 30.
5. Quoted in *ibid.* p. 33.

Chapter 2

1. John Bright, *Hizzoner Big Bill Thompson: An Idyll of Chicago*, New York: Jonathan Cape & Harrison Smith, 1930, p. 14.
2. Quoted in Lloyd Wendt and Herman Kogan, *Big Bill of Chicago*, Indianapolis: The Bobbs-Merrill Company, 1953, p. 39.
3. Quoted in Reinhard H. Luthin,

American Demagogues, Boston: The Beacon Press, 1954, p. 79.

4. Quoted in Wendt and Kogan, *op. cit.*, p. 41.

5. Quoted in Luthin, *op. cit.*, p. 80.

6. Quoted in Wendt and Kogan, *op. cit.*, p. 43.

7. *Ibid.*, p. 44.

8. *Ibid.*, pp. 48–49.

9. In Bill Thompson's day, United States Senators were chosen by state legislatures rather than by popular vote.

10. Quoted in Wendt and Kogan, *op. cit.*, pp. 82–83.

11. Quoted in Bright, *op. cit.*, p. 17.

12. Quoted in Wendt and Kogan, *op. cit.*, p. 87.

13. *Ibid.*

14. *Ibid.*, p. 88.

15. Bright, *op. cit.*, p. 65.

16. Quoted in Wendt and Kogan, *op. cit.*, p. 120.

Chapter 3

1. Quoted in Douglas Bukowski, *Big Bill Thompson, Chicago, and the Politics of Image*, Urbana and Chicago: University of Illinois Press, 1998, p. 37.

2. *Ibid.*

3. Quoted in Lloyd Wendt and Herman Kogan, *Big Bill of Chicago*, Indianapolis: The Bobbs-Merrill Company, 1953, p. 123.

4. Quoted in Douglas Bukowski, "Big Bill Thompson: The 'Model' Politician," in Paul M. Green and Melvin G. Holli (eds.), *The Mayors: The Chicago Political Tradition*, Carbondale: Southern Illinois University Press, 1987, p. 64.

5. Quoted in Wendt and Kogan, *op. cit.*, p. 128.

6. *Ibid.*, p. 126.

7. Richard H. Luthin, *American Demagogues: Twentieth Century*, Boston: The Beacon Press, 1954, p. 86.

8. *Ibid.*

9. Quoted in Bukowski, "Big Bill

Thompson: The 'Model' Politician," p. 66.

10. Quoted in Elmer Davis, "Portrait of an Elected Person," *Harper's Magazine* 155 (July 1927): 177.

11. Quoted in James R. Grossman, *Land of Hope: Chicago, Black Southerners, and the Great Migration*, Chicago: University of Chicago Press, p. 119.

12. *Ibid.*, p. 117.

13. Oscar De Priest left Alabama for Chicago in 1889. He became the first African-American alderman and in 1928 became the first Northern African-American to be elected to Congress.

14. Quoted in John M. Allswang, "The Chicago Negro Voter and the Democratic Consensus: A Case Study, 1918–1936, *Journal of the Illinois State Historical Society* LX (Summer 1967): 154.

15. Bukowski, "Big Bill Thompson: The 'Model' Politician," p. 71.

16. Quoted in Allswang, *op. cit.*, p. 157.

17. *Chicago Defender*, March 5, 1927.

18. Quoted in Wendt and Kogan, *op. cit.*, p. 163.

19. *Ibid.*, pp. 170–171.

20. *Ibid.*, p. 171.

21. *Ibid.*, p. 189.

22. *Ibid.*, pp. 189–190.

23. Quoted in Robert Morse Lovett, "'Big Bill' Thompson of Chicago," *Current History* 1934 (June 1931): 380.

24. Quoted in Wendt and Kogan, *op. cit.*, p. 311.

25. *Ibid.*, p. 198.

26. See Wendt and Kogan, pp. 207–221, for the testimony in this section.

27. Quoted in John Bright, *Hizzoner Big Bill Thompson: An Idyll of Chicago*, New York: Jonathan Cape and Harrison Smith, 1930, p. 198.

Chapter 4

1. Quoted in Lloyd Wendt and Herman Kogan, *Big Bill of Chicago*, Indianapolis: The Bobbs-Merrill Company, 1953, p. 215.

2. *Ibid.*, p. 223.

3. *Chicago Herald-Examiner,* February 23, 1926.

4. Quoted in Wendt and Kogen, *op. cit.,* p. 225.

5. *Ibid.*, p. 227.

6. *Ibid.*

7. Reinhard H. Luthin, *American Demagogues: Twentieth Century,* Boston: The Beacon Press, 1954, pp. 77–78.

8. Quoted in Wendt and Kogan, *op. cit.,* p. 243.

9. *Ibid.*, p. 248.

10. *Chicago Tribune,* March 23, 1927.

11. Quoted in George C. Hoffman, *Big Bill Thompson: His Mayoral Campaigns and Voting Strength,* M.A. thesis, The University of Chicago, 1956, p. 37.

12. Quoted in Hoffman, *op. cit.,* p. 38.

13. Quoted in Wendt and Kogan, *op. cit.,* p. 257.

14. Quoted in Elmer Davis, "Portrait of an Elected Person," *Harper's Magazine* 155 (July 1927): 183.

15. Quoted in Douglas Bukowski, *Big Bill Thompson, Chicago, and the Politics of Image,* Urbana and Chicago: University of Illinois Press, 1998, p. 185.

16. *The New York Times,* November 5, 1927.

17. Luthin, *op. cit.,* p. 96.

18. Bukowski, *op. cit.,* p. 220.

19. *Ibid.*, p. 221.

20. *Ibid.*

21. Wendt and Kogan, *op. cit.,* pp. 281–283.

22. William H. Stuart, *Twenty Incredible Years,* Chicago: M.A. Donohue, 1935, p. 295.

23. *The New York Times,* November 5, 1927.

24. Wendt and Kogan, *op. cit.,* p. 295.

25. Quoted in Dennis Thompson, "The Private Wars of Chicago's Big Bill Thompson," *Journal of Library History* 15 (Summer 1980): 269.

26. Quoted in Wendt and Kogan, *op. cit.,* p. 302.

27. William Hale Thompson, "Are We Victims of British Propaganda?" *The Forum* LXXIX, p. 505.

28. John Bright, *Hizzoner Big Bill Thompson: An Idyll of Chicago,* New York: Jonathan Cape & Harrison Smith, 1930, p. 269.

29. Quoted in Dennis Thompson, *op. cit.,* p. 271.

30. *Ibid.*

31. Quoted in Wendt and Kogan, *op. cit.,* p. 289.

32. *The New York Times,* October 25, 1927.

33. Luthin, *op. cit.,* p. 98.

34. *Ibid.*, p. 99.

35. *Ibid.*

36. *Ibid.*

37. This and the following quotes are quoted in Wendt and Kogan, *op. cit.,* pp. 329–330.

38. Quoted in Mary J. Herrick, *The Chicago Schools: A Social and Political History,* Beverly Hills: Sage Publications, 1971, p. 172.

39. Wendt and Kogan, *op. cit.,* p. 337.

40. Quoted in Wendt and Kogan, *op. cit.,* p. 344.

41. *Ibid.*

42. *Ibid.*, p. 347.

43. Quoted in Bukowski, *op. cit.,* p. 253.

44. *Ibid.*

45. Quoted in Wendt and Kogan, *op. cit.,* p. 355.

46. *Ibid.*, p. 356.

47. *Chicago Daily News,* March 20, 1944.

Chapter 5

1. Thomas F. X. Smith, *The Powertricians,* Secaucus, N.J.: Lyle Stuart, 1982, p. 34.

2. McCarten, *op. cit.,* p. 72.

3. David Dayton McKean, *The Boss: The Hague Machine in Action,* Boston: Houghton Mifflin Company, 1940, p. 35.

4. *Ibid.*

5. Quoted in *ibid.*, p. 39.

6. McCarten, *op. cit.,* p. 69.

7. Quoted in Reinhard H. Luthin,

American Demagogues: Twentieth Century, Boston: The Beacon Press, 1954, p. 128.

8. Quoted in Luthin, *op. cit.*, pp. 127–128.

9. Fleming, *op. cit.*, p. 33.

10. Luthin, *op. cit.*, p. 136.

11. McKean, *op. cit.*, p. 5.

12. *Ibid.*, p. 7.

13. *Ibid.*, p.9.

14. Quoted in Luthin, *op. cit.*, p. 141.

15. *Ibid.*

16. McKean, *op. cit.*, p. 15.

Chapter 6

1. Richard J. Connors, *A Cycle of Power: The Career of Jersey City Mayor Frank Hague*, Metuchen, N.J.: The Scarecrow Press, 1971, p. 34.

2. David Dayton McKean, *The Boss: The Hague Machine in Action*, Boston: Houghton Mifflin Company, 1940, p. 4.

3. Quoted in Russell B. Porter, "Portrait of a 'Dictator' Jersey City Style," *The New York Times Magazine* (February 13, 1938): 16.

4. Quoted in Connors, *op. cit.*, pp. 57–58.

5. *Ibid.*, p. 63.

6. Thomas J. Fleming, "I Am the Law," *American Heritage* XX (June 1969): 37.

7. Quoted in McKean, *op. cit.*, p. 136.

8. Quoted in Fleming, *op. cit.*, p. 38.

9. Quoted in McKean, *op. cit.*, p. 51.

10. *Ibid.*, p. 53.

11. Charles W. Van Devander, *The Big Bosses*, New York: Howell, Soskins, Publishers, 1944, p. 93.

12. McKean, *op. cit.*, p. 207.

13. Quoted in *ibid.*, p. 178.

14. John McCarten, "Evolution of a Problem Child," in *Profiles from The New Yorker*, New York: Alfred A. Knopf, 1938, p. 66.

15. McKean, *op. cit.*, p. 167.

16. *Ibid.*, p. 176.

17. Quoted in Reinhard H. Luthin,

American Demagogues, Boston: The Beacon Press, 1954, p. 141.

18. Quoted in Fleming, *op. cit.*, p. 38.

19. McKean, *op. cit.*, p. 178.

20. McCarten, *op. cit.*, p. 66.

21. Fleming, *op. cit.*, p. 36.

22. McKean, *op. cit.*, p. 181.

23. J. Owen Grundy, *The History of Jersey City*, Jersey City Chamber of Commerce, 1976, p. 56.

24. Quoted in McCarten, *op. cit.*, p. 68.

25. Quoted in McKean, *op. cit.*, p. 218.

26. John Kincaid, *Political Success and Policy Failure: The Persistence of Machine Politics in Jersey City*, Ph.D. dissertation, Temple University, December 1980, p. 451.

27. Quoted in *ibid.*, p. 465.

28. Quoted in McKean, *op. cit.*, p. 96.

29. Quoted in Richard Oulahan, *The Man Who ... The Story of the 1932 Democratic Convention*, New York: The Dial Press, 1971, p. 76.

30. Quoted in Lyle W. Dorsett, "Frank Hague, Franklin Roosevelt and the Politics of the New Deal," *New Jersey History* 94 (Spring 1976): 27.

31. McKean, *op. cit.*, p. 103.

32. Quoted in *ibid.*

33. *Ibid.*

34. Quoted in Sutherland Denlinger, "Boss Hague," *Forum* XCIX (March 1938): 137.

35. Quoted in McKean, *op. cit.*, p. 199.

Chapter 7

1. Quoted in Dayton David McKean, *The Boss: The Hague Machine in Action*, Boston: Houghton Mifflin Company, 1940, p. 80.

2. Quoted in Denis Tilden Lynch, "Her Honor, The Mayor of Washington," *Literary Digest* 119 (March 30, 1935): 24.

3. Quoted in Gary Mitchell, "Women Standing for Women: The Early Political Career of Mary T. Norton," in *New Jersey History* XCVI (Spring-Summer 1978): 27.

4. Dayton David McKean, "Frank Hague," in J.T. Salter (ed.), *Public Men in and Out of Office*, Chapel Hill: The University of North Carolina Press, 1946, p. 451.

5. Quoted in Reinhard H. Luthin, *American Demagogues: Twentieth Century*, Boston: The Beacon Press, 1954, p. 146.

6. *Ibid.*

7. McKean, "Frank Hague," p. 452.

8. *Ibid.*, p. 453.

9. Quoted in Luthin, *op. cit.*, p. 147.

10. *Ibid.*, p. 148.

11. *Ibid.*, p. 150.

12. Quoted in Thomas J. Fleming, "I Am the Law," *American Heritage* XX (June 1969): 45.

13. *Ibid.*

14. McKean, "Frank Hague," p. 454.

15. Willard Wiener, "Hague Is the Law," *New Republic* 110 (January 31, 1944): 145.

16. Richard J. Connors, *A Cycle of Power: The Career of Jersey City Mayor Frank Hague*, Metuchen, N.J.: The Scarecrow Press, 1971, p. 165.

17. John Gunther, *Inside U.S.A.*, New York: Harper and Brothers, 1947, p. 591.

18. Charles W. Van Devander, *The Big Bosses*, Howell, Soskins, Publishers, 1944, p. 105.

19. Dayton David McKean, "The Worst American City," *The American Mercury* LII (February 1941): 212.

20. *Ibid.*, p. 213.

21. *Ibid.*

22. *Newark Sunday Call*, September 22, 1946, p. 4.

23. Sir Walter Scott, "Lay of the Last Minstrel."

Chapter 8

1. Gene Fowler, *Beau James: The Life and Times of Jimmy Walker*, Walker, Clifton, N.J.: Augustus M. Kelley Publishers, 1973, original edition published by Viking Press, 1949 (see notes 1 in Ch. 9 and Ch. 10.), p. 12.

2. Quoted in *ibid.*, p. 13.

3. *Ibid.*, p. 14.

4. Quoted in Louis J. Gribetz and Joseph Kaye, *Jimmy Walker: The Story of a Personality*, New York: Dial Press, 1932, p. 23.

5. Quoted in Fowler, *op. cit.*, p. 58.

6. Quoted in Gribetz and Kaye, *op. cit.*, p. 50.

7. *Ibid.*, p. 51.

8. Quoted in Fowler, *op. cit.*, p. 65.

9. Quoted in Warren Moscow, "Jimmy Walker's City Hall," *New York Times Magazine* (August 22, 1976): 33.

10. Quoted in Fowler, *op. cit.*, pp. 71–72.

11. Quoted in Charles W. Van Devander, *The Big Bosses*, New York: Howell, Soskin Publishers, 1944, p. 12.

12. Quoted in Gribetz and Kaye, *op. cit.*, p. 57.

13. *Ibid.*, p. 58.

14. Fowler, *op. cit.*, p. 74.

15. *Ibid.*, pp. 76–77.

16. Henry F. Pringle, "Portrait of a Mayor at Large," *Harpers Magazine* 150 (February 1928): 316.

17. Quoted in Fowler, *op. cit.*, p. 106.

18. Henry F. Pringle, "Jimmy Walker," *American Mercury* IX (November 1926): 277.

19. Quoted in Alva Johnston, "Profiles; No More Lawyers: George W. Olvany," *The New Yorker* (January 9, 1932): 22.

20. Quoted in Fowler, *op. cit.*, p. 147.

21. Quoted in W. A. Swanberg, *Norman Thomas: The Last Idealist*, New York: Charles Scribner's Sons, 1976, pp. 99–100.

22. Quoted in Harry Fleischman, *Norman Thomas: A Biography: 1884–1968*, New York: W.W. Norton, 1964, p. 104.

23. Fowler, *op. cit.*, p. 152.

Chapter 9

1. Gene Fowler, *Beau James: The Life and Times of Jimmy Walker*, Clifton, N.J.: Augustus M. Kelley Publishers, 1973,

original edition published by Viking Press, 1949, p. 160.

2. "Talking through Silk Shirts," *The New York Times,* January 4, 1926.

3. "Text of Walker's Inauguration Address," *The New York Times,* January 2, 1926.

4. *Ibid.*

5. *The New York Times,* January 4, 1926.

6. Quoted in Fowler, *op. cit.,* p. 190.

7. Henry F. Pringle, "Jimmy Walker," *The American Mercury* IX (November 1926): 272.

8. Quoted in Fowler, *op. cit.,* p. 86.

9. *Ibid.,* pp. 91–92.

10. *Ibid.,* pp. 164–165.

11. Jeff Kisseloff, *You Must Remember This: An Oral History of Manhattan from the 1890s to World War II,* New York: Harcourt, Brace, Jovanovich, 1989, p. 591.

12. Warren Moscow, "The Legend of Jimmy Walker," *Chief Leader* (July 12, 1985): 6.

13. Warren Moscow, "Jimmy Walker's City Hall," *The New York Times Magazine,* August 22, 1976, p. 33.

14. Thomas J. Fleming, "Was It Ever Fun Being Mayor?" *New York* (November 10, 1969): 38.

15. F. Scott Fitzgerald, *The Great Gatsby,* New York: Charles Scribner's Sons, 1925, p. 63.

16. Joseph McGoldrick, "The New Tammany," *The American Mercury* XV (September 1928): 8.

17. *Ibid.,* p. 9.

18. Moscow, "Jimmy Walker's City Hall," p. 32.

19. McGoldrick, *op. cit.,* pp. 11–12.

20. "A New Regime at City Hall," *The Searchlight* XVI (April 1926): 1.

21. McGoldrick, *op. cit.,* p. 11.

22. *Ibid.*

23. "A New Regime at City Hall," *op. cit.,* p. 3.

24. Quoted in "Personal Glimpses: His Honor, 'Jimmy' Walker, Mayor of Europe," *Literary Digest* XCV (October 28, 1927): 39.

25. Quoted in *ibid.,* p. 40.

26. *Ibid.*

27. Quoted in Hector Fuller, *Abroad with Mayor Walker,* New York: Shields Publishing Company, 1928, p. 61.

28. Henry F. Pringle, "Portrait of a Mayor-at-Large," *Harpers Magazine* 156 (February 1929): 313.

29. Quoted in George Walsh, *Gentleman Jimmy Walker: Mayor of the Jazz Age,* New York: Praeger, 1974, p. 131.

30. "Amazing Mayor Early at Work on First Day at Home," *The New York Evening Post,* September 28, 1927, p. 1.

31. Quoted in Thomas J. Fleming, "The First of the Celebrity Mayors," *New York Magazine,* November 10, 1969, p. 42.

32. Fowler, *op. cit.,* p. 243.

33. Quoted in Fowler, *op. cit.,* p. 244.

34. "The City Election," *The Searchlight* XIX (September 1929): 3.

35. "The Mayorality Circus," *The Nation* 129 (October, 23, 1929): 455.

36. Quoted in Fowler, *op. cit.,* p. 245.

37. *Ibid.,* p. 257.

38. Thomas Kessner, *Fiorello H. La Guardia and the Making of Modern New York,* New York: McGraw-Hill, 1989, p. 200.

Chapter 10

1. Quoted in Gene Fowler, *Beau James: The Life and Times of Jimmy Walker,* Clifton, N.J.: Augustus M. Kelly Publishers, 1973, original edition published by Viking Press in 1949, p. 187.

2. "Walker's Administration Turbulent, but Mayor Maintained Wide Popularity," *The New York Times,* September 2, 1932, p. 7.

3. George Walsh, *Gentleman Jimmy Walker: Mayor of the Jazz Age,* New York: Praeger, 1974, p. 107.

4. Quoted in *ibid.,* p. 108.

5. Quoted in Thomas Kessner, *Fiorello H. La Guardia and the Making of Modern New York,* New York: McGraw-Hill, 1989, p. 214.

6. Robert A. Caro, *The Power Broker: Robert Moses and the Fall of New York*, New York: Alfred A. Knopf, 1974, p. 331.

7. *Ibid.*

8. Kessner, *op. cit.*, p. 207.

9. Walsh, *op. cit.*, p. 190.

10. Quoted in Robert A. Caro, *op. cit.*, pp. 338–339.

11. Herbert Mitgang, *Once Upon a Time in New York*, New York: The Free Press, 2000, p. 2.

12. Quoted in Walsh, *op. cit.*, p. 132.

13. Quoted in Kessner, *op. cit.*, pp. 459–460.

14. Fowler, *op. cit.*, pp. 220–221.

15. Thomas H. Gammack, "Trouble Under the Ground," *Outlook and Independent* 151 (April 24, 1929): 653.

16. Quoted in "The Nickel Wins in the Supreme Court," *The Literary Digest* (April 20, 1929): 13.

17. Caro, *op. cit.*, p. 326.

18. Kessner, *op. cit.*, p. 211.

19. Norman Thomas and Paul Blanshard, *What's the Matter with New York: A National Problem*, New York: Macmillan, 1932, p. 41.

20. Kessner, *op. cit.*, p. 211.

21. *Ibid.*, p. 207.

22. Caro, *op. cit.*, pp. 335–336.

23. *Ibid.*, p. 328.

24. Quoted in Walsh, *op. cit.*, p. 208.

25. *The New York Times*, January 3, 1930.

26. Walsh, *op. cit.*, p. 223.

27. Quoted in Thomas J. Fleming, "Was It Ever Fun Being Mayor?" *New York* (November 10, 1969): 42.

28. Milton MacKay, *The Tin Box Parade: A Handbook for Larceny*, New York: Robert M. McBride, 1934, p. 29.

29. Quoted in Fowler, *op. cit.*, p. 288.

30. Quoted in Herbert Mitgang, *The Man Who Rode the Tiger: The Life and Times of Judge Samuel Seabury*, New York: The Fordham University Press, 1996, originally published by Lipincott, Philadelphia, 1963, p. 176.

31. Quoted in Mackay, *op. cit.*, p. 35.

32. William Northrop, *The Insolence of Office*, New York: G.P. Putnam & Sons, 1932, p. 27.

33. Quoted in Walsh, *op. cit.*, p. 236.

34. Quoted in Mitgang, *The Man Who Rode the Tiger*, *op. cit*, p. 200.

35. *Ibid.*, p. 201.

36. Quoted in *ibid.*, pp. 213–214.

37. *Ibid.*, p. 219.

38. Quoted in Walsh, *op. cit.*, p. 302.

39. *Ibid.*, p. 302.

40. Quoted in Mitgang, *Once Upon a Time in New York*, *op. cit.*, p. 148.

41. *Ibid.*, p. 144.

42. Walsh, *op. cit.*, pp. 306–307.

43. *Ibid.*, p. 308.

44. Quoted in *ibid.*, p. 308

45. *Ibid.*, p. 313.

46. Quoted in Fowler, *op. cit.*, p. 313.

47. *Ibid.*, p. 313.

Chapter 11

1. *The New York Times*, September 2, 1932.

2. Quoted in Herbert Mitgang, *Once Upon a Time in New York*, New York: The Free Press, 2000, p. 209.

3. Quoted in *The Literary Digest* (August 13, 1932): 7.

4. *Ibid.*

5. Quoted in Norman Thomas and Paul Blanshard, *What's the Matter with New York: A National Problem*, Appendix II, New York: Macmillan, 1932, p. 350.

6. Quoted in *ibid.*, pp. 350–355.

7. Mitgang, *op. cit.*, p. 170.

8. Quoted in *ibid.*, pp. 169–171.

9. Quoted in Fowler, *op. cit.*, p. 323.

10. *Ibid.*

11. *Ibid.*, p. 324.

12. *Ibid.*, p. 325.

13. *Ibid.*

14. *The New York Times*, September 2, 1932.

15. *Ibid.*

16. Quoted in George Walsh, *Gentleman Jimmy Walker: Mayor of the Jazz Age*, New York: Praeger, 1974, p. 331.

17. Quoted in *ibid.*, p. 333.

18. *Ibid.*, pp. 335–336.
19. Quoted in *ibid.*, p. 337.
20. *Ibid.*, p. 338.
21. Quoted in *ibid.*, p. 339.
22. *Ibid.*, p. 340.
23. *Ibid.*
24. Quoted in *ibid.*, p. 40.
25. Thomas and Blanshard, *op. cit.*, p. 162.
26. *Ibid.*, pp. 162–165.
27. Wallace S. Sayer and Herbert Kaufman, *Governing New York City: Politics in the Metropolis*, New York: Russell Sage Foundation, 1960, p. 697.

Chapter 12

1. Quoted in Peter K. Eisinger, "Ethnic Political Transition in Boston, 1884–1933: Some Lessons for Contemporary Cities," *Political Science Quarterly* 93 (Summer 1978): 220.
2. Eisinger, *op. cit.*, p. 224.
3. John Gunther, *Inside U.S.A.*, New York: Harper & Brothers, 1947, p. 476.
4. James Michael Curley, *I'd Do It Again: A Record of My Uproarious Years*, Englewood Cliffs, N.J.: Prentice-Hall, 1957, p. 38.
5. *Ibid.*, p. 41.
6. *Ibid.*, p. 46.
7. George E. Reedy, *From the Ward to the Whitehouse: The Irish in American Politics*, New York: Charles Scribners' Sons, 1991, p. 76.
8. Quoted in Joseph F. Dinneen, *The Purple Shamrock*, New York: W.W. Norton, 1949, p. 28.
9. Curley, *op. cit.*, p. 45.
10. Oliver E. Allen, *The Tiger: The Rise and Fall of Tammany Hall*, New York: Addison-Wesley, 1993, p. 170.
11. James J. Connolly, *The Triumph of Ethnic Progressivism: Urban Political Culture in Boston, 1900–1925*, Cambridge, Mass.: Harvard University Press, 1998, p. 137.
12. Curley, *op. cit.*, p. 63.

13. Dinneen, *op. cit.*, p. 53.
14. Quoted in Charles H. Trout, "Curley of Boston: The Search for Irish Legitimacy," in Ronald P. Formisano and Constance K. Burns (eds.), *Boston 1700–1980: The Evolution of Urban Politics,* Westport, Conn.: Greenwood Press, 1984, p. 176.
15. Trout, *op. cit.*, p. 177.
16. Dinneen, *op. cit.*, pp. 60–61.
17. Alfred Steinberg, *The Bosses*, New York: Macmillan, 1972, p. 143.
18. Quoted in Jack Beatty, *The Rascal King: The Life and Times of James Michael Curley*, Reading, Mass.: Addison-Wesley, 1992, p. 93.

Chapter 13

1. James Michael Curley, *I'd Do It Again: A Record of All My Uproarious Years*, Englewood Cliffs, N.J.: Prentice-Hall, p. 76.
2. Charles H. Trout, "Curley of Boston: The Search for Irish Legitimacy," in Ronald P Formisano and Constance K. Burns (eds.), *Boston 1700–1980: The Evolution of Urban Politics*, Westport, Conn.: Greenwood Press, 1984, p. 173.
3. Quoted in Jack Beatty, *The Rascal King: The Life and Times of James Michael Curley*, Reading, Mass.: Addison-Wesley, 1992, p. 113.
4. Ray Kierman, "Jim Curley, Boss of Massachusetts," *American Mercury* XXXVII (February 1936): 138.
5. Joseph Dinneen, "The Kingfish of Massachusetts," *Harpers Monthly Magazine* (September 1936): 344.
6. Quoted in Trout, *op. cit.*, p. 179.
7. Beatty, *op. cit.*, p. 127.
8. Herbert Marshall Zolot, *The Issue of Good Government and James Michael Curley: Curley and the Boston Scene from 1897–1918*, Ph.D. Dissertation, State University of New York at Stony Brook, June 1975, p. 98.
9. Quoted in Doris Kearns Good-

win, *The Kennedys and the Fitzgeralds,* New York: Simon and Schuster, 1987, p. 245.

10. Zolot, *op. cit.*, p. 341.

11. Quoted in Zolot, *op. cit.*, p. 344.

12. *Ibid.*

13. *Ibid.*, p. 362.

14. Zolot, *op. cit.*, p. 357.

15. Joseph F. Dinneen, *The Purple Shamrock,* New York: W.W. Norton, 1949, p. 101.

16. *Ibid.*, p. 110.

17. Quoted in Trout, *op. cit.*, p. 181.

18. Alfred Steinberg, *The Bosses,* New York: Macmillan, 1972, p. 150.

19. *The Boston Globe,* January 14, 1914.

20. Steinberg, *op. cit.*, p. 151.

21. Curley, *op. cit.*, p. 128.

22. *Ibid.*, pp. 128–129.

23. Zolot, *op. cit.*, pp. 412–413.

24. *Ibid.*, p. 416.

25. *Ibid.*, p. 422–423.

26. Quoted in Zolot, *op. cit.*, p. 430.

27. *Ibid.*, p. 438.

28. Dinneen, *The Purple Shamrock, op. cit.*, p. 113.

29. Beatty, *op. cit.*, p. 192.

30. *Ibid.*, p. 174.

31. Quoted in *ibid.*, p. 174.

32. *Ibid.*, p. 181.

33. *Ibid.*, p. 182.

34. Zolot, *op. cit.*, pp. 560–561.

35. Beatty, *op. cit.*, p. 200.

Chapter 14

1. Quoted in David A. Yallop, *The Day the Laughter Stopped: The True Story of Fatty Arbuckle,* New York: St. Martin's Press, 1976, p. 67.

2. Yallop, *op. cit.*, p. 68.

3. Jack Beatty, *The Rascal King,* Reading, Mass.: Addison-Wesley, 1992, p. 196.

4. Alfred Steinberg, *The Bosses,* New York: Macmillan, 1972, p. 154.

5. Quoted in Robert Sobel, *Coolidge: An American Enigma,* Washington, D.C.: Regnery Publishing Inc., 1998, p. 144.

6. Quoted in Francis Russell, *A City in Terror: The 1919 Boston Police Strike,* New York: The Viking Press, 1977, pp. 224–225.

7. Sobel, *op. cit.*, p. 130.

8. Steinberg, *op. cit.*, p. 156.

9. Quoted in James Michael Curley, *I'd Do It Again,* Englewood Cliffs, New Jersey: Prentice-Hall, 1957, p. 163.

10. Quoted in Steinberg, *op. cit.*, p. 161.

11. Curley, *op. cit.*, pp. 220–221.

12. *Ibid.*

13. Quoted in Charles H. Trout, *Boston, the Great Depression, and the New Deal,* New York: Oxford University Press, 1977, p. 38.

14. Steinberg, *op. cit.*, p. 167.

15. *The New York Times,* June 2, 1931.

16. Quoted in Steinberg, *op. cit.*, p. 169.

17. Joseph F. Dinneen, *The Purple Shamrock,* W.W. Norton, 1949, p. 183.

18. Quoted in Beatty, *op. cit.*, p. 308.

19. Quoted in Steinberg, *op. cit.*, p. 170.

20. Quoted in William V. Shannon, *The American Irish: A Political and Social Portrait,* Amherst: The University of Massachusetts Press, 1989, p. 221.

21. Quoted in Charles H. Trout, "Curley of Boston: The Search for Irish Legitimacy," in Ronald P. Formisano and Constance K. Burns (eds.), *Boston 1700–1980: The Evolution of Urban Politics,* Westport, Conn.: Greenwood Press, 1984, p. 186.

22. Quoted in Steinberg, *op. cit.*, p. 172.

23. Quoted in Trout, *Boston, the Great Depression and the New Deal, op. cit.*, p. 239.

24. Ray Kierman, "Jim Curley, Boss of Massachusetts," *The American Mercury* XXXVII (February 1936): 137.

25. Reinhard H. Luthin, *American Demagogues,* Boston: The Beacon Press, 1954, p. 36.

26. Kierman, *op. cit.*, p. 150.

27. Steinberg, *op. cit.*, p. 180.

28. Quoted in *ibid.*, p. 185.

29. Curley, *op. cit.*, pp. 310–311.

30. Quoted in Steinberg, *op. cit.*, p. 187.

31. *Ibid.*, p. 189.
32. *Ibid.*, p. 190.
33. *Ibid.*, p. 192.
34. *Ibid.*, p. 193.
35. Shannon, *op. cit.*, p. 231.

Epilogue

1. Quoted in Dennis R. Judd and Tom Swanston, *City Politics: Private Power and Public Policy*, New York: Longmans, 2002, p. 52.
2. "The Capone Era," *Life* 23 (February 10, 1947): 24.
3. Quoted in Robert K. Merton, "Some Functions of the Political Machine," in John A. Gardiner and David J. Olson (eds.), *Theft of the City: Readings on Corruption in Urban America*, Bloomington: Indiana University Press, 1974, p. 412. Italics in original.
4. Lincoln Steffens, *The Shame of the Cities*, New York: Hill and Wong, 1989, p. 8. (Originally published by McClure, Phillips, 1904.)
5. Ella Winter and Granville Hicks, *The Letters of Lincoln Steffens, Vol. I: 1889–1919*, New York: Harcourt, Brace and Company, 1938, p. 222.
6. Merton, *op. cit.*, p. 411.
7. William Riordon, *Plunkett of Tammany Hall*, New York: E.P. Dutton, 1963, p. 17.
8. James Q. Wilson, "Corruption Not Always Scandalous," in John A. Gar-
diner and David J. Olson (eds.), *Theft of the City: Readings in Corruption in Urban America*, Bloomington: Indiana University Press, 1974, p. 32.
9. Theodore J. Lowi, "Gosnell's Chicago Revisited via Lindsay's New York," in John A. Gardiner and David J. Olson (eds.), *Theft of the City: Readings in Corruption in Urban America*, Bloomington: Indiana University Press, 1974, pp. 420–429.
10. Merton, *op. cit.*, p. 411.
11. Edward M. Martin, "William Hale Thompson of Chicago: The Saga of a Sombrero," *National Municipal Review* 17 (November 1928): 664.
12. "Chicago's 'Fighting Judge' Tackles 'Big Bill,'" *The Literary Digest* 108 (January 17, 1931): 9.
13. Kate Sargent, "Chicago, Hands Up!" *The Forum* 58 (October 1927): 522.
14. Douglas Bukowski, *Big Bill Thompson, Chicago, and the Politics of Image*, Urbana: University of Illinois Press, p. 253.
15. William V. Shannon, "Boston's Irish Mayors: An Ethnic Perspective," in Ronald F. Formisano and Constance K. Burns (eds.), *Boston: 1700–1980: The Evolution of Urban Politics*, Westport, Conn.: Greenwood Press, 1984, p. 207.
16. Jack Beatty, *The Rascal King: The Life and Times of James Michael Curley*, Boston: Addison-Wesley, 1992, p. 519.

Further Reading

General

Ellis, Edward Robb. *The Epic of New York City: A Narrative History*. New York: Old Town Books, 1990. Originally published by Coward-McCann, New York, 1966.

Gardiner, John A., and David J. Olson, eds. *Theft of the City: Readings on Corruption in Urban America*. Bloomington: Indiana University Press, 1974.

Holli, Melvin G. *The American Mayor: The Best and Worst Big-City Leaders*. University Park, Pennsylvania State University Press, 1999.

Lankevich, George J. *American Metropolis: A History of New York City*. New York: New York University Press, 1998.

Luthin, Reinhard H. *American Demagogues: Twentieth Century*. Boston: Beacon Press, 1954.

Morris, Lloyd R. *Incredible New York: High Life and Low Life of the Last Hundred Years*. New York: Random House, 1951.

Sayre, Wallace S., and Herbert Kaufman. *Governing New York City: Politics in the Metropolis*. New York: Russell Sage Foundation, 1960.

Shannon, William V. *The American Irish: A Political and Social Portrait*. Amherst: University of Massachusetts Press, 1989. Originally published by Macmillan Company, New York, in 1963.

Steffens, Lincoln. *The Shame of the Cities*. New York: Hill and Wang, 1989. Originally published by McClure, Phillips, 1904.

Steinberg, Alfred. *The Bosses*. New York: Macmillan Company, 1972.

Trout, Charles H. *Boston, the Great Depression, and the New Deal*. New York: Oxford University Press, 1977.

Thompson

Bright, John. *Hizzoner: Big Bill Thompson: An Idyll of Chicago*. New York: Jonathan Cape and Harrison Smith, 1930.

Bukowski, Douglas. *Big Bill Thompson, Chicago, and the Politics of Image*. Urbana and Chicago: University of Illinois Press, 1998.

Gosnell, Harold F. *Machine Politics: Chicago Model*. Chicago: University of Chicago Press, 1937.

Herrick, Mary J. *The Chicago Schools: A Social and Political History.* Beverly Hills: Sage Publications, 1971.
Stuart, William H. *The Twenty Incredible Years.* Chicago: M.A. Donohue & Co., 1935.
Wendt, Lloyd, and Herman Kogan. *Big Bill of Chicago.* Indianapolis: Bobbs-Merrill, 1953.

Hague

Connors, Richard J. *A Cycle of Power: The Career of Jersey City Mayor Frank Hague.* Metuchen, N.J.: Scarecrow, 1971.
Fleming, Thomas J. "I Am the Law." *American Heritage* XX (June 1969): 132–48.
McKean, David Dayton. *The Boss: The Hague Machine in Action.* Boston: Houghton Mifflin, 1940.

Walker

Allen, Oliver E. *The Tiger: The Rise and Fall of Tammany Hall.* Reading, Mass.: Addison-Wesley, 1993.
Fowler, Gene. *Beau James: The Life and Times of Jimmy Walker.* Clifton, N.J.: Augustus M. Kelly Publishers, 1973. Original edition published by Viking Press, New York, 1949.
Gribetz, Louis J., and Joseph Kaye. *Jimmy Walker: The Story of a Personality.* New York: Dial Press, 1932.
MacKay, Milton. *The Tin Box Parade: A Handbook for Larceny.* New York: Robert M. McBride and Company, 1934.
Mitgang, Herbert. *The Man Who Rode the Tiger: The Life and Times of Judge Samuel Seabury.* New York: The Fordham University Press, 1996. Originally published by Lippincott, Philadelphia, 1963.
_____. *Once Upon a Time in New York: Jimmy Walker, Franklin Roosevelt, and the Last Great Battle of the Jazz Age.* New York: The Free Press, 2000.
Walsh, George. *Gentleman Jimmy Walker: Mayor of the Jazz Age.* New York: Praeger, 1974.

Curley

Beatty, Jack. *The Rascal King: The Life and Times of James Michael Curley.* Reading, Mass.: Addison-Wesley, 1992.
Curley, James Michael. *I'd Do It Again: A Record of My Uproarious Years.* Englewood Cliffs, N.J.: Prentice-Hall, 1957.
Dinneen, Joseph F. *The Purple Shamrock: The Hon. James Michael Curley of Boston.* New York: W.W. Norton, 1949.
Harris, Leon A. *Only to God: The Extraordinary Life of Godfrey Lowell Cabot.* New York: Atheneum, 1967.
O'Connor, Edwin. *The Last Hurrah.* Boston: Little, Brown, 1956.
Yallop, David A. *The Day the Laughter Stopped: The True Story of Fatty Arbuckle.* New York: St. Martin's, 1976.

Index